SECOND LANGUAGE ACQUISITION 20
Series Editor: David Singleton, *Trinity College, Dublin, Ireland*

Investigating Tasks in Formal Language Learning

Edited by
María del Pilar García Mayo

MULTILINGUAL MATTERS LTD
Clevedon • Buffalo • Toronto

To Vicente, Vicente Jr. and Irene

Library of Congress Cataloging in Publication Data
Investigating Tasks in Formal Language Learning/Edited by María del Pilar García Mayo.
Second Language Acquisition: 20
Includes bibliographical references and index.
1. Language and languages–Study and teaching. 2. Task analysis in education.
I. García Mayo, María del Pilar.
P53.82.I58 2007
418.007–dc22   2006022421

British Library Cataloguing in Publication Data
A catalogue entry for this book is available from the British Library.

ISBN 1-85359-927-1/EAN 978-1-85359-927-9 (hbk)
ISBN 1-85359-926-3/ EAN 978-1-85359-926-2 (pbk)

Multilingual Matters Ltd
UK: Frankfurt Lodge, Clevedon Hall, Victoria Road, Clevedon BS21 7HH.
USA: UTP, 2250 Military Road, Tonawanda, NY 14150, USA.
Canada: UTP, 5201 Dufferin Street, North York, Ontario M3H 5T8, Canada.

Copyright © 2007 María del Pilar García Mayo and the authors of individual chapters.

All rights reserved. No part of this work may be reproduced in any form or by any means without permission in writing from the publisher.

The policy of Multilingual Matters/Channel View Publications is to use papers that are natural, renewable and recyclable products, made from wood grown in sustainable forests. In the manufacturing process of our books, and to further support our policy, preference is given to printers that have FSC and PEFC Chain of Custody accreditation. The FSC and/or PEFC logos will appear on those books where full accreditation has been granted to the printer concerned.

Typeset by Techset Composition Ltd.
Printed and bound in Great Britain by the Cromwell Press Ltd.

Contents

Foreword

For years, second language (L2) tasks have been providing contexts for language use. Researchers can manipulate tasks to test theoretical claims, and teachers can shape them to promote L2 use and acquisition. As such, tasks have become central to both second language research and pedagogy. In fact, one helpful outcome of the classroom origins of many tasks and their corresponding ecological validity in research has been to provide a fruitful area of common ground between research and practice. Various aspects of tasks, task features, and task complexity are of key interest to today's second language acquisition teachers and researchers, who seek to understand the intricacies of how task-based interaction plays a facilitative role in instructed language development and how research on tasks can inform task-based syllabus design. The widely recognized importance of these linked goals is reflected in the impressive (and increasing) amount of research being carried out in this area. Top-tier journals and conferences on language acquisition now regularly include papers dealing with task-design issues, and several books have appeared providing overviews of task-based learning, teaching, and research concerns (e.g., Ellis, 2003; Nunan, 1989). The collection of work brought together in the current volume adds to this body of work and demonstrates how theory and pedagogy can inform each other regarding shared questions and goals.

A classification and explanation of the effects of task features on learners' L2 production is fundamental to understanding the processes of language acquisition in both research and classroom contexts. In the first chapter of this collection, Peter Robinson points out that many of the intuitive lists of task features (e.g., cognitive load, communicative stress) proposed by teachers and researchers early on were insightful and have been worthwhile; nonetheless, he finds the lack of a single taxonomic system of empirically researched and pedagogically implementable task characteristics problematic. Answers to many of the questions that Rod Ellis usefully raised in his 2003 text can be clarified further: How can tasks be designed to influence language use? In what ways might language acquisition occur as a result? How can tasks be most appropriately used for assessment purposes? Robinson asks these sorts of questions using the lens of his own classification system, focusing on interactional, cognitive, and ability-related criteria, with the goal of ascertaining how task complexity can promote interlanguage development and how tasks can best be sequenced in pedagogical settings. He notes that while certain distinctions have already enjoyed a substantial amount of research (e.g., planned vs. unplanned tasks, open vs. closed solutions), others have not progressed much beyond the proposal stage. Current questions of interest to Robinson include how the procedural and conceptual demands of tasks can affect learners' allocation of attentional resources, noticing of linguistic form, grammaticization of meanings, automatization of access to linguistic knowledge, and, ultimately, attainment of higher levels of L2 proficiency.

Many of the studies following this initial chapter take up a number of Robinson's questions, building on his proposals, testing his claims, and adding new perspectives. Several apply his model of task complexity to the investigation of particular task types and contribute to theorizing based on their results. Indeed, part of the usefulness of this edited collection lies in its bringing together of studies which may allow for a comparison of the effects of design features across a range of task types. Oral and written tasks are represented evenly, and a variety of measures are employed in evaluating learners' on-task L2 use. Several chapters (2, 3, 6, 7, and 8) report on learners' linguistic accuracy, fluency, and complexity, while others focus on aspects of language use such as discourse moves (Chapter 4), focus on form and metatalk (Chapter 5), lexical innovations (Chapter 10), and even the naturally occurring "learning talk" which occurs off-task (Chapter 12). Still others examine vocabulary development and reading comprehension (Chapter 9) and learners' pragmatics knowledge (Chapter 11).

In line with Robinson's research agenda, Craig Lambert and Steve Engler (Chapter 2) explore the effects of the task-design features of goal orientation (open or closed) and information distribution (shared, one-way, or two-way) on learners' oral L2 production, while Roger Gilabert (Chapter 3) examines the effects of planning time and orientation to the *here-and-now* versus the *there-and-then*. Other chapters comparatively evaluate Robinson's (2001, 2003, 2005) Cognition Hypothesis of task complexity against Skehan's (1998, 2001) Capacity Hypothesis, looking empirically at how well their contrasting predictions regarding learners' allocation of attention are borne out. For instance, in order to investigate whether attentional resources exist in multiple non-competitive pools, thereby allowing for simultaneously greater linguistic accuracy and complexity on more complex tasks (as with Robinson), or whether concerns with linguistic accuracy and complexity compete with each other for limited attentional resources (as with Skehan), Folkert Kuiken and Ineke Vedder (Chapter 6) evaluate learners' output on L2 writing tasks which require more or less demanding reasoning. Results such as these have implications not only for theories of attention in SLA, but also for task sequencing in classroom contexts.

Other studies draw inspiration and make important contributions to, research on the value of interaction for language learning. Marisol Fernández García (Chapter 4), for instance, asks how tasks can be designed to promote features of interaction, such as negotiation for meaning, which have been linked to L2 development (Mackey & Gass, 2006). Drawing in part on work by Swain (1995, 1998), Ana Alegría de la Colina and María del Pilar García Mayo (Chapter 5) examine how low-proficiency learners can be pushed to reflect consciously on their own language production, focusing on form and producing metatalk about the target language while conveying meaning in collaborative tasks. Elsa González Álvarez (Chapter 10) investigates learners' problem-solving mechanisms in oral interactions, looking at whether task type influences the extent to which they employ lexical innovation strategies when faced with gaps in their L2 knowledge.

For those readers more interested in classroom concerns, several chapters deal with how task characteristics can be manipulated in relation to learners' needs and motivations. For example, in addition to investigating how task-design features affect learners' linguistic accuracy, fluency, and complexity, Lambert and Engler (Chapter 2) explore their effects on learners' affective engagement in task performance. Alegría de la Colina and García Mayo (Chapter 5) provide pedagogical guidelines for teachers in relation to encouraging learners' metatalk in the implementation of collaborative tasks. In Chapter 8, Neomy Storch and Gillian Wigglesworth examine differences in the writing produced by learners who have completed tasks collaboratively versus individually. The qualitative information they provide regarding the learners' approaches should be useful for educators. In discussing how consciousness-raising tasks can help learners to develop pragmatic awareness about making requests, Eva Alcón (Chapter 11) touches on whether learners show preferences for particular task types. Finally, Marie-Noëlle Lamy (Chapter 12) reconsiders the use of traditional communicative tasks in light of the incidental learning which can occur naturally in learners' conversations on self-selected topics. She highlights L2 learners' resourcefulness and warns that teachers' and researchers' expectations may overlook the educational validity of the "learning-talk" which occurs in off-task communication.

The focus on learner variables which is so important for pedagogy is significant for L2 researchers as well, of course. As Robinson argues, it is important to identify aspects of task complexity which show robust effects on language performance and acquisition across learners, but it is also crucial to investigate how individual differences in abilities and affective variables interact with task conditions so that specific modifications can be made to provide optimal learning opportunities. Along these lines, some of the chapters in this collection take a closer look at learner proficiency in relation to task features, asking, for example, how low-proficiency learners can benefit from metatalk during collaborative tasks (Chapter 5) and how proficiency may mediate the relationship between task characteristics and lexical innovation (Chapter 10). Other chapters investigate how the effects of task complexity might be mediated by language aptitude (Chapter 7) and inferencing skills (Chapter 9).

In sum, this new edited collection provides a rich compendium of work on second language tasks that will be of interest to researchers and students of task-based language learning alike. The book also provides research-based evidence for second language teachers and educators who want to learn about best practices in task-based formal language instruction. Taken as whole, the text provides a broad and balanced overview of the current state of the art in instructed task research, with an impressive range of chapters from leading researchers in the field. The book deals with an interesting variety of target and source languages, modes, contexts and settings, and a range of aspects of task features from multiple complementary perspectives. It makes an important and timely contribution to the field and will be read with interest and profit by any serious task scholar.

Alison Mackey
Georgetown University

References

Ellis, R. (2003) *Task-based Language Learning and Teaching*. New York: Oxford University Press.

Mackey, A. and Gass, S. (2006) Pushing the methodological boundaries in interaction research: An introduction to the special issue. *Studies in Second Language Acquisition, 28* (2) 169–278.

Nunan, D. (1989) *Designing Tasks for the Communicative Classroom*. Cambridge: Cambridge University Press.

Robinson, P. (2001) Task complexity, cognitive resources, and syllabus design: A triadic framework for examining task influences on SLA. In P. Robinson (ed.) *Cognition and Second Language Instruction* (pp. 287–318). Cambridge: Cambridge University Press.

Robinson, P. (2003) Attention and memory during SLA. L.C. Daughty and M.H. Long (eds) *Handbook of Second Language Acquisition* (pp. 631–678). Oxford: Blackwell.

Robinson, P. (2005) Cognitive complexity and task sequencing: Studies in a componential framework for second language task design. *International Review of Applied Linguistics* 43 (1), 1–32.

Skehan, P. (1998) *A Cognitive Approach to Language Learning*. Oxford: Oxford University Press.

Skehan, P. (2001) Tasks and language performance assessment. In M. Bygate, P. Skehan and M. Swain (eds), *Researching Pedagogic Tasks: Second Language Learning, Teaching and Testing* (pp. 167–185). Harlow: Longman.

Swain, M. (1995) Three functions of output in second language learning. In G. Cook and B. Seidlhofer (eds) *Principle and Practice in Applied Linguistics: Studies in Honour of H. G. Widdowson* (pp. 125–144). Oxford: Oxford University Press.

Swain, M. (1998) Focus on form through conscious reflection. In C. Doughty, and J. Williams (eds) *Focus on Form in Classroom Second Language Acquisition* (pp. 64–84), Cambridge: Cambridge University Press.

Contributors

Eva Alcón Soler
Department of English Studies, Campus del Riu Sec, Castelló, Spain

Ana Alegría de la Colina
Dpto. de Filología, Universidad de Cantabria, Santander, Spain

Steve Engler
Faculty of Foreign Studies, The University of Kitakyushu, Kitakyushu-shi, Japan

Marisol Fernández García
Department of Modern Languages, Northeastern University, Boston, USA

María del Pilar García Mayo
Dpto. de Filología Inglesa, Universidad del País Vasco (UPV/EHU), Vitoria, Spain

Roger Gilabert
Blanquerna Communication Studies Department,Universitat Ramon Llull, Barcelona, Spain

Elsa González Álvarez
Facultad de Educación, University of Santiago de Compostela, Spain

Tomohito Ishikawa
Aoyama Gakuin University, Kanagawa, Japan

Folkert Kuiken
Amsterdam Center for Language and Communication, Amsterdam, The Netherlands

Craig P. Lambert
Faculty of Foreign Studies, The University of Kitakyushu, Kitakyushu-shi, Japan

Marie-Noëlle Lamy
Faculty of Education and Languages, The Open University, Milton Keynes, UK

Elke Peters
K.U. Leuven, Faculteit Letteren, Leuven, Belgium

Peter Robinson
Department of English, Aoyama Gakuin University, Tokyo, Japan

Neomy Storch
Department of Linguistics and Applied Linguistics, University of Melbourne, Victoria, Australia

Ineke Vedder
Amsterdam Center for Language and Communication, Amsterdam, The Netherlands

Gillian Wigglesworth
Department of Linguistics and Applied Linguistics, University of Melbourne, Victoria, Australia

Introduction

MARÍA DEL PILAR GARCÍA MAYO

The purpose of this book is to contribute to the growth of interest in task-based language learning and teaching that has been seen in recent years. Numerous publications on this topic (see, among many others, the work by Bygate *et al.*, 2001; Ellis, 2000, 2003, 2005; Lee, 2000; Long & Norris, 2000; Skehan, 1998; Robinson, 2001, 2005; Willis, 1996; the special issue of the journal *Language Teaching Research* vol. 3, 2000) and the first International Conference on Task-Based Language Teaching (held in Belgium in September, 2005) attest to this interest. As is well known, task is a central concept in current second language acquisition (SLA) research, both as a research instrument and as a construct in need of investigation (Ellis, 2003: ix; Seedhouse, 2005). Researchers and teachers consider it of the utmost importance to elicit samples of learner language as this is the basic material that will help us understand how learners restructure their interlanguage over time and design materials accordingly.

As programmes in formal language settings that are currently implementing task-based syllabi seem to be on the increase, there is a need to (i) provide guidelines for task classification, sequencing and design and (ii) determine if this type of approach may actually inform effective teaching practice. The current volume brings together research that focuses on various aspects and effects of pedagogic task design. Eleven of the 12 contributions are data-based studies that use tasks to examine oral interaction, written production, vocabulary and reading, lexical innovation and pragmatics in different formal language learning settings. The number of languages involved (English as a foreign/second language, French/German/Spanish as foreign languages) together with the various aspects of the learning of a language analysed will hopefully provide the reader with different options that can be tested in other contexts, with different language combinations and different groups of learners.

In the opening chapter, 'Criteria for classifying and sequencing pedagogic tasks', Peter Robinson argues for the need of a classificatory system of pedagogic task characteristics. This categorisation will offer guidance as to how to classify and sequence tasks and will introduce order in the data base of findings about tasks effects on L2 learning and performance. Robinson emphasises the importance that the L2 classificatory system meet these constraints: it should be (i) motivated by a theory, (ii) empirically researchable, and (iii) operationally feasible. He reviews interactional, cognitive and ability-determinant criteria for task classification and three proposals (the Skills Hypothesis, the Capacity Hypothesis and the Cognition Hypothesis) for task sequencing, providing a rationale for the two stages in which task complexity is increased in the Cognition Hypothesis.

Chapter 2, 'Information distribution and goal orientation in second language task design' by Craig P. Lambert and Steve Engler, focuses on two task design factors, information distribution and goal orientation, claimed to be related to the nature of discourse learners produce. More specifically, the goal of their paper is to determine the efficacy of those two design factors in supporting a dual-mode processing system. Thirty-six Japanese females with an intermediate level of English participated in the study whose results seem to provide support for shared or open versions of tasks as useful tools '[...] to push L2 development by encouraging more complex language use, whereas one-way versions might subsequently be used to practice and solidify these gains by encouraging more fluent and accurate language use'.

The next three chapters examine tasks and oral production by different groups of learners. In Chapter 3 ('The simultaneous manipulation of task complexity along planning time and [+/− Here-and-Now]: Effects on L2 oral production') Roger Gilabert studies the impact of simultaneously manipulating pre-task planning time and the degree of displaced, past time reference on learners' narrative fluency, complexity and accuracy. A group of 48 English as a Foreign Language (EFL) university students with a lower-intermediate proficiency level were asked to narrate four wordless comic strips under four different levels of task complexity. Findings indicate that planning time has a positive impact on fluency and lexical complexity but no impact on structural complexity and accuracy. Increasing complexity along the [+/− Here-and-Now] variable has a positive effect on accuracy, no effects on structural or lexical complexity and negative effects on fluency. The results are discussed in the light of L1 and L2 production models as well as opposing views of how attentional resources are allocated during task performance (Skehan, 1998; Robinson, 2001).

The study by Marisol Fernández García 'Tasks, negotiation, and L2 learning in a foreign language context' (Chapter 4), examines how two communication tasks (two-way and one-way information gap) contribute to create opportunities for beginner learners of Spanish to engage in the negotiation of meaning. The interaction of 21 dyads was recorded, transcribed and analysed. The overall findings of the study indicate that beginning foreign language learners do not seem to be limited by their linguistic resources and try to make input comprehensible to their partners. They can also provide grammatical feedback by using various forms of modification. The study provides support for the use of tasks with beginner language learners.

In Chapter 5 ('Attention to form across collaborative tasks by low-proficiency learners in an EFL setting') Ana Alegría de la Colina and María del Pilar García Mayo also explore the issue of the use of tasks with low-proficiency learners. The study aims at exploring the facilitating effects of three collaborative tasks (dictogloss, text reconstruction and jigsaw) to promote Focus-on-Form (FonF) and metatalk about the target language. Twenty-four EFL graduate students took part in the study. They were all familiar with the topic of the tasks. The findings reveal that low-proficiency learners can benefit from collaborative tasks provided that they are allowed to carry out metatalk in their L1. The tasks proved to be suitable to draw attention to form as care was taken to free the learners' attention by reducing the cognitive load imposed by the task conditions. Though no great differences were found between the tasks under study, each one focused attention on different linguistic features influenced by the way input was provided.

The next three chapters examine tasks and written production. In Chapter 6 ('Cognitive task complexity and linguistic performance in French L2 writing') Folkert Kuiken and Ineke Vedder focus on the question of whether cognitively more demanding tasks lead to syntactically and lexically more complex written output and whether they promote higher accuracy. Seventy-six Dutch learners of French with different proficiency levels participated in the experiment and two factors of the resource directing dimension (Robinson, 2005): $[+/-$ few elements] and $[+/-$ no reasoning demands] were manipulated. The findings suggest that task complexity does have an effect on linguistic performance as increasing task complexity along resource directing variables results in a more accurate text. No interaction between task complexity and proficiency level was observed in the pool of learners tested.

Chapter 7 'The effect of manipulating task complexity along the $[+/-$ Here-and-Now] dimension on L2 written narrative discourse', by Tomohito Ishikawa, further investigates the issue of task complexity by manipulating the $[+/-$ Here-and-Now] dimension on L2 written discourse. The participants in the study, 54 Japanese low-high intermediate EFL learners, were randomly assigned to two task conditions: [+Here-and-Now] and [−Here-and-Now]. They viewed a cartoon strip for 5 minutes and were given 30 minutes to write about it. The participants in the [−Here-and-Now] condition had to return the strip cartoon to the researcher. The results of the study show multiple significant effects of increasing task complexity along degree of displaced time reference on accuracy, complexity and fluency and, overall, seem to support Robinson's Cognition Hypothesis.

In their study 'Writing tasks: The effects of collaboration' (Chapter 8), Neomy Storch and Gilliam Wigglesworth investigate the process involved in collaborative writing activities and whether there are differences in the product between tasks completed collaboratively and those completed individually. Twenty-four students completed two writing tasks (a report task and an argumentative task) individually and 48 students completed the same tasks in pairs (24 pairs). The students were all advanced EFL learners. The findings point to the merits of collaboration, which afforded the learners the opportunity to generate ideas, give and receive feedback on language. Pairs tended to produce texts with greater grammatical accuracy than individual writers. From a pedagogical perspective, the authors claim that collaborative writing tasks do have a place in the L2 classroom.

In the next chapter of the volume, Chapter 9 ('L2 vocabulary acquisition and reading comprehension. The influence of task complexity'), Elke Peters analyses the issue of the differential effects of task instruction on word retention and reading comprehension when attentional demands are manipulated. The participants of the study were 21 Dutch learners of German as a foreign language, with an intermediate proficiency level. The aspect of task complexity being researched concerned the distinction between single and dual tasks. The results show that students primarily concentrate on text content even when they are set a vocabulary learning task. The data seems to corroborate Skehan's (1998) model pointing towards learners' limited capacity to process incoming information. Furthermore, they confirm VanPatten's (1990) priority for meaning when attending to communicative input: students with a dual task do not score better on the vocabulary tests and on the reading comprehension test, as would be expected within the multiple-resources view put forward by Robinson (2001).

Elsa González Álvarez also investigates lexicon-related issues in Chapter 10 'Task-effect on the use of lexical innovation strategies in interlanguage communication'. The goal of her study is to analyse the use Spanish L2-learners of English make of strategies of lexical innovation or word coinage in oral communication and determine the influence of task type as a contextual variable on the different devices identified in their discourse. Thirty students, placed in three proficiency level groups, took part in the experiment. They were asked to perform three different tasks (picture description, story-telling and interview) with different linguistic, communicative and cognitive demands. The findings show that task-type has an influence on the selection and frequency of use of different strategy types: more controlled and linguistically demanding tasks tend to favor the creation of new terms, whereas less controlled tasks allow for the use of alternative strategies such as reduction and avoidance.

In Chapter 11 ('Fostering EFL learners' awareness of requesting through explicit and implicit consciousness-raising tasks') Eva Alcón Soler focuses on the effect of consciousness-raising tasks on the development of learners' awareness and production of requests. One-hundred and thirty-two high-school EFL learners were assigned to two treatment groups (explicit and implicit) and to a control group. The three groups were exposed to requests as they appeared in selected conversations taken from different episodes of the series *Stargate*. While the explicit group received instructions through direct consciousness raising tasks, the implicit group was required to discover the type of language used in requests through the use of indirect consciousness raising tasks. The findings illustrate that learners' consciousness about requests benefits from the use of consciousness raising tasks and that the effects of explicit instruction seem to be sustained in time more than the effects of implicit instruction.

Distancing herself from the cognitive ways of looking at tasks, Marie-Noëlle Lamy situates her contribution in Chapter 12 ('Interactive task design: Metachat and the whole learner') within the socio-affective and socio-semiotic traditions of task-related research. She provides an ethnographic account of metalinguistic conversations by 40 intermediate-to-advanced learners of French as a foreign language. Lamy explores metachat (a functional interpretation of metalanguage that reflects its interactive and informal qualities) in various controlled, freer, pragmatic and casual contexts with the goal of understanding 'how it constructs the participants' online social world and what learning opportunities it affords them'. The quantitative and qualitative analysis of the data provides evidence that metachat offers interesting possibilities for learners. The author provides ideas about how to integrate this construct into learning programmes and draws implications of her research for task structuring, sequencing and modelling.

The book is addressed to researchers in second language acquisition, as the different types of task used may help in the design of further work along the lines presented in the different contributions, and to teachers who might want to try out the different proposals made adapting them to their particular language learning settings. The book is also addressed to students interested in task-based language learning and teaching.

References

Bygate, M., Skehan, P. and Swain, M. (eds) (2001) *Researching Pedagogic Tasks: Second Language Learning, Teaching and Testing*. Harlow: Longman.

Ellis, R. (2000) Task-based research and language pedagogy. *Language Teaching Research* 4, 193–220.

Ellis, R. (2003) *Task-based Language Learning and Teaching*. Oxford: Oxford University Press.

Ellis, R. (ed.) (2005) *Planning and Task Performance in Second Language*. Amsterdam: John Benjamins.

Lee, J. (2000) *Tasks and Communicating in Language Classrooms*. Boston: McGraw-Hill.

Long, M.H. and Norris, J. (2000) Task-based teaching and assessment. In M. Byram (ed.) *Encyclopedia of Language Teaching* (pp. 597–603). London: Routledge.

Robinson, P. (2001) Task complexity, cognitive resources and syllabus design: A triadic framework for examining task influences on SLA. In P. Robinson (ed.)

Cognition and Second Language Instruction (pp. 287–318). Cambridge: Cambridge University Press.

Robinson, P. (2005) Cognitive complexity and task sequencing: Studies in a componential framework for second language task design. *International Review of Applied Linguistics in Language Teaching* 43 (1), 1–33.

Seedhouse, P. (2005) "Task" as a research construct. *Language Learning* 55 (3), 533–570.

Skehan, P. (1998) *A Cognitive Approach to Language Learning*. Oxford: Oxford University Press.

VanPatten, B. (1990) Attending to form and content on the input. *Studies in Second Language Acquisition* 12, 287–301.

Willis, J. (1996) *A Framework for Task-Based Learning*. Harlow: Longman.

Chapter 1

Criteria for Classifying and Sequencing Pedagogic Tasks

PETER ROBINSON

Introduction: Task Taxonomy, Classification and Programme Design

A fundamental pedagogic question underlies much of the research done into second language (L2) tasks. How do teachers design and deliver a *sequence* of tasks that sustains learner effort to use the L2, from beginning to end, and which simultaneously leads to L2 learning and development? The Bangalore Project, described by Prabhu (1987) was the first large-scale attempt to operationalise an answer to this question following a syllabus based entirely on tasks. The Bangalore Project's criteria for grading and sequencing tasks, as described by Prabhu, were intuitive, based on teacher decisions about whether and to what degree their 'reasoning demands' posed a 'challenge' to learners. But while intuitions can be shared, often they are not. Consequently, subsequent research has examined these, and other, claims made for the proposed effects of task demands on L2 learning and performance – the aim being to establish an empirical (non-intuitive) basis for decision-making about L2 task design and sequencing. Some characteristics, such as whether tasks are planned (Ellis, 2005); whether there is no fixed solution (open) versus only one (closed) (Long, 1989); or whether the task involves reference to events happening in a currently shared context (Here-and-Now) versus in the past, elsewhere (There-and-Then) (Robinson, 1995), have been quite extensively studied. Other characteristics have been less researched, and a number still remain at the proposal stage. While replications of what empirical findings there are, and some standardisation of measures used to arrive at them, continue to be needed, what has become clear is that there are multiple task effects on L2 learning and performance, as has also been found in the many task domains studied in the broader fields of behavioual, and psychological science.

Task taxonomy

What is still unclear, however, is how these different characteristics relate to each other *categorically*, and what effects they might have in *combination* during classroom performance – issues which are essential to theoretically and empirically informed L2 task and programme design. For example, giving learners time to plan, or designing a task where only one solution is possible, or a task that requires reference in the Here-and-Now, all seem to be characteristics that are different in 'kind'. And giving learners time to plan an open versus a closed task, or a Here-and-Now versus a There-and-Then task may produce very different results. Do these different 'kinds' of task characteristic, or combinations of them, affect not only performance, but also second language acquisition (SLA) processes in different ways? And how do we go from information like this – if we knew it – to using it in the design of pedagogic tasks for groups of L2 learners? What is needed to help promote answers to such questions is a *classificatory system* which introduces order into the current data base of findings, enabling *categories* of the learning and performance demands of tasks to be related to SLA processes, and also to be used in instructional programme design.

Taxonomic descriptions in many areas, such as personality traits (Matthews & Deary, 1998); educational objectives (Bloom, 1956); or cognitive abilities (Carroll, 1993), provide theoretically motivated, testable, rationales for how findings from laboratory studies can be generalized across each other, and to operational settings (e.g. clinical diagnoses of personality; formal settings for L2 instruction). Taxonomic descriptions can therefore guide research and application, but they must also develop to accommodate findings, and theoretical progress. In the early period of SLA research into tasks, many lists of characteristics thought to affect learning and performance were proposed. Understandably, at that time, these lacked to varying degrees, either theoretically motivated taxonomic structure, or empirical support. One notable exception was a taxonomy described by Pica *et al.* (1993) which classified task characteristics on the basis of interactional criteria, such as the goal of the task (open versus closed) and the direction of information flow (from one person to another, or mutually, both ways). This taxonomy was motivated by theoretical claims, and research into them, about the value of interaction for SLA. Since that taxonomy was proposed, SLA theory and research in information processing frameworks (e.g. Johnson, 1996; Robinson, 1996; Skehan, 1998) has resulted in a number of quite different proposals for relevant and operationalisable L2 task characteristics. These 'cognitive criteria' now need to be accommodated with 'interactional criteria' in an expanded taxonomic description of L2 tasks. With these issues in mind a taxonomy described later in this chapter identifies categories of L2 task characteristics that have been researched (as well as some, so far, only proposed), and classification criteria that can be drawn on to systematically assign them to one category or another.

Three approaches to task classification

One specific outcome of such a categorisation of pedagogic task character-istics is that it should offer guidance as to how to classify and sequence tasks in task-based approaches to syllabus design. Task classification is log-ically prior to task sequencing, but at least three different approaches to classifying tasks are apparent in the broader educational and psychologi-cal research literature on developing taxonomies of human learning and performance. A choice of one best methodology, however, is not a problem, since all are necessary, and complement each other conceptually, being most appropriate (though not exclusively so) at three different stages, and levels, of implementing L2 instruction, as is illustrated in Table 1.1.

In *behaviour descriptive* approaches to task classification, categories of tasks are based on observation (both participant and non-participant) and descriptions (which may be elicited by structured, or unstructured inter-views from job performers, supervisors, etc.) of what people actually do while performing a task. Examples of these approaches are *behavioural typology* analysis (Williams, 1977); classification of *common denominators* of task performances required across industrial or other workplace jobs (McCormick, 1979); and descriptions of jobs on the basis of *worker functions* or behaviours (Fine, 1974). Behaviour descriptive approaches to identifying *target tasks*, their *subtasks*, and the *steps* needed to perform them (together with a sampling of target domain discourse), are important at the Needs Analysis stage and level of Table 1.1, as input to L2 course design (see e.g. recent papers in Long, 2005), and also to performance-referenced testing of abilities to accomplish either steps in, sub-tasks of, or global target tasks (for placement or achievement purposes) to some criterion measure of success (e.g. Norris *et al.*, 1998; Robinson & Ross, 1996).

Information-theoretic approaches adopt a different level of description, classifying tasks in terms of the information processing stages, and the cognitive processes involved in mediating input to the task performer and

Table 1.1 Stage, domain, analyses and outcomes of task classification and sequencing procedures

Stage	Domain	Analyses	Outcomes
Needs identification	Real-world L2 use and performance	Behaviour and discourse descriptive	Target task and performance-referenced test specifications
Syllabus design	Target task descriptions	Information-theoretic	Pedagogic task sequences
Learner assessment	Pedagogic tasks	Ability requirements	Task aptitude profiles

the output (spoken, written, and/or other behavioural responses) required for successful task completion. These cognitive-task analytic approaches have been the focus of attempts at task classification, and proposals for task sequencing both outside (e.g. Hollnagel, 2003; Seamster *et al.*, 1997) and within the L2 literature (e.g. Bygate *et al.*, 2001; Robinson, 1996, 2001a, 2005a; Robinson *et al.*, 1995; Skehan, 1998, 2001). While sharing the same information-theoretic approach to describing task characteristics, not all of these proposals share the assumption that classification of pedagogic tasks be based on the target tasks identified in the needs analysis, as will be described below.

A third approach to task classification, the *ability requirements* approach, classifies tasks in terms of the human cognitive abilities required to perform them effectively (Carroll, 1993; Snow *et al.*, 1984). Clearly, L2 learners differ in their strengths in abilities drawn on during information processing (such as working memory capacity), and these differences, as well as differences in the information processing demands of pedagogic tasks themselves, will affect the outcomes of pedagogic task performance for individuals. Research into interactions between L2 learner information processing abilities, and the information processing demands of tasks has begun to be systematically approached in recent years, and this will be important to identifying aptitudes for different kinds of task performance and L2 processing, and so to matching learners to, or supporting performance on, various pedagogic task types and practice sequences, as will also be described below.

Programme design

Articulating L2 task classification and sequencing decisions, using these analytic methodologies and across the stages and levels of programme design illustrated in Table 1.1, therefore presents a number of implementational challenges. Based on the description of target tasks, pedagogic tasks need to be designed, classified using information-theoretic criteria, then sequenced so as to increase L2 processing demands to target task levels. These decisions themselves need to be formatively evaluated, and revised, based on evidence of whether and to what extent they lead to success on target task assessments. Aptitude profiles, once developed, need to be used to adjust sequencing decisions for individual learners, perhaps by increasing amounts of task practice for (some) learners low in the abilities (some) task demands draw on. The following sections further address issues introduced here: (1) articulating classification and sequencing decisions with needs analysis and assessment of learner abilities; (2) other constraints on pedagogically relevant classificatory systems, and a taxonomic description of L2 pedagogic task characteristics which aims to meet them; and (3) some implications of this taxonomy, and the classification criteria it includes, for task sequencing and L2 syllabus design.

Formal Settings for L2 Instruction: Articulating Needs, Task and Learner Analyses

An instructional-design theory offers explicit guidance on how to effectively articulate learner needs, instructional tasks, and learner abilities, and on how to implement and evaluate programmes of instruction, across a variety of formal settings (Reigeluth, 1999). Theories differ over how this articulation is best achieved. Similarly, various proposals for L2 instruction afford an important role to tasks but differ in their rationales for how task-based instruction can promote SLA processes, and also with respect to which of the stages in Table 1.1 are necessary to, and so should be articulated during programme delivery and evaluation. These theoretical and implementational differences are summarised below, since they have each led to a variety of proposals for L2 task classification and sequencing, some of which are complementary, and some of which are not.

Needs analysis

Depending on the domain, and so content to be learned, instructional-design theories differ in their recommendations for how units of instruction be classified and sequenced, but many agree that an important first step is the analysis of learner needs and that subsequent classification and sequencing of instructional units be based on it. For example, Gagne *et al.* (2005) describe the first two steps in the 'Analysis' component of their ADDIE (Analyse, Design, Develop, Implement, Evaluate) model of instructional design as follows: '1. First determine the needs for which instruction is the solution. 2. After identifying the needs to be served by the course and some of the situational factors, then conduct an instructional analysis ... an important outcome [of which] is task classification' (Gagne *et al.*, 2005: 24–25). Consistent with this, Long (1998) has argued that methodological choice of *task* as a unit of analysis in the identification of learner needs and in syllabus design allows both of these stages of programme development to be articulated in theoretically coherent, and practically complementary ways, identifying six operational steps involved in the design and delivery of task-based language teaching: (1) conduct a needs analysis; (2) from the needs analysis identify target tasks; (3) from the target tasks derive pedagogic task types; (4) grade and sequence the pedagogic tasks; (5) deliver instruction using appropriate methodology; (6) evaluate instruction using criterion-referenced measures of task performance.

Needs analysis and pedagogic task classification

Articulating task-based needs analysis and task design has two consequences for task classification criteria. They should be consistent with (that is, map on to, in conceptually coherent, and operationally feasible ways) the *behaviours* involving language use identified by the needs analysis.

And using the criteria to grade and sequence pedagogic tasks should facilitate both language *performance* (access to and effective deployment of existing L2 knowledge under increasingly demanding processing conditions) as well as language *development* (since in many cases learners will not only have to execute what they know of the L2 more effectively to be successful on target tasks, but also acquire new L2 knowledge).

While accepting that needs analysis is necessary, however, other approaches to L2 instructional design adopt different units of analysis, classifying the language (not tasks) needed to communicate in a 'purposive domain', and then using this (sociolinguistic, rhetorical functional) linguistic classification as a basis for the syllabus (e.g. Crombie, 1985; Munby, 1978). Consistent, in methodological principle, with language-based needs analyses some recent approaches to task-based instruction advocate using tasks as a means of delivering a linguistically (at least in part) specified and sequenced syllabus (Johnson, 1996; Nunan, 2004; Willis, 1990). Others have argued that a needs analysis, of any kind, is not necessary, opting to base syllabus design, and task classification decisions on intuitively determined estimates of the difficulty of pedagogic tasks (Prabhu, 1987), or on decisions about how sequences of tasks can lead to the balanced development of linguistic accuracy, fluency and complexity, defined independently of specific target task demands (Skehan, 1998).

Task classification and ability assessment

Proposals for the use of tasks in instructed L2 settings differ not only with respect to the nature, or necessity, of needs analysis, but also in the importance they attach to, and so the provision they make for, assessing learner abilities and individualising instruction. While task-based approaches have often been claimed to be learner-centred (e.g. Candlin, 1987; Nunan, 1993) very few have described in any detail how pedagogic tasks could be articulated with ability-requirement analyses, with the aim of matching learners to, and supporting performance during, instructional options in task practice, and sequencing. Elsewhere a distinction has been made (Robinson, 2001a, 2001b) between *task complexity* (dependent on differences in the intrinsic processing demands of tasks, such as simple addition versus calculus, or exchanging business cards, versus conducting business meetings in the L2) and *task difficulty* (dependent on the abilities learners bring to tasks, such as aptitude for math, or for L2 learning and use). Task complexity, and levels of cognitive abilities affecting perceptions of task difficulty clearly *interact* in differentiating success on tasks for L2 learners, and also the linguistic outcomes (accuracy, fluency and complexity) of L2 task performance. However, the relative lack of progress in researching the important issues of how they do interact, and of which abilities are most widely predictive of differential L2 success, and variation in linguistic performance, no doubt hinges on the absence of currently agreed criteria for classifying, and distinguishing between, the most pedagogically relevant information processing demands of tasks. This itself partly reflects the absence of an agreed set of superordinate task categories and a classificatory system that relates them to SLA processes and L2 performance demands in a principled way. This is the issue to which we turn next.

Constraints on Classificatory Systems and Criteria for Classifying Tasks

A classificatory system has structure, providing a means of ordering or arranging entities and phenomena (e.g. plants, or pedagogic tasks) into groups or sets (e.g. green or not green, requiring one-way or two-way information exchange) on the basis of properties groups or sets share (see Sokal, 1974). In the cases just given, the classificatory criteria are simply assigned, to plants and to tasks, on the basis of descriptive properties they share, such as colour, or direction of information flow. But such descriptive taxonomies are inadequate when it comes to explaining, for example, why some plants when eaten lead to sickness or not, or why some tasks lead to learning or not. In the case of L2 pedagogic tasks, therefore, the first constraint a classificatory system should attempt to accommodate is that it be *motivated by a theory* of how performing tasks, and in a particular order, using the system, has causal effects on learning and development, and also on improvements in L2 performance and use. Meeting this constraint should help ensure that research into task classification is not simply descriptive, and that if tasks do have predicted effects, then deeper theoretical principles guiding their design can be generalised to other aspects of classification and sequencing.

For operational reasons it is also important that the L2 task classificatory system meet two other constraints. It should be *empirically researchable*, identifying characteristics and dimensions that predict effects found in controlled experimental settings, formal classroom settings, and in contexts of real world use of the L2. Meeting this constraint allows confidence in decision-making about the articulation of target task demands and pedagogic task design, and promotes understanding of the extent to which the abilities developed during classroom performance on tasks sharing a characteristic, transfer, and generalise beyond it. Thirdly, the classificatory system should be *operationally feasible*, permitting classification and design of a wide range of pedagogic tasks reliably and consistently, by researchers and teachers, in a way that relates to a wide range of target task performances. Meeting this constraint ensures the system is not unmanageably broad, and that task classification in one programme, by one group of teachers/designers, is comparable to decisions made by others elsewhere using the same system.

Early lists of task characteristics

Currently, no classificatory system is accepted as a shared basis for research or educational decision-making by task-based language learning researchers, programme designers and teachers. In the absence of research findings, early proposals for task characteristics affecting the 'difficulty' of tasks resulted in intuitive, often insightful, lists of factors such as cognitive load, communicative stress, and code complexity (Candlin, 1987); lack of cultural knowledge, confidence and motivation (Brindley, 1987); and the transition from easier information gap, to reasoning gap, to more difficult opinion gap activities (Prabhu, 1987; see Robinson, 2001b for an extensive review). More recent empirical research into task effects on language production has led to further proposals for pedagogically relevant task characteristics. For example, Skehan (2001) describing his analyses of learner production on three 'task types' (a personal task, a narrative task, and a decision-making task – chosen because they represent common task types in EFL coursebooks) identified five characteristics that seemed to significantly affect performance across them, including the degree of structure the task has, whether it was dialogic or monologic, and whether the required outcome was complex or not.

Bearing in mind the theoretical, researchable and feasible constraints on classificatory systems described above, three broad categories of criteria emerge from these, and other, proposals so far made for classifying L2 task characteristics and their demands on learners. These can each be further divided into subcategories, having a systematic hierarchical relation to each other; *interactional* criteria, *cognitive* criteria, and *ability-determinant* criteria. Table 1.2 illustrates these categories, and describes the criteria and analytic procedures to be followed in assigning task characteristics to one or the other.

Interactional criteria for classifying L2 tasks

Most of the early work (which of course continues today) on identifying acquisitionally relevant characteristics of L2 tasks focused on *interactional criteria* for distinguishing them, following proposals by Hatch (1978), Long (1983) and others that interaction is an important context and opportunity for activating processes thought to contribute to SLA. Characteristics of tasks studied for their contribution (both quantitative and qualitative) to opportunities for L2 interaction can be further subclassified into those distinguished on the basis of participation variables (the nature of the solution to, and direction of information flow on, tasks) and on the basis of participant variables (how different configurations of participants affect the amount and quality of interaction). Task characteristics distinguished on the basis of *participation* variables include: (1) whether the solution to the task is optional (open) or fixed (closed); (2) whether information exchange goes from A to B (one-way), or is reciprocal (two-way); (3) whether agreement is required (convergent) or the opposite (divergent); (4) whether there

Table 1.2 Pedagogic L2 task classification – categories, criteria, analytic procedures, and characteristics

Task complexity	*Task condition*	*Task difficulty*
(Cognitive factors)	(Interactive factors)	(Learner factors)
(Classification criteria: cognitive demands)	(Classification criteria: interactional demands)	(Classification criteria: ability requirements)
(Classification procedure: information-theoretic analyses)	(Classification procedure: behaviour descriptive analyses)	(Classification procedure: ability assessment analyses)
Sub-categories:	Sub-categories:	Sub-categories:
(a) Resource-directing variables making cognitive/conceptual demands	(a) Participation variables making interactional demands	(a) Ability variables and task relevant resource differentials
+/− here and now (Robinson, 1995)	+/− open solution (Long, 1989)	h/1 working memory (Mackey *et al.*, 2002)
+/− few elements (Kuiken *et al.*, 2005)	+/− one way flow (Pica *et al.*, 1993)	h/1 reasoning (Stanovitch, 1999)
−/+ spatial reasoning (Becker & Carroll, 1997)	+/− convergent solution (Duff, 1986)	h/1 task-switching (Monsell, 2003)
−/+ causal reasoning (Robinson, 2005a)	+/− few participants (Crookes, 1986)	h/1 aptitude (Robinson, 2005b)
−/+ intentional reasoning (Baron-Cohen, 1995)	+/− few contributions needed (McGrath, 1984)	h/1 field independence (Skehan, 1998)
−/+ perspective-taking (MacWhinney, 1999)	+/− negotiation not needed (Long, 1983)	h/1 mind-reading (Langdon *et al.*, 2002)

(continued)

Table 1.2 (*Continued*)

Task complexity	*Task condition*	*Task difficulty*
(b) Resource-dispersing variables making performative/procedural demands	(b) Participant variables making interactant demands	(b) Affective variables and task relevant state-trait differentials
+/– planning time (Skehan, 1998)	+/– same proficiency (Yule & MacDonald, 1990)	h/l openness (Costa & Macrae, 1985)
+/– prior knowledge (Urwin, 1999)	+/– same gender (Pica et al., 1991)	h/l control of emotion (Mayer et al., 2000)
+/– single task (Robinson et al., 1995)	+/– familiar (Plough & Gass, 1993)	h/l task motivation (Dornyei, 2002)
+/– task structure (Skehan & Foster, 1999)	+/– shared content knowledge (Pica et al., 1993)	l/h processing anxiety (MacIntyre & Gardner, 1994)
+/– few steps (Fleishman & Quaintance, 1984)	+/– equal status and role (Yule & MacDonald, 1990)	h/l willingness to communicate (MacIntyre, 2002)
+/– independency of steps (Romiszowski, 1988)	+/– shared cultural knowledge (Brindley, 1987)	h/l self-efficacy (Bandura, 1997)

are few, or many participants in the interaction; (5) whether only one or a few individual contributions to the interaction are needed, versus more; (6) and whether contributions to interaction require no, or little, versus extensive negotiation.

Task characteristics distinguished on the basis of *participant* variables include: (1) whether learners are the same, or different proficiency level; (2) the same or different gender; (3) familiar or unfamiliar with each other; (4) whether they share, or do not share, knowledge of a domain; (5) whether they have the same role in a task with respect to status, institutional/social standing, position in the workplace, seniority, etc., or not; (6) and whether they share, or do not, relevant cultural knowledge about how interactions are conducted in the L2. All of these characteristics can be identified using the behaviour descriptive analytic procedures used at the needs analysis stage of target task description, mentioned above (cf. Table 1.1). Table 1.2 summarises these subcategories, and task characteristics relevant to each, together with cited representative studies and/or theoretical discussion of them.

Cognitive criteria for classifying tasks

Following on from studies of the effects of task characteristics on stimulating interaction, and influenced by cognitive processing accounts of SLA by amongst others McLaughlin (1987), Schmidt (1990), and Bialystok (1994) current research has proposed *cognitive criteria* for distinguishing task characteristics (where, by 'cognitive', what is meant is the extent to which task characteristics can affect the allocation of an individual's attention, memory, reasoning and other processing resources). These characteristics are identified using the information-theoretic task analytic procedures referred to above, and can be further divided into two subcategories (see Table 1.2).

The first subcategory distinguishes task characteristics on the basis of the concepts that the task requires to be expressed and understood (e.g. relative time, spatial location, causal relationships, and intentionality). Elsewhere these are called 'resource-directing' cognitive dimensions of tasks (Robinson, 2003). Clearly, conceptualisation is more or less demanding of cognitive resources. This is evidenced, for example, by the staged emergence of conceptual abilities – and their linguistic expression – in childhood (Cromer, 1991), and by similar stages in the ability to mark and code them linguistically in the L2 during adult naturalistic second language acquisition (Perdue, 1993). Expending the mental effort needed to make more demanding *cognitive/conceptual* distinctions in language should therefore prime learners – and direct their attentional and memory resources – to aspects of the L2 system required to accurately understand and convey them, thereby facilitating 'noticing' of these, and so speeding up L2 grammaticisation in conceptual domains. Proposed resource-directing variables distinguishing task characteristics include: (1) whether the task requires reference to events happening now, in a mutually shared context (Here-and-Now) versus to events that occurred in the past, elsewhere (There-and-Then); (2) reference to few, easily distinguished, versus many similar elements; (3) reference to spatial location, where easily identifiable and mutually known landmarks can be used, versus reference to location without this support; (4) simple information transmission, versus reasoning about causal events and relationships between them; (5) simple information transmission, versus reasoning about other people intentions, beliefs and desires and relationships between them; (6) and whether the task requires the speaker/listener to take just one first-person perspective on an event, or multiple second, and third person perspectives.

In contrast to resource-directing variables are those that make increased *performative/procedural* demands on participants' attentional and memory resources, but do not direct them to any aspect of the linguistic system which can be of communicative value in performing a task. Meeting these demands during pedagogic task performance therefore should facilitate not development, and acquisition of new L2 form-concept mappings (what Bialystok, 1994, has called 'analysis'), but rather automatic access to an already established interlanguage system (what Bialystok has called 'control'). These resource-dispersing (Robinson, 2003) variables include those that distinguish task characteristics on the basis of: (1) giving planning time (and so increasing resource availability) versus not giving it; (2) providing background knowledge needed for task performance, versus not giving it; (3) tasks requiring only one thing to be done, versus those requiring two (dual) or many (multiple) things to be done simultaneously; (4) tasks where there is a clear structure available to help on deciding which steps are needed to complete it, versus those without one; (5) tasks where one or few steps are needed to complete it, versus those requiring many steps; (6) and tasks where there is no necessary sequence or 'chain' in which steps are followed, versus those which require participants to follow a strictly chained sequence, in which one step must be performed before another.

The cognitive factors, and subcategories of task characteristics described here, therefore expand on some previous proposals for pedagogically relevant task characteristics mentioned above. For example, Candlin's (1987) 'cognitive load' (which he argued makes tasks more difficult) has been divided into two theoretically motivated subcategories of resource-directing, and resource-dispersing variables, which are proposed to have differential effects on learning, and performance. Resource-directing variables distinguish task characteristics on the basis of the conceptual demands they make, while resource-dispersing variables distinguish task characteristics on the basis of the procedural demands they make. Brindley's 'lack of relevant cultural knowledge' characteristic, which he argued makes tasks more difficult, is captured in the distinction made between tasks where background knowledge (whether cultural or not) is available versus absent. And Skehan's '+ task structure' characteristic, making tasks less difficult, has been accommodated, alongside other related characteristics that affect performative/procedural demands, such as the number of steps a task requires to be performed, and whether these are strictly sequenced.

Ability-determinant criteria for classifying tasks

Early lists of characteristics thought to affect second language task performance and learning also included various *affective* variables, such as 'communicative stress' (Candlin, 1987), and 'confidence and motivation' (Brindley, 1987). Undoubtedly these are likely, in many cases, to be related to task-based learning and performance in both negative and positive ways, but they cannot be used to make *a priori* sequencing decisions about tasks for groups of learners, since learners in any one group will vary greatly from each other with respect to each of them. Similarly, learners will differ from each other with respect to their strengths in cognitive *abilities*, such as working memory capacity, drawn on during task performance. Task classification and design, and sequencing based on the interactive factors (Task Conditions), and cognitive factors (Task Complexity) in Table 1.2 are, therefore, the logical basis of L2 syllabuses for *groups* of learners.

Information about learner factors, and how they relate to success in meeting the cognitive and interactional demands pedagogic tasks make, is essential to optimising the chances of success for learners, and for program level decisions about individualising instruction, but as yet there is little research into this. Once the relevant learner factors are identified, and their interaction with various cognitive and interactive characteristics of tasks established, this information could be used to deliver level 3 of programme design illustrated in Table 1.1, i.e. matching learners to, and/or supporting their performance on the various tasks specified in the syllabus. Table 1.2 makes some proposals for likely relevant ability and affective variables. On the whole, *ability* variables would seem to be most strongly related to the perceived 'difficulty' of performance on tasks making cognitive demands, and contributing to their cognitive *task complexity*, in Table 1.2. Suggested relevant ability variables include the ability to switch quickly between component tasks during tasks requiring dual and multiple-task performance; and also working memory capacity; reasoning abilities; various abilities proposed to underlie L2 learning aptitude; field independence; and mind-reading, i.e. the ability to successfully attribute intentions to others in conversational interaction.

In contrast, *affective* variables would seem to be more predictive of the perceived 'difficulty' of *interactional task demands*. Possibly predictive affective variables include willingness to communicate; input, processing and output anxiety; openness to experience; self-regulation and the ability to control emotion; task specific motivation; and self-efficacy. These are each described as high (h), or low (l) in Table 1.2, but clearly in most usual, non-selected instructed L2 populations individual differences will be distributed normally and continuously. And even in non-usual populations (because, for example, they are selected for language training on the basis of specific occupationally relevant abilities and dispositions, such as doctors and nurses) variance in such ability and affective variables can be population-normed and related to task-based learning outcomes.

Interactions of abilities, affect, and task demands

Some research has begun to examine the influence of several of these variables on the linguistic outcomes of pedagogic task performance (amount of interaction, uptake, utterance complexity, etc.) (see e.g. Dornyei, 2002, on task-specific motivation, and Niwa, 2000, on working memory capacity). However, much more research, and conceptualisation, is clearly needed. A coherent way for this to proceed is to examine the influence of ability and affective variables on interaction, uptake of focus on form, and the accuracy, fluency and complexity of speech while performing tasks having one or another of the cognitive and interactional characteristics listed in Table 1.2. This will be not only of practical value, but will also help clarify the facts surrounding some theoretical claims that have been made about the effects of task characteristics on L2 speech production and learning. For example, Skehan (1998) has argued that increasing the cognitive, and so attentional demands of tasks in ways described above will have negative effects on the accuracy, fluency and complexity of learner production. I agree that this will likely be so for resource-dispersing variables, such as planning time, or single task, since these make increased *performative/procedural demands*, relative to less cognitively demanding counterpart characteristics, and so cause problems for learners attempting to 'access' their current interlanguage system. But in contrast to Skehan, and consistent with claims of the Cognition Hypothesis of task-based learning and task sequencing (Robinson, 2001b, 2005a), I argue that increasing task complexity by making increased *cognitive/conceptual demands*, such as + causal reasoning, will lead learners to complexify their speech to meet the increased conceptual and functional demands of the task. Such increases should also lead to greater attempts at L2 grammaticisation, and greater accuracy relative to simpler versions. However, these effects may perhaps be strongest in learners high in the abilities the particular resource-directing variable draws on, such as causal reasoning (see Stanovitch, 1999). Within group variance in these abilities would therefore mask these predicted effects. Some of these issues are briefly taken up in the section which follows.

Task Classification and Sequencing

The categories and task characteristics described in Table 1.2 are integral to the 'Cognition Hypothesis' of task classification and sequencing, referred to above. But these categories and characteristics can also be related to two other proposals for sequencing tasks, the 'Skills Hypothesis' (Johnson, 1996), and the 'Capacity Hypothesis' (Skehan, 1998). Each of these differs in theoretical SLA motivation for pedagogic task sequencing decisions. They also differ over which task characteristics in Table 1.2 are to be used in the design and sequencing of tasks; and with respect to how sequencing decisions are related to needs analysis and target task performance. A brief summary of these differences is offered here.

The Skills Hypothesis and task sequencing

The first of these is a proposal for adding a 'processing dimension' to the linguistic criteria used in grading and sequencing tasks, to facilitate the skilled learning of content identified in a language-based needs analysis (e.g. Munby, 1978). Johnson claims that functions, structures and other linguistic units need to be presented to learners in sequences of activities (called tasks) that facilitate the *automatisation* of declarative knowledge of these forms. To do this, following initial focus on forms learners should be put 'in a position where they have less attention available (one unit less, as it were) than they actually need to perform a task with comfort' (Johnson, 1996: 139). This is done by shifting the focus of exercise sequences making up 'tasks' to more demanding conceptual content, thereby withdrawing attention from forms and facilitating automatic access to them during 'task' performance. In terms of Table 1.2 (although Johnson does not describe task characteristics in these ways), this would involve initially presenting exercises low in the cognitive/procedural demands (e.g. + planning time, + single task) and in their conceptual/communicative demands (e.g. + few elements, + no reasoning) and then gradually presenting exercises higher in both these categories of task complexity.

The Capacity Hypothesis and task sequencing

Johnson's proposal is one for using tasks to deliver a linguistic syllabus, and sequencing is based on theories of automaticity and skill acquisition. Skehan's 'Capacity Hypothesis' makes a similar proposal, i.e. more demanding tasks 'consume more attentional resources ... with the result that less attention is available for focus on form' (Skehan, 1998: 97), therefore sequencing tasks from less cognitively demanding to more demanding optimises opportunities for attention allocation to language form. Task design is also seen as a means to promote 'balanced language development' in the areas of accuracy, fluency and complexity of production. This can be done because certain task characteristics 'predispose learners to channel their attention in predictable ways, such as clear macrostructure towards accuracy, the need to impose order on ideas towards complexity, and so on' (Skehan, 1998: 112). However, due to scarcity of attentional resources, tasks can lead either to increased complexity, or accuracy of production, but not

WATERFORD INSTITUTE OF TECHNOLOGY LIBRARY CLASS 418·007 ACC. NO 147701 to both. Tasks should therefore be sequenced by choosing those with characteristics that lead to each, at an appropriate level of difficulty, as determined by three factors: (1) *code complexity* is described in 'fairly traditional ways', as in descriptions of structural syllabuses, or developmental sequences (Skehan, 1998: 99); (2) *cognitive complexity* is the result of the *familiarity* of the task, topic or genre, and the *processing* requirements; information type, clarity and organisation, and amount of computation required; and (3) *communicative stress* involves six characteristics including time pressure, number of participants, and opportunities to control interaction. Unlike Johnson, Skehan does not use tasks to deliver and practice a linguistic syllabus, and tasks are sequenced from less to more difficult to minimise what he argues are the negative effects, given limited attentional capacity, of increased cognitive and attentional demands on linguistic performance. The goals of task-based instruction are to promote language development in the areas of accuracy, fluency and complexity of speech, as well as comprehension, and task selection and classification is not constrained by the need to articulate pedagogic tasks with target tasks identified in a needs analysis.

The Cognition Hypothesis and task sequencing

Despite some similarity of emphasis on the information processing demands of tasks, unlike these proposals, the Cognition Hypothesis assumes behaviour descriptions of target tasks for populations of learners are the starting point for pedagogic task design, as illustrated in Table 1.1. Based on behaviour descriptions the interactional demands of target tasks are classified using the task characteristics in Table 1.2, distinguishing them in terms of participation and participant variables. Similarly, the cognitive demands are classified using those characteristics distinguishing them in terms of cognitive/conceptual, and performative/procedural demands. These classifications are the basis on which pedagogic tasks are designed and subsequently sequenced.

Interactional demands of pedagogic tasks *are not graded and sequenced*. The task conditions, e.g. $+/-$ one way flow, $+/-$ equal status and role, are replicated each time pedagogic task versions are performed. A rationale for this, offered only briefly here, is that holding task conditions constant is important to ensuring transfer of training to real-world contexts. The more task conditions are practiced in pedagogic versions, the more elaborate and consolidated the scripts become for real-world performance, and on which successful transfer will draw, outside the classroom. *Cognitive demands* of pedagogic tasks, however, *are graded and sequenced*. Simpler versions with respect to all relevant cognitive demand characteristics are performed first, and then task complexity (i.e. cognitive demands) is gradually increased on subsequent versions to target task levels. Task complexity is therefore the *sole* basis of pedagogic task sequencing.

There are *two stages* in which task complexity is increased, and which are decision points for task and syllabus design. In each sequence of pedagogic tasks, relevant resource-dispersing variables are first increased in complexity (so if the target task requires dual task performance, without planning time, then planning time is provided, and the dual task characteristics are performed separately). The rationale for this is to first promote access to, and consolidate the learner's current L2 interlanguage system during pedagogic task performance. Subsequently increasing performative and procedural demands to target task levels, thereby promotes increased automatic access to, and learner 'control' over, the current system in responding to pedagogic task demands.

In the second stage, once the performative/procedural demands have reached target like levels, then cognitive/conceptual demands are gradually increased to target like levels. As described above, I argue these can direct learners attentional and memory resources to aspects of the L2 system needed to code increasingly complex concepts, and to meet increasingly complex functional demands requiring their expression in language. This promotes analysis and development of the current interlanguage system. Increasing these demands should lead to more *accurate* and *complex* learner production, more *noticing* of task relevant input, and heightened memory for it, and so lead to more *uptake* of forms made salient in the input through various focus on form interventions.

More complete rationales for these claims, both developmentally, and in terms of attentional and memory theory, are given elsewhere (Robinson, 2001b, 2003, 2005a). Of course, increasing task complexity in the way just described during pedagogic task performance is not the only way more accurate and complex learner production, and more noticing and uptake of forms in the input, can be promoted. But it is consistent with a theory of how task-based learning and syllabus design can promote all four through sequencing decisions. Whether these proposals for L2 instructional design, and the claims of the Cognition Hypothesis which support them, are empirically substantiable and feasible are issues both practice, and research into the effects of task characteristics described in this chapter, will resolve together.

References

Bandura, A. (1997) *Self-Efficacy: The Exercise of Control*. New York: W.H. Freeman & Co.

Baron-Cohen, S. (1995) *Mindblindness*. Cambridge, MA: MIT Press.

Becker, A. and Carroll, M. (eds) (1997) *The Acquisition of Spatial Relations in a Second Language*. Amsterdam: Benjamins.

Bialystok, E. (1994) Analysis and control in the development of second language proficiency. *Studies in Second Language Acquisition* 16, 157–168.

Bloom, B.S. (1956) (ed.) *Taxonomy of Educational Objectives: Handbook 1, Cognitive Domain*. New York: McKay.

Brindley, G. (1987) Factors affecting task difficulty. In D. Nunan (ed.) *Guidelines for the Development of Curriculum Resources* (pp. 45–56). Adelaide National Curriculum Resource Centre.

Bygate, M., Skehan, P. and Swain, M. (eds) (2001) *Researching Pedagogic Tasks: Second Language Learning, Teaching and Testing.* Harlow: Longman.

Candlin, C. (1987) Towards task-based language learning. In C. Candlin and D. Murphy (eds) *Language Learning Tasks* (pp. 5–22). London: Prentice Hall.

Carroll, J.B. (1993). *Human Cognitive Abilities: A Survey of Factor-Analytic Studies.* New York: Cambridge University Press.

Costa, P.T. and McCrae, R.R. (1985) *The NEO Personality Inventory Manual.* Odessa, FL: Psychological Assessment Resources, Inc.

Crombie, W. (1985) *Discourse and Language Learning: A Relational Approach to Syllabus Design.* Oxford: Oxford University Press.

Cromer, R. (1991) *Language and Thought in Normal and Handicapped Children.* Oxford: Blackwell.

Crookes, G. (1986) *Task Classification: A Cross-Disciplinary Review.* Center for Second Language Classroom Research, Technical Report # 4, University of Hawaii.

Dornyei, Z. (2002) The motivational basis of language learning tasks. In P. Robinson (ed.) *Individual Differences and Instructed Language Learning* (pp. 137–158). Amsterdam: Benjamins.

Duff, P. (1986). Another look at interlanguage talk: Taking task to task. In R. Day (ed.) *Talking to Learn: Conversation in Second Language Development* (pp. 147–181). Rowley, MA: Newbury House.

Ellis, R. (ed.) (2005) *Planning and Task Performance in a Second Language.* Amsterdam: Benjamins.

Fine, S.P. (1974) Functional job analysis: An approach to technology for manpower planning. *Personnel Journal* 11, 813–818.

Fleishman, E.A. and Quaintance, M.K. (1984) *Taxonomies of Human Performance: The Description of Human Tasks.* New York: Academic Press.

Gagne, R.M., Wager, W.W., Golas, K.C. and Keller, J.M. (2005) *Principles of Instructional Design* (5th edn). Belmont, CA: Thomson, Wadsworth.

Hatch, E. (1978) Discourse analysis and second language acquisition. In E. Hatch (ed.) *Second Language Acquisition: A Book of Readings* (pp. 402–435). Rowley, MA: Newbury House.

Hollnagel, E. (ed.) (2001) *Handbook of Cogniitive Task Analysis.* Mahwah, NJ: Erlbaum.

Johnson, K. (1996) *Language Teaching and Skill Learning.* Oxford. Blackwell.

Kuiken, F., Mos, M. and Vedder, I. (2005) Cognitive task complexity and second language writing performance. In S. Foster-Cohen, M.P. García-Mayo and J. Cenoz (eds) *Eurosla Yearbook* (Vol. 5) (pp. 195–222). Amsterdam: Benjamins.

Langdon, R., Coltheart, M., Ward, P. and Catts, S. (2002) Disturbed communication in schizophrenia: The role of pragmatics and poor theory-of-mind. *Psychological Medicine* 32, 1273–1284.

Long, M.H. (1983) Native speaker/non native speaker conversation and the negotiation of comprehensible input. *Applied Linguistics,* 4, 126–141.

Long, M.H. (1989) Task, group, and task-group interactions. *University of Hawai'i Working Papers in ESL* 8, 1–25.

Long, M.H. (1998) Focus on form in task-based language teaching. *University of Hawaii Working Papers in ESL* 16, 49–61.

Long, M.H. (ed.) (2005) *Second Language Learning Needs Analysis.* Cambridge: Cambridge University Press.

MacIntyre, P. (2002) Motivation, anxiety and emotion in second language acquisition. In P. Robinson (ed.) *Individual Differences and Instructed Language Learning* (pp. 45–64). Amsterdam: Benjamins.

MacIntyre, P. and Gardner, R. (1994) The subtle effects of language anxiety on cognitive processing in the second language. *Language Learning* 44, 283–305.

Mackey, A., Philp, J., Egi, T., Fujii, A. and Tatsumi, T. (2002) Individual differences in working memory, noticing of interactional feedback and L2 development. In P. Robinson (ed.) *Individual Differences and Instructed Language Learning* (pp. 181–210). Amsterdam: Benjamins.

MacWhinney, B. (1999) The emergence of language from embodiment. In B. MacWhinney (ed.) *The Emergence of Language* (pp. 213–256). Mahwah, NJ: Erlbaum.

Matthews, G. and Deary, I. (1998) *Personality Traits.* Cambridge: Cambridge University Press.

Mayer, J.D., Salovey, P. and Caruso, D. (2000) Models of emotional intelligence. In R.J. Sternberg (ed.) *Handbook of Intelligence* (pp. 396–420). New York: Cambridge University Press.

McCormick, E.J. (1979) *Job Analysis: Methods and Applications.* New York: AMACOM Publishing.

McGrath, J. (1984) *Groups: Interaction and Performance.* Englewood Cliffs, NJ: Prentice Hall.

McLaughlin, B. (1987) *Theories of Second Language Learning.* London: Arnold.

Monsell, S. (2003) Task switching. *Trends in Cognitive Sciences* 7 (3), 134–140.

Munby, J. (1978) *Communicative Syllabus Design.* Cambridge: Cambridge University Press.

Niwa, Y. (2000). Reasoning demands of L2 tasks and L2 narrative production: Effects of individual differences in working memory, intelligence and aptitude. Unpublished MA dissertation, Department of English, Aoyama Gakuin University, Japan.

Norris, J., Brown, J.D., Hudson, T. and Yoshioka, J. (1998) Developing second language performance tests. University of Hawaii Second Language Teaching and Curriculum Center Technical Report # 19: University of Hawaii Press.

Nunan, D. (1993) Task-based syllabus design: Selecting, grading and sequencing tasks. In G. Crookes and S. Gass (eds) *Tasks in a Pedagogic Context: Integrating Theory and Practice* (pp. 55–68). Clevedon: Multilingual Matters.

Nunan, D. (2004) *Task-based Language Teaching.* New York: Cambridge University Press.

Perdue, C. (ed.) (1993) *Adult Language Acquisition: Crosslinguistic Perspectives Vol. 2: The Results.* Cambridge: Cambridge University Press.

Pica, T., Holliday, L., Lewis, N., Berducci, D. and Newman, J. (1991) Language learning through interaction: What role does gender play? *Studies in Second Language Acquisition* 13, 343–376.

Pica, T., Kanagy, R. and Falodun, J. (1993) Choosing and using communication tasks for second language teaching and research. In G. Crookes and S. Gass (eds) *Tasks and Language Learning: Integrating Theory and Practice* (pp. 1–34). Clevedon, Avon: Multilingual Matters.

Plough, I. and Gass, S. (1993) Interlocutor and task familiarity: Effects on Interactional structure. In G. Crookes and S. Gass (eds) *Tasks and Language Learning: Integrating Theory and Practice* (pp. 95–122). Clevedon, Avon: Multilingual Matters.

Prabhu, N.S. (1987) *Second Language Pedagogy.* Oxford: Oxford University Press.

Reigeluth, C.M. (1999) What is instructional-design theory and how is it changing? In C.M. Reigeluth (ed.) *Instructional-Design Theories and Models* (Vol. II) (pp. 5–30). Mahwah, NJ: Erlbaum.

Robinson, P. (1995) Task complexity and second language narrative discourse. *Language Learning* 45, 99–140.

Robinson, P. (1996) Connecting tasks, cognition and syllabus design. In P. Robinson (ed.) *Task Complexity and Second Language Syllabus Design: Data-Based Studies and Speculations* (pp. 1–16). Brisbane: University of Queensland Working Papers in Applied Linguistics.

Robinson, P. (2001a) Task complexity, task difficulty, and task production: Exploring interactions in a componential framework. *Applied Linguistics* 22, 27–57.

Robinson, P. (2001b) Task complexity, cognitive resources, and syllabus design: A triadic framework for investigating task influences on SLA. In P. Robinson (ed.) *Cognition and Second Language Instruction* (pp. 287–318). Cambridge: Cambridge University Press.

Robinson, P. (2003) Attention and memory during SLA. In C. Doughty and M.H. Long (eds) *Handbook of Second Language Acquisition* (pp. 631–678). Oxford: Blackwell.

Robinson, P. (2005a) Cognitive complexity and task sequencing: A review of studies in a Componential Framework for second language task design. *International Review of Applied Linguistics in Language Teaching* 43 (1), 1–33.

Robinson, P. (2005b) Aptitude and second language acquisition. *Annual Review of Applied Linguistics* 25, 45–73.

Robinson, P. and Ross, S. (1996) The development of task-based testing in English for Academic Purposes programs. *Applied Linguistics* 17, 523–549.

Robinson, P., Ting, S. and Urwin, J. (1995) Investigating second language task complexity. *RELC Journal* 25, 62–79.

Romiszowski, A.J. (1988) *Designing Instructional Systems: Decision Making in Course Planning and Curriculum.* Abingdon, UK: RoutledgeFarmer.

Schmidt, R. (1990) The role of consciousness in second language learning. *Applied Linguistics* 11, 127–158.

Seamster, T.L., Redding, R.E. and Kaemf, G.L. (1997) *Applied Cognitive Task Analysis in Aviation.* Avebury, UK: Ashgate Publishing.

Skehan, P. (1998) *A Cognitive Approach to Language Learning.* Oxford: Oxford University Press.

Skehan, P. (2001) Tasks and language performance assessment. In M. Bygate, P. Skehan and M. Swain (eds) *Researching Pedagogic Tasks* (pp. 167–185). London: Longman.

Skehan, P. and Foster, P. (1999) The influence of task structure and processing conditions on narrative retellings. *Language Learning* 49, 93–120.

Snow, R.E., Kyllonen, P.C. and Marshalek, B. (1984) The topography of ability and learning correlations. In R.J. Sternberg (ed.) *Advances in the Psychology of Human Intelligence* (pp. 47–103). Hillsdale, NJ: Erlbaum.

Sokal, R.R. (1974) Classification: Purposes, principles, progress, prospects. *Science,* 185, 1115–1123.

Stanovitch, K. (1999) *Who is Rational: Studies of Individual Differences in Reasoning.* Mahwah, NJ: Erlbaum.

Urwin, J. (1999) Second language listening task complexity. Unpublished PhD dissertation, Monash University, Melbourne, Australia.

Williams, R.G. (1977) A behavioral typology of educational objectives for the cognitive domain. *Educational Technology* 17 (6), 418–431.

Willis, D. (1990) *The Lexical Syllabus: A New Approach to Language Teaching.* London: Collins.

Yule, G. and MacDonald, M. (1990) Resolving referential conflicts in L2 interaction: The effect of proficiency and interactive role. *Language Learning* 40, 539–556.

Chapter 2

Information Distribution and Goal Orientation in Second Language Task Design

CRAIG P. LAMBERT and STEVE ENGLER

Introduction

In task-based approaches to second language (L2) education, communication tasks typically require learners to work together and use the L2 functionally in order to solve problems that approximate to some degree the real-world tasks that they have to accomplish outside of the classroom (cf. Long, 2000: 189; Skehan, 1996: 38). Certain factors in the design of such tasks may enable teachers and materials planners to manipulate the nature of the discourse required to complete them and thus improve learning outcomes (see Robinson, 2001; Skehan, 1996: 55). The two design factors investigated in the present study are connected with 'information gap' tasks and are widely used in L2 materials design on the assumption that they facilitate learning. The way in which they do so, however, is far from clear.

Long (1989) argues that information distribution and goal orientation are two task design factors that are directly related to the nature of the discourse learners produce on task. The first of these refers to the way in which the information required to complete the task is distributed at the outset. In contrast to tasks in which the essential information is shared by the participants completing it, Long distinguishes between distributions which produce a one-way and a two-way flow of information. In a one-way configuration, all of the task-essential information is allotted to one learner who must communicate it to the other(s). In a two-way configuration, on the other hand, the task-essential information is distributed between all of the learners who must share and integrate it (Long, 1989: 13). The second design factor Long discusses pertains to the way in which the task orients learners toward the goal of completing it. For an open goal orientation, learners know that there is no correct solution to the task, whereas for a closed goal orientation they know that there is only one or a small range of possible solutions (Long, 1989: 18).

The present study aims to determine whether either of these design factors may be useful for sequencing tasks to support a dual-mode learning system. Skehan (1996) posits fluency, accuracy and complexity as goals for L2 instruction: accuracy is the capacity to handle a current level of interlanguage (IL); fluency is the capacity to use such an IL system in real time; and complexity is the elaboration of an IL system. As attention is essential for learning, and the capacity to pay attention to things while learning is limited, an L2 learner will not be able to meet the demands of real time communication and pay attention to new L2 forms at the same time. It thus seems likely that there will be a trade-off effect between the fluency and the complexity of production. Furthermore, as the tasks employed in task-based L2 courses generally focus learners' attention on meaning, fluency development can dominate at the expense of IL development over time. It is thus important that task-based instruction support a dual-mode system, consisting of both rule-based learning and exemplar-based learning. Rule-based processing will be characterised by complex production, a slower speech rate, reformulations, hesitations and redundancies. Exemplar-based processing, on the other hand, will be characterised by fluent and accurate production of known forms or expressions and avoidance of new or partially mastered forms. For balanced language development, instruction thus needs to provide learners with constant cycles of such analysis and synthesis by sequencing tasks so that an emphasis on restructuring is followed by an emphasis on fluency and accuracy. In this way, the learner's IL system can continue to develop until it is consistent with native-speaker norms, and learners will retain the ability to, '. . . operate a dual-mode system in which well-organized exemplars are available to respond to real-time pressures, but a rule-based system can still be accessed when the need for precision or creativity arises' (Skehan, 1996: 49). If task design factors can be found which produce a trade-off effect between the fluency and the complexity of production, they can be used to support a dual-mode processing system in which rule-based and exemplar based learning, 'combine in a synergistic manner so that the learning outcomes are more than the sum of the parts' (Skehan, 1996: 43). The present study aims to determine the efficacy of information distribution and goal orientation in supporting such a system.

Information distribution

Empirical interest in information distribution began in the early 1980s. At least five studies have appeared which have dealt with its effects on L2 production in one way or another (Crookes & Rulon, 1985; Doughty & Pica, 1986; Foster, 1998; Gass & Varonis, 1985; Pica *et al.*, 1989). The insurmountable problem with these early studies, however, is that information distribution was not examined independently from the tasks used, and there may have been inherent differences in the nature or content of these tasks which could have resulted in any or all of the observed results. This shortcoming severely limits the usefulness of these results in formulating hypotheses about the effects of the information distribution factor itself on L2 production.

In spite of the lack of empirical evidence on the effects of information distribution, however, it is the primary factor in the design of information-gap tasks, which continue to be a staple in L2 classrooms and course books. In light of the continued pervasiveness with which this factor has been employed in L2 teaching and materials design over the past two decades, research is needed which: (1) configures single tasks for each information distribution condition studied so that the effects of information distribution can be observed independently of task type; (2) considers these conditions across at least three distinct task types, most importantly to ensure that the observed results are not task-specific, but also to test the robustness of any observed effects across a range of typical tasks; and (3) provides a comprehensive perspective on all levels of the factor (shared, one-way and two-way) on each task to determine whether these distinctions are meaningful. The present study has been designed to meet these requirements.

Goal orientation

Duff (1986) brought the importance of goal orientation to the attention of L2 researchers in her study of the effects of convergent and divergent tasks on production. Convergent tasks require learners to work together to reach a common solution, whereas divergent tasks require them to defend opposing views. Duff analysed the production of eight participants completing two convergent tasks and two divergent tasks. The convergent tasks required them to select items to prepare for an extended stay on a desert island and to rank characters in a story according to responsibility. The two divergent tasks required them to debate whether television had a positive or negative role in society and whether there is any connection between age and wisdom. It was found that the convergent tasks used resulted in more words and c-units per task, as well as more confirmation checks, referential questions and total questions. The divergent tasks used, on the other hand, resulted in more words per turn, more words per c-unit and more s-nodes per c-unit. There thus seems to have been a trade-off between fluency and complexity in Duff's study, but it is difficult to say whether this resulted from goal orientation or inherent differences in the tasks themselves.

By the 1990s, studies on the effects of open and closed goal orientation on L2 production began to appear. The first two of these replicate the same design with learners of different L2s (English and Spanish). In the first, Rankin (1990) compared the production of 16 learners of English on an open and a closed version of a criterion-based selection task. The open version required them to discuss who of a number of people should survive, and the closed version required them to determine who of a number of people was guilty of a crime. It was found that the closed version resulted in more complex discourse (relative clauses) and incorporatation input than the open version. However, no differences were observed for complexity (s-nodes per t-unit) or accuracy (target-like use of articles). Furthermore, when Mannheimer (1993) replicated Rankin's study with 20 learners of Spanish, it was again found that the closed version of the task resulted in more complex discourse (s-nodes per t-unit) and incorporation of input with no differences in accuracy (target-like use of the *a personal* and the subjunctive). Unfortunately, no attempt was made to measure fluency in either of these studies.

Rankin (1995) then conducted a second study with 30 learners of German on an open and a closed version of a descriptive task. In the open version, participants each had four pictures of an eight picture set of gifts and had to describe them and choose between them. In the closed version, they each had four items on an eight item matrix board and had to describe and place them correctly. This time, however, no differences were found for either complexity (s-nodes per c-unit) or accuracy (appropriate adjective endings per attributive adjective phrase). However, on the open version of the task participants did speak more (total c-units) and engage in more morphological avoidance, whereas on the closed version they engaged in more negotiation of meaning and repaired more morphological mistakes.

Finally, Rahimpour (1997) compared the production of 50 learners of English on an open and a closed version of a narrative task. The open version required them to tell a story based on a picture strip. The closed version required them to do the same thing while someone tried to correctly order the pictures. It was found that the closed version resulted in more fluent speech than the open version (number of words per pause). However, no differences were observed for complexity (s-nodes per t-unit and content words per t-unit) or accuracy (error-free t-units and target-like use of articles).

Thus, the results of previous research on goal orientation are mixed. It even seems possible that the observed effects may have been task-specific: Rankin (1990) and Mannheimer (1993) found similar results when using the same task, but Rankin (1995) and Rahimpour (1997) found quite different results when using different tasks. A study is needed which considers the effects of open and closed goal orientation across task types to ensure that any results are not task-specific and to test their robustness. The present study has been designed to address this need.

Methodology

Design

The present study employed a two-by-three repeated-measures design. The two-level factor was learners' goal orientation, and the levels were 'open' and 'closed'. The three-level factor was information distribution, and the levels were 'shared', 'one-way', and 'two-way'. These conditions were counterbalanced into six treatment orders to control for performance effect and the design was repeated three times with different participants and a different task each time.

Participants

The study was conducted at a private two-year women's college in Japan. The college is rated highly for English education among two-year colleges, and it might be argued that the student body represents a relatively high-motivation subgroup of the population of tertiary-level Japanese English majors. The English programme admitted approximately 250 English majors per year from an annual pool of approximately 1200 applicants. Approximately 500 majors were thus enrolled at any given time. All learners had at least six years of English instruction in secondary school following the structural syllabus of the Japanese Board of Education. In addition, many had supplemented their English education with private classes at cram schools or English conversation schools. Some had also studied, traveled or lived in English-speaking countries. Institutional TOEFL scores typically ranged between about 380 and 520 with outliers at higher levels.

In sampling participants from this population, payment in cash was used as an incentive for participation. Five-hundred copies of a flyer were circulated. The flyer explained that the purpose of the project was to investigate the effectiveness of different types of oral communication tasks for learning English. Participation would require the completion of six communication tasks with a partner similar to those used in regular oral English classes and would take approximately 90 minutes. Participants had to be English majors enrolled at the college, willing to do their best on the tasks, reliable and punctual, willing to be recorded, and available at one of the scheduled times. Those participants meeting these requirements registered on a first come, first serve basis at the researcher's office. Each registered for one of three sessions based on their availability. When 12 learners had registered for a session, it was closed. Thirty-six participants, who received 1200 yen (approximately US$ 12) for their time, registered for the study. All were Japanese females between the ages of 18 and 21.

Materials

Three tasks were used in the study: (1) sequencing pictures into stories; (2) determining who is responsible; (3) arranging times to meet.

Six versions of each of these tasks were created: (1) shared, open; (2) shared, closed; (3) one-way, open; (4) one-way, closed; (5) two-way, open; (6) two-way, closed. The three materials sets were configured for six dyads each and individual booklets were created which counterbalanced the six versions of each task into treatment orders, producing a diagram-based

Latin square design. They also kept the roles of information giver and receiver in the one-way versions of the tasks consistent to control for individual differences. The booklets were translated into Japanese by a native-speaker of the language who was a certified translator to ensure that participants clearly understood their role in the study and how to perform each version of the task in turn.

Task 1: This task required participants to sequence four pictures into a story. The pictures for the different versions were taken from practice versions of an English proficiency test used in Japan (EIKEN) which requires the narration of a story based on a picture strip by continuing a one-sentence prompt. The four-frame picture stories contained Japanese and foreign men, women and children in common social situations (e.g. work, holiday, dining out, etc.) and identical characters were used in many of the stories. Japanese picture strips were chosen as they were more intuitive for the participants and controlled for culturally unfamiliar meanings and situations. Stories were selected for all six versions which contained two distinct primary characters such as a man and a woman or an adult and a child as well as two secondary characters to control for number of elements and referent similarity across conditions.

The closed versions of the task operated on pictures from one original story in a scrambled order. The task was to determine the original order. The directions stressed that there was an original story and thus only one correct solution to the task. The open versions, by contrast, operated on pictures taken from four different stories, but involving similar looking characters. The task was to order them to create a plausible story. The directions stressed that there was no original story and that any order could be a possible solution.

For the shared versions of the task, all four pictures were printed in the same order in both participants' booklets. The directions informed them of this and asked them to show this page of their booklets to one another as they completed it. For the one-way versions, the four pictures were printed in one participant's booklet only and the other's was blank. The directions informed them of this and explained that they must complete the task without showing each other their booklets. Finally, for the two-way versions, two of the pictures were printed in each of the booklets, and the instructions informed them of this, explaining that they must complete the task without showing each other their booklets.

Task 2: This task required participants to determine who was responsible in an unfortunate scenario. The six scenarios all involved loss of life, property or personal injury. Each scenario involved four characters that were specified at the top. The facts of each case were then divided into four parts of similar length (approximately 3 to 4 lines each). The six versions of the task were translated into Japanese to control for L2 reading variables.

The three closed versions involved deliberate crimes and the loss was the direct responsibility of one person. The task was to consider the facts provided in the four parts and determine which of the four suspects was guilty. The directions stressed that only one person committed the crime and that the other three were innocent. There was thus only one correct solution to the task. For the three open versions, the loss was the result of an unintentional mishap in which four characters were all involved in different ways. The task was to determine who was the most responsible. The directions stressed that no one was clearly innocent and that all were partially responsible. There was thus no correct solution to the task. The distribution of the four parts of the information was handled in the same way as in Task 1 above. The directions concerning its use were also identical.

Task 3: This task required participants to arrange times for four people with divergent schedules to meet. Each of the four schedules was represented by a four-by-four grid with times of the day along the vertical axis and days of the week along the horizontal axis. Each schedule had three different time slots filled with an event. If all four schedules were combined, there were only four time slots left in which all four people were free. There were then four events to schedule for the four people. These were specified at the top. All six versions of the task thus operated on four schedules and four events.

The closed versions of the task operated on events which were only appropriate for specific times of the day and week. They could thus only be scheduled into the time slots which were open on the four schedules in a specific combination, and the task was to find that combination. The directions stressed that there was only one solution. For the open versions, the four events were appropriate for any time. They could thus be scheduled into any slot open on all four schedules in any combination. Any solution was equally acceptable, and the directions stressed that there was no correct solution. The distribution of the four schedules was handled in the same way as in Tasks 1 and 2 above. The directions concerning the use of this information were also identical.

Procedures

The data were collected in three sessions. The seating and tape recorders were prepared in the designated room prior to each session. There were six stations arranged for two participants each with a cassette recorder. Participants took seats at separate stations as they arrived until all six stations had one participant at it. The next six participants were then randomly paired with these as they arrived.

All participants were familiar with the room and used to having classes in it. The researcher was a full-time teacher at the college, and the participants knew him. Although the participants were not familiar with the tasks used in the study, they were accustomed to completing oral communication tasks in pairs and small groups in their regular classes. They had been informed that their performances would be recorded and seemed quite prepared for it. At no point during the data collection or analysis did the researchers find reason to suspect that the participants had not been at ease during the study or that their performance had been affected by the presence of the tape recorders or the research environment.

After participants had been allocated to treatments, the booklets were distributed, and they were asked to read the initial set of instructions carefully. They were given time to do this and to ask questions. These instructions oriented them to the project and what was expected of them. In brief, they were informed that: (1) they should not think of the project as a test, but rather as a chance to discuss some problems with a friend in English; (2) they should discuss each problem as much as possible as though they felt it very important; (3) they must try to agree on a solution to each problem; (4) they would have 10 minutes for each task: two minutes to read the directions quietly and eight minutes to speak; (5) they must follow the directions for each task carefully; (6) they must work on the task specified for the eight minutes without going backward or forward in their booklets; (7) they must speak only English during those eight minutes; and (8) if they finish early, they should review or confirm their solution, discussing the task until the eight minutes were finished.

Each recording session lasted exactly one hour. During this time the researcher timed the performances carefully and ensured that all six tape recorders were turned on and off according to schedule. The researcher also ensured that the directions regarding information sharing were followed by all six pairs.

Analysis

The data base for the study consisted of 18 48-minute tapes containing 108 eight-minute task performances. These were transcribed. Each participant turn was then divided into AS-units (analysis of speech units, Foster *et al.*, 2000) against which complexity, fluency and accuracy were calculated.

AS-units: The guidelines of Foster *et al.* (2000) for a 'level two' analysis were followed closely in dividing the discourse into AS-units. Independent clauses and subordinate clauses, as well as independent sub-clausal units which could be elaborated into full clauses, were counted as AS-units. Minor utterances which did not add referential meaning to the discourse, such as echo responses or non-elicited feedback to show comprehension or agreement (e.g. *uh-huh, yeah, right, okay*), were not coded. In more difficult cases, pauses and intonation contours were taken into consideration as the governing principle was whether or not a piece of discourse constituted a single chunk of micro-planning.

Complexity: This was measured as the ratio of clauses (s-nodes) to AS-units. Clauses were tensed or untensed verbs which were not functioning as noun phrases. The guidelines provided by Foster *et al.* (2000) were followed closely in coding clauses. Generally, non-finite verbs were only coded when they were accompanied by a subject, object, complement or adverbial to verify their clausal status. The number of clauses produced by each participant during a given task performance was divided by the number of AS-units the participant produced to arrive at the complexity ratios.

Fluency: This was measured as the ratio of dysfluency markers (pauses and repetitions) to AS-units. Dysfluent pauses were those in which participants seemed to be searching for language or which otherwise seemed due to a deficiency in L2 skill. Pauses which set off planned chunks or which were used for rhetorical effect were not coded as dysfluency markers. AS-unit breaks were thus never double coded as dysfluent pauses. Dysfluent repetitions were cases in which participants repeated a word or phase until they could put together the necessary language to continue. Repetitions used for functional purposes within the discourse context, such as when a speaker wanted to stress something or make sure that the listener understood, were not coded as dysfluencies. The number of AS-units produced by each participant during a given performance was divided by the number of dysfluencies that the participant produced to create an inverse relationship in the fluency ratios. In this way, the ratio increased as number of dysfluencies decreased and vice versa.

Accuracy: This was measured by the proportion of error-free AS-units. The number of error-free AS-units produced by each participant during a given task performance was divided by the total number of AS-units the participant produced to arrive at the accuracy scores.

Both researchers independently coded the third tasks performance in each treatment from the three data sets. These 18 performances thus represented all participants, tasks, and conditions. Pearson product-moment correlation coefficients were calculated to establish interrater reliability on AS-units ($r = 0.972$, $p < 0.01$, $n = 36$), clauses ($r = 0.971$, $p < 0.01$, $n = 36$), error-free AS-units ($r = 0.921$, $p < 0.01$, $n = 36$), and dysfluency markers ($r = 0.953$, $p < 0.01$, $n = 36$). These correlations were deemed acceptable. One researcher coded the remainder of the data base. The scores were then tallied and two-way GLM repeated-measures tests for within subjects effects were conducted for main effects and interactions using SPSS 11.0 for Windows.

Results

Table 2.1 summarises the results of the statistical test for main effects and interaction of the two factors on the complexity of participants' production.

Information distribution had a significant effect on the complexity of participants' production overall ($p < 0.01$), accounting for nearly 22% of the variance (partial eta squared = 0.218). *Post hoc* paired-sample *t*-tests revealed that this effect was due to significant differences between the

Table 2.1 Within-subjects effects for complexity

Factors	Type III SS	df	ms	F	Sig	Partial eta²	Obs. Power p = 0.05
Info	0.374	2	0.187	9.767	0.000	0.218	0.979
		1.768	0.211		0.000		0.967
		1.855	0.202		0.000		0.972
		1.000	0.374		0.004		0.860
Goal	0.267	1.000	0.267	12.763	0.001	0.267	0.935
Info × goal	2.466	2	1.233	0.594	0.555	0.017	0.145
		1.521	1.621		0.512		0.132
		1.526	1.565		0.517		0.134
		1.000	2.466		0.446		0.116

shared and one-way versions of the tasks ($t = 3.418$, $df = 35$, $p < 0.01$) and the shared and two-way versions of the tasks ($t = 3.746$, $df = 35$, $p < 0.01$). Production was significantly more complex on the shared versions of the tasks (mean = 1.28) than on the one-way versions (mean = 1.19). Likewise, production was significantly more complex on the shared versions than on the two-way versions (mean = 1.19). There was no difference in complexity between the one-way and two-way versions of the tasks.

Goal orientation also had a significant effect on the complexity of participants' production overall ($p < 0.01$), accounting for almost 27% of the variance (partial eta squared = 0.267). Production was significantly more complex on the open versions of the tasks (mean = 1.26) than on the closed versions (mean = 1.19).

Table 2.2 summarises the results of the statistical test for main effects and interaction of the two factors on the fluency of participants' production.

Table 2.2 Within-subjects effects for fluency

Factors	Type III SS	df	ms	F	Sig	Partial eta²	Obs. Power p = 0.05
Info	16.270	2	8.139	4.163	0.020	0.106	0.716
		1.025	15.880		0.048		0.516
		1.027	15.845		0.048		0.517
		1.000	16.279		0.049		0.510
Goal	2.647	1.000	2.647	0.004	0.947	0.000	0.050
Info × goal	1.427	2	0.713	1.441	0.244	0.40	0.299
		1.068	1.336		0.240		0.221
		1.074	1.338		0.240		0.222
		1.000	1.427		0.238		0.215

Information distribution had a significant effect on the fluency of participants' production overall ($p < 0.05$), accounting for approximately 11% of the variance (partial eta squared = 0.106). *Post hoc* paired-sample *t*-tests revealed that this effect was due to significant differences between the one-way and shared versions of the tasks ($t = 2.129, df = 35, p < 0.05$). Production was significantly more fluent on the one-way versions (mean = 1.33) than the shared versions (mean = 0.73). There was no significant difference in fluency between the shared and two-way versions or between the one-way and two-way versions.

No significant main effects were found for the goal orientation factor on the fluency of participants' production overall. Production was equally fluent on the open and the closed versions of the tasks. However, *post-hoc* analyses revealed a significant difference between the open and closed versions of Task 2 ($t = 2.458, df = 11, p < 0.05$). Production was thus significantly more fluent on the closed versions of Task 2 (mean = 0.74) than they on the open versions (mean = 0.55).

Table 2.3 summarises the results of the statistical test for main effects and interaction of the two factors on the accuracy of participants' production.

Information distribution had a significant effect on the accuracy of participants' production overall ($p < 0.05$), accounting for approximately 12% of the variance (partial eta squared = 0.116). *Post hoc* paired-sample *t*-tests revealed that this effect was due to significant differences between the one-way and shared versions of the tasks ($t = 2.770, df = 35, p < 0.01$) and the two-way and shared versions ($t = 2.144, df = 35, p < 0.05$). Production was significantly more accurate on the one-way versions (mean = 0.52) than on the shared versions (mean = 0.45). Likewise, production was significantly more accurate on the two-way versions (mean = 0.50) than on the shared versions. There was no significant difference in accuracy on the one-way

Table 2.3 Within-subjects effects for accuracy

Factors	Type III SS	df	ms	F	Sig	Partial eta²	Obs. Power p = 0.05
Info	0.179	2.000	8.930	4.600	0.013	0.116	0.761
		1.888	9.461		0.015		0.743
		1.992	8.966		0.013		0.760
		1.000	0.179		0.039		0.550
Goal	2.816	1.000	2.816	1.612	0.213	0.044	0.235
Info × goal	6.556	2	3.278	2.545	0.086	0.068	0.493
		1.896			0.089		0.479
		2.000			0.086		0.493
		1.000			0.120		0.342

and two-way versions overall. However, *post-hoc* analyses revealed a significant difference in accuracy between the one-way and two-way versions of Task 3 ($t = 3.061$, $df = 11$, $p < 0.05$). Production was significantly more accurate on the one-way versions of Task 3 (mean = 0.69) than on the two-way versions (mean = 0.59).

No significant effects were found for goal orientation on the accuracy of participants' production. Production was equally accurate on the open and the closed versions of the all three tasks.

Information distribution: This factor resulted in a relatively consistent trade-off effect between complexity, on the one hand, and fluency/accuracy, on the other. The shared versions of all three tasks resulted in more complex production than both the one-way and the two-way versions, whereas the one-way versions resulted in more accurate and more fluent production than the shared versions across all three tasks. The two-way versions also resulted in more accurate production across tasks, but not more fluent production as would be predicted. This seems to be largely due to production on Task 1, as the means on Tasks 2 and 3 tend toward the two-way versions being more fluent than the shared (see Table 2.4).

As can be seen in the task-level means in Table 2.4, the trade-off effect was not as pronounced on Task 1 as it was on either Task 2 or Task 3.

The crucial division for this trade-off effect was between the shared versions and the divided (one-way and two-way) versions of the tasks. There were no significant differences between the one-way and two-way versions for fluency, accuracy or complexity overall. However, *post hoc t*-tests revealed that the one-way versions of Task 3 did result in more accurate production than the two-way versions. Surprisingly, there was also a trend toward the one-way versions resulting in more fluent discourse than the two-way versions (see Table 2.4), but none of these differences were significant.

Goal orientation: This factor did not result in a consistent trade-off effect. Overall, the open versions resulted in significantly more complex production than the closed versions, but the closed versions did not result in more fluent or more accurate production. Although there were clearly no effects

Table 2.4 Information distribution means

	Complexity			Fluency			Accuracy		
	Shared	1-way	2-way	Shared	1-way	2-way	Shared	1-way	2-way
Overall	1.28	1.19	1.19	0.73	1.33	0.78	0.45	0.52	0.50
Task 1	1.23	1.20	1.20	0.78	1.85	0.76	0.40	0.42	0.43
Task 2	1.40	1.27	1.27	0.51	0.85	0.57	0.42	0.45	0.47
Task 3	1.21	1.09	1.11	0.89	1.3	1.02	0.54	0.69	0.59

Information Distribution and Goal Orientation

Table 2.5 Goal orientation means

	Complexity		Fluency		Accuracy	
	Open	*Closed*	*Open*	*Closed*	*Open*	*Closed*
Overall	1.26	1.19	0.95	0.94	0.50	0.48
Task 1	1.22	1.21	1.32	0.94	0.44	0.39
Task 2	1.37	1.26	0.55	0.74	0.46	0.43
Task 3	1.18	1.09	0.99	1.15	0.60	0.61

on accuracy, the lack of effect on fluency was largely a result of Task 1. *Post-hoc* analyses revealed that the closed versions of Task 2 resulted in more fluent production than the open versions, and this is supported by a non-significant trend in Task 3 (see Table 2.5).

Task 1 had resulted in a less pronounced trade-off effect for information distribution, and it can be seen in Table 2.5 that the main effect for the open versions of the tasks on complexity is also largely due to participants' performances on Tasks 2 and 3, as the difference on Task 1 was nominal (see Table 2.5).

Task type: Post-hoc analyses were also conducted on the between-subjects differences in complexity, fluency and accuracy at the task level. It was found that task type was an additional factor that resulted in a relatively consistent trade-off effect between the complexity and the fluency/accuracy of production. Both Task 1 ($t = 2.564$, $df = 11$, $p < 0.05$) and Task 2 ($t = 4.125$, $df = 11$, $p < 0.01$) resulted in more complex discourse than Task 3. Task 3, on the other hand, resulted in more fluent production than Task 2 ($t = 4.728$, $df = 11$, $p < 0.01$) and more accurate production than both Task 1 ($t = 6.969$, $df = 11$, $p < 0.01$) and Task 2 ($t = 6.134$, $df = 11$, $p < 0.01$). Task 3 did not result in more fluent production than Task 1 as would be predicted (see Table 2.6).

The crucial division for this trade-off effect was thus between Tasks 1 and 2, on the one hand, and Task 3, on the other. There were no significant differences between Task 1 and Task 2 for fluency or accuracy. However, Task 2 did result in more complex discourse than Task 1 ($t = 3.178$, $df = 11$, $p < 0.01$).

Table 2.6 Task means

	Task 1: ordering pictures	Task 2: deciding responsibility	Task 3: arranging times
Complexity	1.21	1.31	1.14
Fluency	1.13	0.64	1.07
Accuracy	0.42	0.45	0.61

Discussion

The results of the study provide some evidence for a connection between information distribution and a trade-off between complexity and fluency/accuracy in at least one population of ESL learners. Allowing participants to share task-essential information resulted in more complex production, whereas dividing this information for a one-way flow of information resulted in both more fluent and more accurate production. All other things being equal, the results thus provide support for information distribution as a potentially useful design factor for promoting dual-mode processing in task-based L2 instruction. Furthermore, in allotting task-essential information, the important distinction seemed to be between allowing learners to share the information or not. Although a one-way configuration produced a somewhat more consistent trade-off effect than a two-way configuration in the present study, the effects of these conditions did not differ greatly in other respects.

The goal orientation factor did not result in a clear trade off on production. Although the open versions resulted in more complex production, the closed versions did not result in more fluent production except in the case of one of the three tasks observed. The factor had no effect on accuracy. Although these results are not inconsistent with goal orientation potentially having some role in dual-mode processing, more research on the extent to which this factor interacts with task is necessary.

The tasks used in the study also resulted in a trade-off between complexity and fluency/accuracy. Tasks 1 and 2 resulted in more complex production than Task 3, and Task 3 in more fluent and accurate production than Task 2 and more accurate production than Task 1. These results are not particularly surprising as Task 1 (ordering pictures to make a story) and Task 2 (determining who is most responsible) are clearly more difficult than Task 3 (arranging times to meet) in at least two respects. In terms of code complexity, Tasks 1 and 2 require structures and lexicon to express and support ideas and opinions, whereas Task 3 only requires short, simple pieces of information to be confirmed or disconfirmed. Furthermore, in terms of content complexity, Task 1 and Task 2 require more on-line computation as participants have to actively think through each new piece of information in relation to the others to arrive at a solution. Task 3, on the other hand, involves the repetition of the same process for each new piece of information. The reasoning demands of Tasks 1 and 2 are thus higher than those of Task 3. These results thus also provide some evidence for a connection between task difficulty and a trade-off between complexity and fluency/accuracy in at least one population of ESL learners. Easier tasks in terms of code and content complexity resulted in more fluent and accurate production, whereas more demanding tasks resulted in more complex production. Task difficulty may thus also have a role to play in promoting dual-mode processing in task-based instruction.

However, there are several limitations to be kept in mind. First, it seems that there are other factors inherent in the nature of specific tasks that interact with the factors observed here. If only Tasks 2 and 3 had been used in the study, it is very likely that there would have been significant differences supporting a very clear trade-off effect with shared/open/complex versions resulting in more complex production, and divided/closed/simple versions resulting in more fluent and more accurate production. Task 1, however, behaved quite differently than the other two tasks in spite of the carefully planned and controlled design used across them. More research is thus required to determine the extent to which the effects observed are task-specific.

In addition to task variables, however, participant variables should also be taken into account when interpreting the results of this study. As mentioned earlier, the participants were a relatively homogenous group of high-motivation learners in Japan. Motivation, in terms of willingness to invest time, energy and personal resources into the completion of L2 communication tasks, is an important variable in predicting performance. Rankin (1995) may have been on the right track when he observes that:

> A closed task ... may be so easy for participants that little if any creativity is fostered. once a problem-solving heuristic was agreed upon by the participants, the solution – and the language needed to achieve it – was highly predictable. The open task, on the other hand, allowed for considerable creativity. Opinions were shared and weighed, refined, rejected; humor sometimes played a role ... Closed tasks may discourage such creativity as they focus attention on the problem or puzzle at hand. (Rankin, 1995: 7)

In other words, open versions of tasks may allow more freedom to engage in different types of conversation based on individual needs and interests, make creative contributions, and arrive at original solutions. This freedom may have beneficial effects on the performance of relatively motivated learners who could be expected to take advantage of such opportunities to push their language abilities on their own initiative and produce more complex discourse as a result. Closed versions, by contrast, may discourage them from taking this initiative and stick with the requirements of the task as set. By the same token, the freedom provided by open tasks may have negative effects on the performance of low-motivation learners who might use it to finish as quickly as possible without regard for precision and produce less complex discourse as a result. The more highly-constrained nature of closed tasks may result in more complex discourse in such as case. Although it is impossible to do more than speculate, these or related difference may account for the opposite results for goal orientation obtained in the present study and in the previous research on goal orientation (i.e. Mannheimer, 1993; Rahimpour, 1997; Rankin, 1990).

However, if there is an interaction between task design factors and motivation level, it may be a systematic and predictable one that could be understood and controlled in developing tasks for different groups. In Japan, for example, class groups are often maintained year after year, and dynamics typically develop which determine the group's willingness to do communicative work in the classroom and which allow the instructor to plan materials accordingly. Research is thus needed to determine in what way, if any, the efficacy of these design factors to support dual-mode processing is dependent on learners' disposition toward completing tasks in general.

Proficiency level is another participant variable which should be taken into account in interpreting the results of this study. Rankin (1995: 10) also speculates that closed tasks may be most useful at the novice level and of more limited use with advanced learners. Unfortunately, at the time that the data were collected for the present study, the participants' institution TOEFL scores were either between a year and two years old. However, the participants were all between a low-intermediate and high-intermediate communicative ability. They could communicate effectively, but not always efficiently, and could still benefit from practice using the language for its own sake. The results obtained at higher or lower proficiency levels may have been quite different. Future research might address the ways in which the efficacy of these design factors to support dual-mode processing is dependent on proficiency from the beginning level to the advanced level.

Thus, the results of the present study provide some evidence that, in the case of relatively motivated young-adult Japanese females who are at a broadly intermediate level of English proficiency, shared or open versions of tasks, all other things being equal, might be used to push L2 development by encouraging more complex language use, whereas one-way versions might subsequently be used to practice and solidify these gains by encouraging more fluent and accurate language use. In addition, tasks which place higher code and content demands on these learners, all other things again being equal, might be expected to result in more complex language use, whereas those that place lower code and content demands on them might be expected to result in more fluent and accurate language use. However, within the broader context of task-based L2 learning, the relationship between task design and L2 production is likely to be far more complex than the variables observed here. A few of the variables that might be taken into account in predicting the effects of task design on L2 production were discussed. It seems that the motivation and proficiency level of the learners may be an essential consideration. Divided or closed versions of tasks, for example, may be more effective at lower levels where attention is burdened simply by mobilising the L2 to communicate. Shared or open versions, on the other hand, may be more effective as proficiency is gained and attention is freed for creative and more socially-aware communication. At the same time, however, learners of lower motivation may continue to benefit from divided or closed versions of tasks even at higher levels, whereas more motivated learners may benefit from shared or open versions at any level. In addition, it must be kept in mind that other differences inherent in tasks may also interact with these design factors in as yet unpredictable ways. In short, effective use of information distribution and goal orientation in task L2 task design and sequencing will require teachers and materials planners to take a broader range of variables in both the tasks themselves and education environment into account rather than adopting them uncritically in all situations. It is hoped that the present study scratches the surface of the research that will be required to understand these variables

References

Crookes, G. and Rulon, K.A. (1985) Incorporation of corrective feedback in native speaker/non-native speaker conversation. University of Hawaii (mimeo).

Doughty, C. and Pica, T. (1986) "Information gap" tasks: Do they facilitate second language acquisition? *TESOL Quarterly* 20 (2), 305–325.

Duff, P. (1986) Another look at interlanguage talk: Taking task to task. In R. Day (ed.) *Talking to Learn* (pp. 147–181). Rowley: Newbury House.

Foster, P. (1998) A classroom perspective on the negotiation of meaning. *Applied Linguistics* 19 (1), 1–23.

Foster, P., Tonkyn, A. and Wigglesworth, G. (2000) Measuring spoken language: A unit for all reasons. *Applied Linguistics* 21 (3), 354–375.

Gass, S.M. and Varonis, M. (1985) Task variation and non-native/non-native negotiation of meaning. In S.M. Gass and C.G. Madden (eds) *Input in Second Language Acquisition* (pp. 149–161). Boston, Heinle and Heinle.

Long, M.H. (1989) Task, group and task-group interactions. In S. Anivan (ed.) *Language Teaching Methodology for the Nineties* (pp. 31–50). Singapore: SEAMEO Regional Language Centre.

Long, M.H. (2000) Focus on form in task-based language teaching. In R.D. Lambert and E. Shohamy (eds) *Language Policy and Pedagogy* (pp. 181–196). Philadelphia: John Benjamins.

Mannheimer, R. (1993) Close the task, improve the discourse. *Estudios de Linguistica Aplicada* 17, 18–40.

Pica, T., Holliday, L., Lewis, N. and Morgenthaler, L. (1989) Comprehensible output as an outcome of linguistic demands on the learner. *Studies in Second Language Acquisition* 11, 63–90.

Rahimpour, M. (1997) Task condition, task complexity and variation on oral L2 discourse. PhD thesis, University of Queensland.

Rankin J. (1990) A case for close-mindedness: Complexity, accuracy and attention in closed vs. open tasks. University of Hawaii (mimeo).

Rankin J. (1995) The effects of task design on accuracy and self-monitoring. American Association of Applied Linguistics (mimeo).

Robinson, P. (2001) Task complexity, cognitive resources and second language syllabus design. In P. Robinson (ed.) *Cognition and Second Language Instruction* (pp. 287–318). Cambridge: Cambridge University Press.

Skehan, P. (1996) A framework for the implementation of task-based learning. *Applied Linguistics* 17 (1), 38–62.

Chapter 3

The Simultaneous Manipulation of Task Complexity Along Planning Time and (+/− Here-and-Now): Effects on L2 Oral Production

ROGER GILABERT

Introduction

The objective of this study is to analyse the effects of manipulating the cognitive complexity of tasks on L2 narrative oral production. It specifically addresses the issue of how the three dimensions of production (i.e. fluency, complexity, and accuracy) compete for attention during L2 task performance by establishing four levels of cognitive complexity which are achieved by simultaneously manipulating two widely researched variables: pre-task planning time and the degree of displaced, past time reference.

In the last few years, considerable attention has been devoted to task design and task-based syllabus design. Basically, two different agendas have inspired research into task features. The first one is an interactionist perspective which has been concerned with establishing what modifications can be applied to tasks in order for them to generate specific conversational episodes which, generally, have been regarded as negotiation of meaning. These studies have been particularly interested in whether task design can lead to interactive production episodes that have been referred to as clarification requests, confirmation checks, and comprehension checks. These episodes have been claimed to lead to second language acquisition (Long, 1985, 1989, 2000).

From an information-processing perspective concerned with performance, questions have been asked as to how task manipulation can lead to differentials in the areas of fluency, complexity, and accuracy. A number of researchers have investigated the effects of task on production along their degree of familiarity (Bygate, 1999, 2001; Foster & Skehan, 1996; Plough & Gass, 1993; Robinson, 2001a); their number of elements (Kuiken *et al.*, 2005;

Robinson, 2001a); single and dual task performance (Niwa, 2000); the pre-task and on-line planning time allotted to them (Crookes, 1989; Ellis, 1987; Foster & Skehan, 1996; Mehnert, 1998; Ortega, 1999; Skehan & Foster, 1997; Wigglesworth, 1997; Yuan & Ellis, 2003); and their degree of complexity along displaced, past time reference (Iwashita *et al.*, 2001; Robinson, 1995; Rahimpour, 1997). These studies have been concerned with how a balanced performance in the three areas of production can potentially lead to more effective language use and acquisition, as well as with how such information can be used to make sequencing decisions in syllabus design.

It is the preoccupation with sequencing tasks in a syllabus in a principled way that has given rise to the concept of *task complexity*. A great divide has traditionally existed between models which argue that decisions in syllabus construction should be motivated by findings in second language acquisition (SLA) (Long, 1985; Long & Crookes, 1992; Robinson, 1998; Skehan, 1998) and those who suggest criteria which are not necessarily informed by SLA (Ellis, 1997; Nunan, 1989; Willis, 1990). In synthetic syllabi, whether structural, lexical, or functional-notional, grading of syllabus units is quite an intuitive activity which depends on various notions of 'difficulty', 'usefulness' or 'frequency' (see Robinson, 1998). Within analytic syllabi with an almost exclusive focus on meaning, procedural syllabi (Prabhu, 1987) have had quite a random selection and sequencing of tasks, which were taken from other subjects. Finally, in process syllabi (Breen, 1984; Candlin, 1984) tasks are jointly negotiated between teachers and learners and therefore organised according to learners' wants and needs. In content-based syllabi, sequencing is the result of incorporating the intuition of experts in the subject matter into syllabus design.

Task Complexity and L2 Oral Production

The concept of task complexity, then, springs from the need to establish criteria for sequencing tasks in a syllabus from easy/simple to difficult/complex in a reasoned way that will foster interlanguage development. Rather than looking at the linguistic features of language activities, syllabi that have used tasks as their units have focused on task design in order to find out how tasks impose cognitive demands on learners. In this way, task design has allowed researchers to speculate about the effects that increasing task difficulty or complexity may have on L2 task performance. With some exceptions (Kuiken *et al.*, 2005), the majority of these studies have been concerned with oral production.

The concept of task complexity

Beyond early attempts at sequencing tasks from simple to complex in a syllabus (Brown *et al.*, 1984; Prahbu, 1987), Skehan (Skehan, 1998; Skehan

& Foster, 2001) and Robinson (2001a, 2001b, 2003, 2005a) have identified a series of task design factors that can be manipulated along a continuum in order to achieve different levels of difficulty or complexity.

From a communicative approach to language teaching, which has been concerned, among other issues, with how task and syllabus design can contribute to interlanguage development, Skehan (Skehan, 1998; Skehan & Foster, 2001) suggests that both task manipulation and sequencing for syllabus design should be based not just on intuitions about difficulty but on empirical findings. For Skehan and Foster (2001: 196): 'Task difficulty has to do with the amount of attention the task demands from the participants. Difficult tasks require more attention than easy tasks.' Having evidence of the effects of task demands on production can be used to direct learners' efforts toward different areas of performance separately or simultaneously. In addition to that, if links are established between production and acquisition, research evidence can be used to manipulate tasks to maximise the effectiveness of language learning.

Skehan (Skehan, 1998; Skehan & Foster, 2001) suggests a three-way distinction of difficulty, to which learner factors can also be added: *code complexity* (vocabulary load and variety; linguistic complexity and variety); *cognitive complexity* (familiarity topic, discourse or task; amount of computation and organization, and sufficiency of information); *communicative stress* (time pressure; scale; number of participants; length of text; modality; stakes; opportunity for control); and *learner* factors (intelligence; breadth of imagination; personal experience).

He suggests that information should be collected regarding the effects of task manipulation on the areas of fluency, accuracy, and complexity. Skehan takes linguistic complexity to be a 'surrogate' of learners' willingness to stretch their interlanguage by experimenting with more difficult forms and by trying out more elaborate language. In his view, the information obtained from the manipulation of task features can be used to establish longer-term pedagogic goals in which both meaning and form can be attended to, and in which interlanguage development can be integrated into fluent performance. Regarding sequencing, Skehan and Foster (2001: 193–194) propose that: 'the individual task has to be located, in a principled way, in longer-term instructional sequences which seek to promote balanced development, such that improvement in one area will be consolidated by improvements in others'. Skehan and Foster (2001), however, make no specific suggestions as to which dimension should be used for making prospective sequencing decisions, and their 'principled way' is in need of further exploration.

Acknowledging the rich research tradition in the interactive dimension of tasks, Robinson has shifted the focus to the cognitive processes involved in task production. Robinson (2001a: 28) states that: 'task complexity is the result of the attentional, memory, reasoning, and other information processing demands imposed by the structure of the task on the language learner. These differences in information processing demands, resulting from design characteristics, are relatively fixed and invariant'. Robinson proposes a three-dimensional model that distinguishes between three different types of factors: *cognitive complexity* factors (resource-directing ones such as [+/− few elements], [+/− Here-and-Now], and [+/− no reasoning demands]; resource-dispersing ones such as [+/− planning], [+/− single task], and [+/− prior knowledge]); *interactive* factors (participation variables such as one way/two way, convergent/divergent, open/closed; participant variables such as gender, familiarity, power/solidarity); and *leaner* factors (affective variables such as motivation, anxiety, and confidence; ability variables such as aptitude, proficiency, and intelligence).

In Robinson's view, task complexity should be the sole basis for making prospective sequencing decisions, since task conditions (participation and participant variables) and task difficulty (affective and ability variables) often cannot be predicted before a course starts and can therefore only inform on-line decisions. In his view, task performance conditions are determined by a needs analysis. Information about the effects of task complexity on production should help syllabus designers to organise pedagogic tasks from simple to complex so that they progressively approximate real world target tasks. According to Robinson (2001b: 301), increasing the cognitive complexity of tasks 'will facilitate the "means" of language learning, and therefore lead to a transition in the learner's knowledge states'.

Production as mediated by complexity and attention

These two different but complementary conceptions of complexity make different predictions about the fluency, complexity, and accuracy of L2 production during task performance.

Skehan (Skehan, 1998; Skehan & Foster, 2001) understands difficulty as the amount of attention the task demands from the participants. Skehan's view of how the three areas of production interact during performance is based on a limited-capacity view of attention in which more difficult tasks demand more attention than easy tasks, and such higher demands for attention have specific consequences for performance. Skehan bases his predictions on a limited-capacity conception of attention, which suggests that when task demands are high, attention can only be allocated to certain aspects of performance to the detriment of others. His conception of attention resembles the models of early selection and limited capacity, like the one advanced by Kahneman's (1973) in which there is a single volume of attention that 'runs out' of resources. Of the three dimensions of performance, Skehan believes that complexity and accuracy are in competition for attention, a statement that he has supported with evidence from a number of studies on pre-task planning, which will be reviewed in the following section.

Robinson (2001a, 2001b, 2003, 2005a), however, has a contrasting view regarding cognitive complexity. He proposes that attention, as suggested by models such as Wickens' (1989, 1992), can draw on multiple resources. Wickens' (1989) model of dual-task performance proposes breaking the single volume of attentional resources into a series of dichotomical dimensions. The dichotomy affecting processing stages opposes the per-ceptual/cognitive dimension (i.e. encoding and central processing) to the response dimension. For codes of processing, the spatial is opposed to the verbal. In the case of modality, auditory perception is opposed to visual per-ception, and responses can be manual or vocal. Wickens (1989, 1992) claims that because these different dimensions draw on different resource pools, competition for attention may not necessarily happen. There is competition when two tasks or two dimensions of the same task feed on the same resource pool. For example, having two conversations simultaneously would lead to competition of resources and poor performance since they would both draw on the same 'verbal' resource pool. On the other hand, driving home while simultaneously singing or verbalising thoughts would draw on the 'manual' and 'vocal' dimensions of performance, and there-fore no competition for attention would occur. Thus, the model predicts that the amount of interference will depend on the number of shared lev-els on all three dimensions (i.e. codes, modalities, and responses).

Robinson believes that manipulating task complexity by increasing the cognitive demands of tasks can lead to simultaneous improvement of accu-racy and complexity. He distinguishes between resource-directing and resource-dispersing dimensions. Manipulating Task Complexity along the first group of task variables ([+/− elements], [+/− Here-and-Now], [+/ − reasoning demands]) directs attention to a wide range of functional and linguistic requirements. Increasing complexity along resource-dis-persing dimensions ([+/− planning time], [+/− prior knowledge], [+/− single task]) reduces attentional and memory resources with negative con-sequences for production, a position which is in agreement with Skehan's. Despite such negative consequences, progressively increasing complexity along resource-dispersing variables is also important in order to approx-imate the complexity conditions under which real-world tasks are performed.

Planning Time and (+/− Here-and-Now) Studies

This section reviews the literature on the variables of planning time and +/− Here-and-Now, as they are crucial for this study. I specifically focus on the issue of attention during oral performance and discuss the different findings. For a more detailed review of planning time studies see Ellis (2005) and for a review of both planning time and +/− Here-and-Now studies see Gilabert (2005).

Planning time studies

What research evidence has shown so far is that giving learners extended planning time before task performance seems to have beneficial effects for fluency and complexity, while the picture for accuracy is not so clear. As we will see below, providing extended 'on-line' (i.e. during performance) planning time has shown to have positive effects for accuracy (Yuan & Ellis, 2003).

From a variationist stance, Ellis (1987) looked into how different levels of planned discourse affect learners' written and oral performance. He operationalised three different degrees of planned discourse, and hypothesised that access to forms that have not been fully automatised, such as the third person '-s' or regular past '-ed', would benefit from planning time. Ellis found that the accuracy in the use of irregular past forms was not affected by the different levels of planning. His main conclusion was that increased planning time leads to higher accuracy of rule-based language, while unplanned discourse is more lexical in nature.

Foster and Skehan (1996) manipulated planning time on three different task types: a personal information gap task, a narrative task, and a decision-making task. Foster and Skehan found a significant effect for two measures of fluency, number of pauses and total silence, and reported that the personal task triggered the most fluent speech; complexity, in terms of sentence nodes per C-units, was higher for the detailed planning group (i.e. 10 minutes plus guidance as to how to plan) than for the undetailed planning group (i.e. 10 minutes without guidance). The undetailed planning group, in turn, triggered higher levels of complexity than the group without planning. The researchers, however, obtained mixed results for accuracy, the undetailed planning group obtaining more error-free clauses. The narrative task triggered the most complex speech but the lowest levels of accurate language. Foster and Skehan concluded that there are 'tradeoff' effects between complexity and accuracy, especially with narrative tasks, in which attention devoted to complexity has negative effects for accuracy. This was not the case with decision-making tasks, in which accuracy and complexity were more balanced.

In a subsequent study, Skehan and Foster (1997) used the same kind of task types as in their 1996 study. This time, however, they operationalised a post-task requirement in which learners were told that they would go public, which they predicted would result in higher levels of accuracy. This second time their results showed that planning could be associated with greater fluency and accuracy in the narrative task, while they did not find greater complexity associated with increased planning. Skehan and Foster suggested once again that accuracy and complexity are in competition for attentional resources when task demands are increased along planning time. They therefore concluded that planning time can only be channeled to one of the aspects (either accuracy or complexity), and not to the two dimensions simultaneously.

Mehnert (1998) confirmed Skehan and Foster's (1997) limited capacity model of attention. In a study with two task types varying in complexity, a simple instruction task and a complex exposition task, Menhert compared the effects of allotting no planning time, one minute, five minutes, and 10 minutes to four different groups. His overall results showed that engaging in extended planning time before carrying out a task had positive effects for performance. Regarding each specific measure, he found that planners who had 10 minutes were more fluent, more accurate, and more lexically dense than non-planners, with no significant differences in structural complexity. He found, however, that when learners had a short time for planning (one minute), they focused more on accuracy, whereas when they had longer time to prepare (10 minutes), they tried to produce more complex speech at the expense of accuracy, suggesting that any gains in accuracy and complexity are not achieved simultaneously.

In contrast to previous suggestions, Ortega (1999) questioned the limited processing capacity model in which the three dimensions of production enter into competition, arguing that previous studies had neglected the investigation of the planning process. In a study of oral narrative discourse under a 10-minute planning condition and a no-planning condition with learners of Spanish, Ortega found results similar to previous studies regarding production. Her results showed that complexity and fluency were enhanced by pre-task planning, whereas mixed results were found for accuracy. She went beyond previous studies and included retrospective interviews in order to find out more about the quality of pre-task planning, in term of focus on form and strategic planning. Ortega concluded that a number of factors affect the quality of planning. Firstly, she suggested that task complexity may play a role in the sense that cognitively complex tasks may benefit more from planning than simple ones. Secondly, she suggested that the operationalisation of planning is important in the sense that developmental readiness and task essentialness need to be taken into account. Thirdly, learner orientation towards form or meaning also plays a role. In the fourth place, learner proficiency needs to be brought into the picture since she speculated that higher level students may benefit more and differently from planning than lower-level students. Finally, she suggested that proficiency should be a moderating factor in the limited processing capacity model.

Springing from a concern with the mixed findings regarding accuracy, Yuan and Ellis (2003) operationalised the construct of 'online' planning, which they presented in contrast with no planning and pre-task planning. Using an oral narrative in their study, Yuan and Ellis found that whereas pre-task planning time promoted higher complexity and lexical variety, it did not have significant effects on accuracy, in line with what several previous studies had also reported. Extended on-line planning with no pre-task planning, despite having negative effects for lexical variety, also had a beneficial effect for complexity and, most importantly, for accuracy. Learners who were given unlimited time during performance were less fluent but reformulated and self-corrected their speech more, by drawing on their explicit knowledge, which as a consequence led to a more accurate performance. They also confirmed the trade-off effect in language production, especially of learners with limited L2 proficiency. Since they found that both pre-task planning and on-line planning promote higher accuracy, they concluded that the main trade-off effect is between fluency and accuracy. If learners are given time to plan prior to task performance, they prioritise fluency. If they are given time to plan on-line, they may pay more attention to accuracy at the expense of fluency. Finally, Yuan and Ellis detailed the trade-off effect further by showing that pre-task planning increases lexical variety but not grammatical accuracy, whereas on-line planning improves grammatical accuracy over lexical variety.

Here-and-Now studies

In general, previous studies have shown that tasks in the There-and-Then are more cognitively demanding than tasks performed in the Here-and-Now, with specific consequences for production.

Robinson (1995) investigated the impact of manipulating Here-and-Now on three different narratives. In the Here-and-Now condition, learners were asked to narrate a comic strip in the present tense while looking at it. The There-and-Then was operationalised by having the students narrate the story in the past tense and without visual support during performance. Such operationalisation was based on both L1 and SLA findings that had shown that displaced, past time reference is more complex and therefore appears later than present, context-supported reference. Robinson predicted less fluent speech but higher lexical and structural complexity as well as accuracy for There-and-Then tasks. Robinson found that the most complex narrative, performed in displaced past time reference, elicited more accurate speech and more lexical complexity than the narrative performed in the Here-and-Now. It also showed a trend for greater dysfluency but showed no significant differences for structural complexity.

Rahimpour (1997) extended Robinson's research by crossing a complexity variable (Here-and-Now) with a condition variable (open vs. closed). Rahimpour operationalised three levels of complexity by including a narrative in the Here-and-Now, one in the There-and-Then, and one in the Here-and-Now/There-and-Then. This researcher hypothesised that the Here-and-Now/There-and-Then narrative would be more complex that the other versions of the task. His results showed that learners who carried out the most complex versions of the task were significantly less fluent, with no significant differences regarding either structural or lexical complexity, and with significant improvements with regard to error-free units but not target-like use of articles.

From an interest in language testing, Iwashita *et al.* (2001) investigated the effects of manipulating complexity on L2 learners' fluency, complexity, and accuracy. They established eight levels of complexity along four dimensions: (i) [+/− perspective], that is, whether the learner was speaking as if the story had happened to her or not; (ii) [+/− immediacy], that is, in the Here-and-Now or in the There-and-Then; (iii) [+/− adequacy], that is, whether the set of pictures was complete or incomplete; (iv) [+/− planning time], which they operationalised as either 3.5 minutes or 0.5 minutes. Following Foster and Skehan's (1996) predictions for task difficulty, the researchers hypothesised that less difficult versions of tasks would trigger more fluency and accuracy but less complex speech. They found that there were no significant differences between easy and difficult versions of tasks except for accuracy. In the case of immediacy, they found that the more difficult version of tasks, that is, in There-and-Then, triggered higher levels of accuracy, which went against their prediction.

Questions and hypotheses

This study is motivated by, firstly, the fact that research evidence is needed regarding the synergistic effects of crossing planning time and the degree of displaced, past time reference, two widely researched task factors which so far have been investigated in isolation. Secondly, it is also motivated by the need to explore the different, and sometimes contradictory, conceptions of attention and predictions regarding the effects of increasing the cognitive demands of tasks on production. This study therefore aims at answering the following general question: How does increasing the cognitive complexity of tasks along simultaneously planning time and the Here-and-Now variable affect the fluency, complexity, and accuracy of production?

On the basis of previous studies, I entertain the following hypotheses:

Hypothesis 1: Increasing the cognitive complexity of tasks along planning time will have negative effects for all three areas of production, while reducing cognitive complexity by providing pre-task planning time will have positive effect for fluency and structural complexity but not for lexical complexity or for accuracy.

Hypothesis 2: Increasing the cognitive complexity of tasks along the degree of displaced, past time reference will generate dysfluency but higher structural and lexical complexity and accuracy.

In addition, this research will investigate the synergistic effects of manipulating both dimensions of complexity ([+/− planning time] and [+/− Here-and-Now]) simultaneously. No hypotheses will be advanced regarding the manupulation of the two variables since there is a lack of studies that combine them.

Experimental Design

This study draws on data that are part of a larger study on the effect of manipulating task complexity on L2 narrative oral production (Gilabert, 2005) and addresses the issue of competition for attention. In what follows I provide information regarding participants and experimental design.

Participants

Forty-eight (48) first- and second-year university students with a lower-intermediate proficiency level of English participated in the study on a volunteer basis. They had been placed in the same level of English class by an internal placement test of the Blanquerna Communication Studies programme at Universitat Ramon Llull, in Barcelona, Spain. However, since the reliability of such a test has never been statistically tested, homo-geneity regarding proficiency levels was also controlled for by means of a C-test.[1] Learners' years of instruction ranged from six to 12 and their ages were between 18 and 22.

Design

A repeated-measures design was used in which the within-subjects fac-tor was task complexity. As far as the independent variable is concerned, four levels of Task Complexity were analysed:

Condition 1: Planned Here-and-Now
Condition 2: Unplanned Here-and-Now
Condition 3: Planned There-and-Then
Condition 4: Unplanned There-and-Then

Repeated-measures analyses of variance (ANOVA) of the dependent variables were carried out. These include: pruned speech rate for fluency, the Guiraud's Index of lexical richness for lexical complexity, the S-Nodes per T-units for structural complexity, and the percentage of self-repairs for accuracy.

In order to counterbalance any carryover effects, the following measures were taken:

- Subjects were only given two stories in each session; stories 1 and 2 in the first session, and stories 3 and 4 in the second one. Sessions were two days apart.
- All students narrated the four stories in the same order, but a Latin square design[2] was used to counterbalance the effects of sequence of condition presentation.

Repeated measures ANOVAs for each measure displayed neither dif-ferences among stories nor interaction between conditions and sequence of presentation.

Tasks and procedures

The four stories used in this research were thought to be especially useful for data collection because they were all wordless comic strips, they all contained a small number of characters who were involved in the action, and they had a clear climax and resolution. All plots worked in a similar way: in the first vignettes a number of expectations were generated which were reversed towards the end of the story, with the aim of achieving a humorous effect. Finally, despite the fact that all the social events represented by the comic strips were exaggerated and distorted by the artist's sense of humour, they were all thought to refer to situations all students could be familiar with within their cultural parameters.

Following several studies (Foster & Skehan, 1996; Mehnert, 1998; Ortega, 1999; Skehan & Foster, 1997), operationalisation of planning time was 10 minutes for planned narratives and 50 seconds for unplanned ones (enough to understand the story). When planning time was available, subjects were encouraged to take notes on what to say and how to say it as they planned, but were told they would not be allowed to keep their notes during task performance.

Regarding the Here-and-Now/There-and-Then distinction, this research followed Robinson's (1995) operationalisation. For Here-and-Now, learners were asked to narrate the story in the present while they looked at the strips. For There-and-Then, learners were asked to narrate the story in the past tense, and they were not allowed to look at the pictures as they performed the task.

Production measures

In this study, the rate of pruned speech was chosen to code and measure each narrative. The main advantage of this kind of measure is that it in fact includes both the amount of speech and the length of pauses, since it takes into account the number of syllables and the total number of seconds in the narrative (Griffiths, 1991). In pruned speech rate, as opposed to unpruned speech rate, repetitions, reformulations, false starts, and asides in the L1 are eliminated from the calculation (Lennon, 1991). The formula used for the calculation of pruned speech rate is the number of syllables divided by the total number of seconds and multiplied by 60.

The type/token ratio has been shown to be extremely sensitive to differences in text length, since the higher the number of tokens, the lower the ratio (Vermeer, 2000). Here the Guiraud's index of lexical richness is used. The advantage of such a measure is that by including the square root of the tokens it compensates for differences in text length. Hence, the Guiraud's Index of lexical richness was calculated by dividing the number of types by the square root of the number of tokens.

Three basic units of analysis have been used by production researchers for measuring syntactic complexity in oral production: the C-unit, the T-unit, and the utterance.[3] In this study the T-unit was preferred over the C-unit, since it dealt with one-way, monologic narratives which were expected to trigger no elliptical answers. Syntactic complexity was measured by counting the number of S-Nodes and dividing it by the total number of T-units.

Regarding accuracy, this research operationalises a new measurement: the percentage of self-repairs. There are a number of arguments that can be advanced in order to justify its use: firstly, self-repairs, whether other-initiated or self-initiated (Schegloff *et al.*, 1977), denote students' awareness of form (Kormos, 1999), revision of their hypotheses about the target language (Lyster & Ranta, 1997), and noticing (Swain, 1998), and can be interpreted as learners' attempts at being accurate. All these functions of self-repairs have been said to potentially lead to acquisition, and they have been pointed out in order to defend the benefits of certain types of corrective feedback. Self-initiated repairs, which serve the same purposes as other-initiated repairs, are the result of the speakers' monitoring of their own speech (Levelt, 1989).

Secondly, while the percentage of error-free units and the target-like use (TLU) of articles, which have been traditionally used by both planning time and Here-and-Now studies, provide information about the accuracy of the 'finished' product of learner's performance, this new measure presents accuracy 'in process' as learners try to correct and improve their own speech. Thirdly, Yuan and Ellis (2003: 17) reported a higher proportion of self-repairs under certain planning conditions, and they stated that during on-line planning learners engage 'more fully in searching their linguistic repertoires and in monitoring their speech production'. In the present study, the percentage of self-repairs is calculated by taking the number of self-repairs[4] and dividing it by the total number of errors[5] and multiplying the results by 100.

Statistical instruments

This study has used repeated-measures ANOVA for the comparison of stories and conditions and *post hoc* Scheffe's comparisons to identify the exact location of differences. Outliers were detected by means of box plots and eliminated from the calculation in order to achieve the sphericity of the data, which was confirmed by means of Mauchly's test.

Both intrarater and interrater measures were used in the transcription and coding of the narratives. The transcription of the narratives was carried out by the researcher and a research assistant. Intrarater reliability reached 97%, and interrater agreement, which was calculated by means of percentage agreement, out of a randomly selected sample of 10% percent of the data, reached 93.7%.

Results

Results in this section are presented according to the order of the hypotheses advanced previously. Table 3.1 below shows the descriptive statistics for all the measures. After that, the effects of manipulating planning time on the three dimensions of production are presented first, and the effects of increasing complexity along the Here-and-Now variable are presented second.

Effects of increasing task complexity along planning time on production

There was a reliable main effect for pruned speech rate $F(117,3) = 14.767$, $p < 0.01$, which suggests that fluency was affected by the different degrees of complexity (see Table 3.2). *Post hoc* Scheffe's tests showed that that both simple Here-and-Now and complex There-and-Then tasks generated significantly higher speech rate when performed under conditions of 10 minutes planning time. Planned Here-and-Now tasks triggered significantly more fluent speech ($p < 0.01$) than unplanned Here-and-Now tasks. There-and-Then tasks performed under planned conditions were also significantly more fluent ($p < 0.05$) than tasks performed under unplanned conditions (see Table 3.3 and Figure 3.1).

Regarding lexical and structural complexity, there was a significant main effect for the Guiraud's index of lexical richness $F(114,3) = 18.873, p < 0.01$ (see Table 3.2). *Post hoc* Scheffe's tests showed that Here-and-Now tasks performed under planned conditions generated a significantly higher level of lexical richness ($p < 0.05$) than under unplanned conditions. There-and-Then narratives also generated a higher lexical richness ($p < 0.05$) when performed under planned conditions than under unplanned ones. Contrary to what Hypothesis 1 predicted, results show that increasing planning time generates significantly higher levels of lexical complexity (see Table 3.3 and Figure 3.2). As for structural complexity, there was no significant main effect for structural complexity $F(123,3) = 1.711, p = 0.168$. In both simple and complex tasks, providing time caused a slightly higher level of structural complexity. Nevertheless, these differences were not significant for either Here-and-Now or There-and-Then narratives. It can therefore be concluded that none of the four combinations of the $+/-$ planning and $+/-$ Here-and-Now variables had any significant impact on structural complexity (see Table 3.2 and Figure 3.3).

With regard to the measure of accuracy, there was a significant main effect for both the percentage of self-repairs $F(123,3) = 5.617, p < 0.01$. Simple tasks performed in the Here-and-Now with 10 minutes' planning generated a slightly higher percentage of self-repairs than tasks performed with minimal planning time. This was similar for There-and-Then tasks, which again caused a lower proportion of self-repairs in unplanned tasks

Table 3.1 Descriptive statistics of conditions: means, standard deviations, skewness, and kurtosis

Dependent Variable	Condition 1 Planned Here-and-Now				Condition 2 Unplanned Here-and-Now				Condition 3 Planned There-and-Then				Condition 4 Unplanned There-and-Then			
	M	SD	Sk	K	M	SD	Sk	K	M	SD	Sk	K	M	SD	Sk	K
Pruned speech rate (n = 43)	107.81	24.22	0.349	−0.578	97.08	23.42	0.023	−0.599	96.33	22.77	0.323	−0.025	89.75	24.04	0.299	−0.627
Guiraud's Index (n = 41)	5.24	0.609	0.099	0.045	4.79	0.614	0.127	−0.973	5.08	0.573	0.116	−0.513	4.59	0.597	0.171	−0.146
S-nodes per T-units (n = 47)	1.55	0.272	0.312	0.205	1.50	0.271	0.335	0.053	1.46	0.228	0.329	−0.178	1.45	0.221	0.145	−0.086
% of self-repairs (n = 45)	14.21	9.44	0.328	−0.465	13.90	9.47	0.417	−0.426	19.84	8.99	0.033	−0.431	18.45	11.74	0.110	−0.467

M = mean; SD = standard deviation; Sk = skewness; K = kurtosis.

Table 3.2 Repeated measures ANOVA by condition: main effects obtained for different levels of Task Complexity for all measures

General measure	Dependent variable	Mauchly's sphericity	Df	Sum of Squares	F-value	p-value	η^2
Fluency	Pruned speech rate	n.s.	117,3	8246.048	14.767	0.000**	0.281
Complexity	Guiraud's Index (lexical)	n.s.	111,3	8.738	18.873	0.000**	0.338
	S-nodes per T-units (structural)	n.s.	123,3	0.277	1.711	n.s.	n.s.
Accuracy	% of self-repairs	n.s.	123,3	1439.946	5.617	0.001**	0.120

Df = degrees of freedom; η^2 = partial eta squared (effect size).
*$p < 0.05$; **$p < 0.01$.

Table 3.3 Hypothesis 1. Fluency, lexical and structural complexity, and accuracy measures: Mean differences between planned and unplanned tasks under both simple Here-and-Now and complex There-and-Then conditions

Comparison	Fluency pruned speech rate	Complexity Guiraud's Index	Complexity sentence nodes per T-units	Accuracy percentage of self-repairs
Planned Here-and-Now (Condition 1) vs Unplanned Here-and-Now (Condition 2)	10.01**	0.45**	0.04	0.31
Planned There-and-Then (Condition 3) vs Unplanned There-and-Then (Condition 4)	6.58*	0.49*	0.01	1.39

*$p < 0.05$.

as compared to planned ones. None of these differences, however, reached statistical significance (see Table 3.2 and Figure 3.4).

We can therefore conclude that the manipulation of planning time again had a significant impact on fluency and lexical complexity but not on structural complexity or accuracy, hence only partially confirming Hypothesis 1.

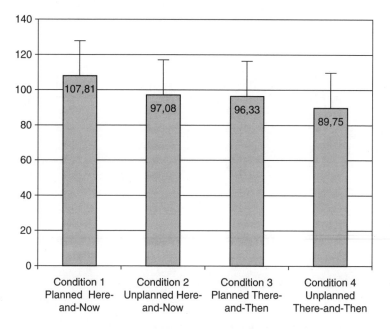

Figure 3.1 Fluency measure: pruned speech rate

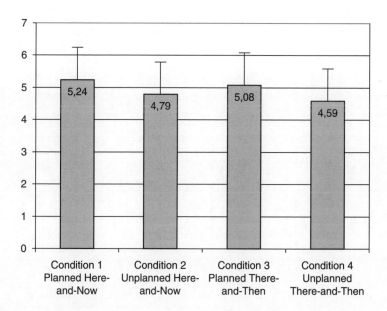

Figure 3.2 Lexical complexity measure: Guiraud's Index of lexical richness

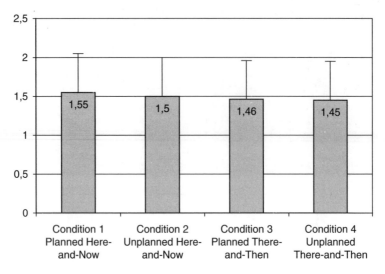

Figure 3.3 Structural complexity measure: S-nodes per T-units

Effects of increasing task complexity along (+/− Here-and-Now) on production

Hypothesis 2 was devised to investigate the impact of increasing complexity along the [+/− Here-and-Now] variable under both planned and unplanned conditions. It was predicted that such increase would reduce

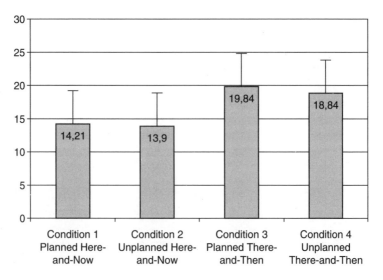

Figure 3.4 Hypothesis 1. Accuracy measure: percentage of self-repairs

Table 3.4 Hypothesis 2. Fluency, lexical and structural complexity, and accuracy measures: Mean differences between simple Here-and-Now and complex There-and-Then tasks under both planned and unplanned conditions

Comparison	Fluency pruned speech rate	Complexity Guiraud's Index	Complexity sentence nodes per T-units	Accuracy percentage of self-repairs
Planned Here-and-Now (Condition 1) vs Planned There-and-Then (Condition 3)	12.58*	0.13	0.05	−5.89*
Unplanned Here-and-Now (Condition 2) vs Unplanned There-and-Then (Condition 4)	7.30*	0.18	0.01	−5.20*

fluency but would have a positive impact on the complexity, both lexical and structural, and accuracy of learners' production.

Regarding pruned speech rate, learners were significantly more fluent ($p < 0.05$) when narrating tasks in the Here-and-Now than when doing so in the There-and-Then under planned conditions. This behaviour was the same when planning time was 50 seconds, which caused learners to be significantly more fluent ($p < 0.05$) when producing Here-and-Now narratives than when producing narratives in the There-and-Then (see Table 3.4 and Figure 3.1).

With regard to lexical complexity, the results of the Guiraud's Index of lexical richness show that complexity is reduced by increasing task demands along the [+/− Here-and-Now] variable, hence contradicting what was hypothesized in Hypothesis 1 (see Table 3.4 and Figure 3.2). As for structural complexity, this was the same between simple and complex tasks performed with 50 seconds' planning time. Hypothesis 2, predicted that tasks in the There-and-Then would also generate higher levels of structural complexity than those in the Here-and-Now. Hypothesis 2 was not confirmed (see Table 3.4 and Figure 3.3).

The results for accuracy regarding Hypothesis 2 differ considerably from the ones obtained for Hypothesis 1. While providing time had a limited, non-significant effect on learners' accuracy, increasing complexity along the [+/− Here-and-Now] variable had a strong, positive effect on learners' accuracy. The percentage of self-repairs showed higher levels of attention to form when tasks were performed in the There-and-Then than when produced in the Here-and-Now. Hence, complex tasks in the There-and-Then triggered a significantly ($p < 0.05$) higher proportion of self-repairs than Here-and-Now tasks when performed after 10 minutes of planning. This was also the case when task demands were made higher by reducing planning time to less than a minute, which caused more episodes of self-repair when learners spoke in the past and without looking at the pictures than when narrating the stories in the Here-and-Now. Hypothesis 2 was therefore confirmed for accuracy (see Table 3.4 and Figure 3.4).

Discussion

The first part of the discussion deals with the results of the different dimensions of production. It does so by considering production as affected by the different degrees of task complexity. The second part focuses on the issue of competition for attention during task performance.

Production results

In general, increasing complexity along pre-task planning time brings learners closer to the 'real' processing conditions under which narrative discourse in conversation often takes place, that is, without previous preparation and often using displaced, past time reference. However, the results reported in this chapter lead us to draw the conclusion that these increases in complexity do not seem to direct learners' attention to any particular grammatical features of their language. If, on the contrary, pre-task planning time is provided, as it is often the case in instructional contexts, learners will achieve a more lexically rich and varied performance as well as a more fluent one. On the other hand, increasing complexity along the [+/− Here-and-Now] variable makes learners reduce their rate of speech but also pushes them to focus on how they code their messages. Reducing complexity along this latter variable only produces a minor improvement in fluency.

Under Condition 1, that is, with the support of the context (i.e. comic strips) and in the present, pre-task planning time had the effect of ensuring a fluent and lexically complex performance but did not particularly draw the learners' attention to how they encoded their messages. In this sense I would agree with Yuan and Ellis (2003: 7) who conclude that: 'It follows that pre-task planning does not greatly assist formulation, especially of grammatical morphology. Thus, the linguistic correlate of effort put into conceptualizing what to say is enhanced complexity and fluency rather than accuracy.' [sic]. Furthermore, the fact that planning time improves lexical complexity but does not improve accuracy does not necessarily have to be explained in terms of limited attention or competition for attention. It may also be explained by the fact that providing planning time *per se* does not guide learners towards more accurate speech. Although it has been shown that during pre-task planning time, attention to form can and does take place, the results described in this study as well as in some previous ones show that pre-task planning time does not focus learners on form during performance in any particular way.

For Condition 2, which keeps tasks simple at the level of contextual support and present time reference but makes them complex by reducing planning time, all dimensions of production are negatively affected, which confirms both Skehan's and Robinson's predictions. Speech rate is significantly slower than in that of its planned counterpart. If anything, and as shown by protocol analysis reports, under this condition, learners use their resources to find the words they need to communicate their message, which still generates a low percentage of lexical words and low ratio of lexical to function words, as well as a minimal level of monitoring and self-repairs.

Condition 3, which makes tasks simple along planning time but complex along displaced, past time reference, triggers lexically complex language as well as increased attention to form, with only fluency being affected negatively. Under planned conditions, the effects of increasing task complexity along the +/− Here-and-Now on fluency were stronger than when doing so along unplanned ones. This means that when comparing Condition 1 to Condition 3, in Condition 3 attention was geared towards both complexity and accuracy with negative consequences for fluency. Going from Condition 2 to Condition 4, that is, from an unplanned Here-and-Now task to an unplanned There-and-Then one, led learners only to focus on self-repairs under Condition 4, and hence the mean difference in fluency was lower than between planned tasks. This also conforms to Robinson's predictions for monologic tasks, which suggests that if tasks are kept simple along resource-dispersing variables (e.g. planning time) but are made more complex along resource-directing variables (e.g. +/− Here-and-Now), attention may be allotted to complexity and accuracy simultaneously. These findings are also coherent with those of Yuan and Ellis (2003).

Finally, Condition 4 makes tasks complex at both levels, which has negative effects for fluency and complexity and only has positive effects for monitoring of learners' own speech. This conforms to both Skehan's and Robinson's prediction that if tasks are made more complex along planning time, attention will be drawn to either complexity or accuracy, but not both simultaneously.

The competition for attention issue

During the review of both planning time and Here-and-Now studies, we saw that some authors suggested that trade-off effects exist between accuracy and complexity, while others concluded that trade-off effects took place between fluency and accuracy.

First of all, despite the fact that the metaphor that has prevailed is one of limited capacity in which the three dimensions of production compete equally for attention, I would argue that fluency should be considered to be separate from complexity and accuracy. This research has shown that fluency is reduced when processing demands are high. If processing load is reduced, for example, by the effect of providing pre-task planning time, fluency increases. These two facts show fluency to be clearly sensitive to processing. But the results of this experiment present quite a complex picture of how fluency interacts with complexity and accuracy, a picture which depends on the direction in which planning time is manipulated. When extended pre-task planning time is provided, significant gains are found for fluency and lexical complexity at the expense of attention to structural complexity or accuracy. When task demands are made higher by reducing planning time, resources do not seem to be employed to improve performance in any of the other areas, as seen by the results of lexical and structural complexity, and accuracy. Nevertheless, I would like to suggest that fluency does not require attention in the same way that complexity and accuracy do. Differences in fluency are the consequence of what happens with complexity and accuracy, but fluency does not diminish because of the lack of attentional control. In other words, higher fluency is not the consequence of attention allocation policies, as complexity and accuracy would be, but the consequence of more efficient message planning and faster lexical access and selection (Levelt, 1989).

Wickens (1989: 73) suggests that when two tasks are being carried out simultaneously, confusion between the tasks may lead to poor performance. However, a number of strategies can be applied, and he adds: 'One such strategy may be to continue to try to perform the two activities in parallel but at some lower rate of performance, perhaps by being more careful, in a manner that will slow the rate of responses. This strategy will be effortful and extract a toll on resources, but will reduce the degree of confusion that results.' In contrast, planning utterances, finding the words to express meaning, and coding them grammatically and phonologically, all involve conscious attention allocation, at least in the case of L2 speakers, with detrimental effects for fluency.

I believe that the results obtained for Condition 3 disprove the argument that there are not enough attentional resources to focus on complexity and accuracy simultaneously. As we saw in the previous section, if tasks are made simple along resource-dispersing dimensions but made complex along resource-directing ones, a simultaneous focus on accuracy and complexity is possible. Even people who have drawn on multiple source models have come to the conclusion that complexity and accuracy compete for attention. Kormos (2000: 348), who uses Wickens' (1989) model as a reference, has argued that the different dimensions of production draw on the same resource pool: 'Upon processing their speech, L2 learners need to rely on the same verbal resource pool; therefore the various phases of speech production need to compete with each other for attentional resources.'

Maybe the explanation lies in the fact that the concept 'resource pool' has not been sufficiently defined. In this sense, Robinson (2003: 646) indicated that: 'codes would have to be representationally specified, as would resource pools'. I would add that, regarding performance, we also need to clarify the nature of the dimensions of accuracy and complexity. If we see them as just two dimensions of a single task (i.e. speaking) that draw on a single pool of resources and therefore compete, as Skehan (1998) and Kormos (2000) suggest, then we need to define what the limits of such capacity are and account for how time-sharing can be achieved, as in Condition 3 of this experiment where learners paid attention to both meaning and morphosyntactic forms. If we take a multiple-resource approach, it remains to be proven that what happens during speech is that accuracy and complexity are two tasks (i.e. in a dual-task conception like Wickens' (1989) that draw on different resource pools and can therefore be attended to simultaneously.

One of the strongest arguments against the limited-capacity conception of attention has been advanced by Robinson (2003, 2005b). Based on attention models that go beyond the limited capacity idea, Robinson suggests that:

> [...] explanations linking relative ease or difficulty of L2 comprehension, or different characteristics of L2 production, to task demands may be more legitimately framed in terms of confusion and cross-talk between codes (of L1, interlanguage, and L2 syntax, morphology, semantics, and phonology/orthography) within specific resource pools during task performance, rather than in terms of global capacity limitations. (Robinson, 2003: 646)

As a way of conclusion, this study has been an attempt at understanding how different degrees of cognitive complexity affect narrative oral production. In my view, task complexity, both as operationalised in this study as well as in previous ones, stands out as a robust and testable construct for task and syllabus design. Findings obtained from task-based research on production and acquisition lend themselves to not just task-based syllabus construction but also to other approaches such as process or content-based teaching. Besides that, the experimental operationalisation and manipulation of different task features can be easily transferred to pedagogic contexts in order to achieve specific effects on production and, possibly, learning.

Finally, further research should bring individual differences into the picture. Some task-based studies have started to cross complexity and learner factors in interesting ways. For example, Niwa (2000) has looked into how individual differences such as aptitude, intelligence, and working memory can differentiate complex task performance. For a detailed review of such studies see Robinson (2005b).

Notes

1. C-tests have been described as having high reliability and validity indices and have often been adopted as instruments for testing learner proficiency. See Klein-Braley (1997), Jafarpur (1999), and Babaii and Ansary (2001).
2. In a Latin square design, treatments are assigned at random within rows and columns, with each treatment once per row and once per column, in order to control for variation in two directions. In this case the two directions are condition and sequence (Steel & Torrie, 1980).
3. Other alternatives have been suggested more recently. Foster *et al.* (2000) suggest the AS-Unit (the Analysis of Speech Unit) which corrects some of the shortcomings of T-Units, C-Units, and utterances. In this study the T-Unit was chosen because of the one-way, non-interactional nature of the narratives used, and for the sake of comparability to previous studies.
4. Self-repairs exclusively refers to error-repairs in this study since no protocol analysis was used to neither detect different repairs nor appropriateness repairs (Kormos, 1999). Also, phonological self-repairs were not considered either, even if they are relatively easy to detect. The reason is to be found in the difficulty to reach an agreement between raters as to what constitutes a phonological error. An example of a lexical self-repair would be: 'OK one day eh this eh man #men eh saw hair eh in in a comb a combing comb a combing combing *comb* REPAIR.' An example of a morphosyntactic self-repair would be: 'eh the man go to eh go went the man *went* REPAIR in a a doctor eh in a doctor's room'.
5. The definition of error is adopted from Lennon (1991: 182): 'a linguistic form or combination of forms, which in the same context and under similar conditions of production would, in all likelihood, not be produced by the speakers' native speaker counterparts'.

References

Babaii, E. and Ansary, H. (2001) The C-test: A valid operationalization of reduced redundancy principle? *System* 29, 209–219.

Breen, M.P. (1984) Process syllabuses for the language classroom. In C.J. Brumfit (ed.) *General English Syllabus Design: ELT Documents No. 118* (pp. 47–60). London: Pergamon Press and The British Council.

Brown, G., Anderson, A., Shillcock, R. and Yule, G. (1984) *Teaching Talk: Strategies for Production and Assessment.* Cambridge: Cambridge University Press.

Bygate, M. (1999) Task as context for the framing, reframing and unframing of language. *System* 27 (1), 33–48.

Bygate, M. (2001) Effects of task repetition on the structure and control of oral language. In M. Bygate, P. Skehan and M. Swain (eds) *Researching Pedagogic Tasks. Second Language Learning, Teaching, and Testing* (pp. 23–48). Harlow: Longman.

Candlin, C.N. (1984) Syllabus design as a critical process. In C.J. Brumfit (ed.) *General English Syllabus Design: ELT Documents No. 118* (pp. 29–46). London: Pergamon Press and The British Council.

Crookes, G. (1989) Planning and interlanguage variation. *Studies in Second Language Acquisition* 11 (4), 367–383.

Ellis, R. (1987) Interlanguage variability in narrative discourse: Style shifting in the use of the past tense. *Studies in Second Language Acquisition* 9, 1–20.

Ellis, R. (1997) *SLA Research and Language Teaching.* Oxford: Oxford University Press.

Ellis, R. (2005) *Planning and Task Performance in a Second Language.* Amsterdam: John Benjamins.

Foster, P. and Skehan, P. (1996) The influence of planning and task type on second language performance. *Studies in Second Language Acquisition* 18, 299–323.

Foster, P., Tonkyn, A. and Wigglesworth, G. (2000) Measuring spoken discourse: A unit for all reasons. *Applied Linguistics* 21 (3), 333–353.

Gilabert, R. (2005) Task complexity and L2 narrative oral production. PhD thesis, Universitat de Barcelona.

Griffiths, R. (1991) Pausological research in an L2 context: A rationale and review of selected studies. *Applied Linguistics* 12, 345–364.

Iwashita, N., McNamara, T. and Elder, C. (2001) Can we predict task difficulty in an oral proficiency test? Exploring the potential of an information-processing approach to task design. *Language Learning* 51 (3), 401–436.

Jafarpur, A. (1999) Can the C-test be improved with classical item analysis? *System* 27, 79–89.

Kahneman, D. (1973) *Attention and Effort*. Englewood Cliffs, NJ: Prentice-Hall.

Klein-Braley, C. (1997) C-tests in the context of reduced redundancy testing: An appraisal. *Language Testing* 14, 47–84.

Kormos, J. (1999) Monitoring and self-repair in L2. *Language Learning* 49 (2), 303–342.

Kormos, J. (2000) The role of attention in monitoring second language speech production. *Language Learning* 50, 343–384.

Kuiken, F., Mos, M. and Vedder, I. (2005) Cognitive task complexity and second language writing performance. In S. Foster-Cohen, M.P. García-Mayo and J. Cenoz (eds) *EUROSLA Yearbook 5* (pp. 195–222). Amsterdam: John Benjamins.

Lennon, P. (1991) Error: Some problems of definition, identification and distinction. *Applied Linguistics* 12, 180–195.

Levelt, W.J.M. (1989) *Speaking: From Intention to Articulation*. Cambridge, MA: Massachusetts Institute of Technology Press.

Long, M.H. (1985) A role for instruction in second language acquisition: Task-based language teaching. In K. Hyltenstam and M. Pienemann (eds) *Modelling and Assessing Second Language Acquisition* (pp. 77–79). Clevedon: Multilingual Matters.

Long, M.H. (1989) Task, group, and task-based interactions. *University of Hawaii Working Papers in ESL* 8 (2), 1–26.

Long, M.H. (2000) Focus on form in task-based language teaching. In R.D. Lambart and E. Shohany (eds) *Language Policy and Pedagogy* (pp. 179–192). Amsterdam/Philadelphia: John Benjamins.

Long, M.H. and Crookes, G. (1992) Three approaches to task-based syllabus design. *TESOL Quarterly* 26, 27–56.

Lyster, R. and Ranta, L. (1997) Corrective feedback and learner uptake. *Studies in Second Language Acquisition* 19, 37–66.

Mehnert, U. (1998) The effects of different lengths of time for planning on second language performance. *Studies in Second Language Acquisition* 20, 52–83.

Niwa, Y. (2000) Reasoning demands of L2 tasks and L2 narrative production: Effects of individual differences in working memory, intelligence, and aptitude. Unpublished MA dissertation, Aoyama Gakuin University.

Nunan, D. (1989) *Designing Tasks for the Communicative Classroom*. Cambridge: Cambridge University Press.

Ortega, L. (1999) Planning and focus on form in L2 oral performance. *Studies in Second Language Acquisition* 21, 109–148.

Plough, I. and Gass, S. (1993) Interlocutor and task familiarity: Effects on interactional structure. In G. Crookes and S. Gass (eds) *Tasks and Language Learning: Integrating Theory and Practice* (pp. 33–56). Clevedon: Multilingual Matters.

Prabhu, N.S. (1987) *Second Language Pedagogy*. Oxford: Oxford University Press.

Rahimpour, M. (1997) Task condition, task complexity and variation in L2 discourse. Unpublished PhD dissertation, University of Queensland.

Robinson, P. (1995) Task complexity and second language narrative discourse. *Language Learning* 45, 99–140.

Robinson, P. (1998) State of the art: SLA theory and second language syllabus design. *The Language Teacher* 22 (4), 7–14.

Robinson, P. (2001a) Task complexity, task difficulty, and task production: Exploring interactions in a componential framework. *Applied Linguistics* 22 (1), 27–57.

Robinson, P. (2001b) Task complexity, cognitive resources, and syllabus design: A triadic framework for examining task influences on SLA. In P. Robinson (ed.) *Cognition and Second Language Instruction* (pp. 287–318). Cambridge: Cambridge University Press.

Robinson, P. (2003) Attention and memory. In C. Doughty and M.H. Long (eds) *Handbook of Second Language Acquisition* (pp. 631–678). Oxford: Blackwell.

Robinson, P. (2005a) Cognitive complexity and task sequencing: Studies in a componential framework for second language task design. *IRAL* 44 (1), 1–32.

Robinson, P. (2005b) Aptitude and second language acquisition. *Annual Review of Applied Linguistics* 25 (1), 46–73.

Schegloff, E., Jefferson, G. and Sacks, H. (1977) The preference of self-correction in the organization of repair in conversation. *Language* 53, 361–382.

Skehan, P. (1998) *A Cognitive Approach to Language Learning.* Oxford: Oxford University Press.

Skehan, P. and Foster, P. (1997) Task type and task processing conditions as influences on foreign language performance. *Language Teaching Research* 1 (3), 185–211.

Skehan, P. and Foster, P. (2001) Cognition and tasks. In P. Robinson (ed.) *Cognition and Second Language Instruction* (pp. 183–205). Cambridge: Cambridge University Press.

Steel, R.G.D. and Torrie, J.H. (1980) *Principles and Procedures of Statistics.* New York: McGraw-Hill.

Swain, M. (1998) Focus on form through conscious reflection. In C. Doughty and J. Williams (eds) *Focus on Form in Classroom SLA* (pp. 64–81). New York: Cambridge University Press.

Vermeer, A. (2000) Coming to grips with lexical richness in spontaneous speech data. *Language Testing* 17, 65–83.

Wigglesworth, G. (1997) An investigation of planning time and proficiency level on oral test discourse. *Language Testing* 14, 85–106.

Wickens, C. D. (1989) Attention and skilled performance. In D.H. Holding (ed.) *Humans Skills* (pp. 71–105). New York: John Wiley.

Wickens, C.D. (1992) *Engineering Psychology and Human Performance.* New York: Harper Collins.

Willis, D. (1990) *The Lexical Syllabus.* London: Collins.

Yuan F. and Ellis, R. (2003) The effects of pre-task planning and on-line planning on fluency, complexity, and accuracy in L2 monologic oral production. *Applied Linguistics* 24 (1), 1–27.

Chapter 4

Tasks, Negotiation, and L2 Learning in a Foreign Language Context

MARISOL FERNÁNDEZ GARCÍA

Introduction

In the last few decades, theoretical perspectives on the role of interaction in the second language acquisition (SLA) process have focused on a particular variety of interaction referred to as negotiation (Gass & Varonis, 1985, 1986, 1989; Pica, 1987, 1992, 1994; Varonis & Gass, 1985a, 1985b). Negotiation has been claimed to create conditions for second language (L2) development as it offers learners opportunities to obtain L2 input that is adjusted to their comprehension needs, get feedback on production, produce modified output, and focus learners' attention to relevant L2 structural and semantic relationships.

While it is widely accepted that opportunities for interaction and for negotiation of meaning are crucial for learners to advance in the L2 learning process, much of the evidence comes from research with learners of English in a second language (ESL) context, where interaction with native speakers (NSs) is readily available to them. There is almost no research that examines the oral interactions of learners in foreign language contexts (see García Mayo & Pica, 2000, for an exception), where interaction with other learners and with non-native-speaking instructors is the norm rather than the exception. Although a few recent studies on synchronous written interactions have focused on interaction and negotiation in a foreign language context (e.g. Fernández-García & Martínez-Arbelaiz, 2002, 2003; Pellettieri, 2000), most of it is not easily comparable with the ESL research given the different media, tasks and settings used across studies.

This study explores how learners' interaction with each other affects their learning in a foreign language situation, where learners are regularly each other's resource for language learning, by investigating two different though related facets of negotiation. First, this research examines how two communication tasks contribute to create opportunities for learners to engage in the negotiation of meaning. In the second part, the study analyses the type of modified input, feedback, and modified output that beginning foreign language learners can provide to each other while engaged in negotiation exchanges.

Research Background

Negotiation and second language acquisition

Since the early work of Hatch (1978) and Long (1983a, 1983b), the role that interaction and negotiation play in the language learning process has been an important thrust of research in second language acquisition (SLA) studies. A growing body of research has provided evidence showing that learners often engage in negotiation exchanges among themselves or with native speakers whereby they work collaboratively towards mutual understanding (among others, Gass & Varonis, 1985, 1986, 1989; Pica, 1987, 1992, 1994; Varonis & Gass, 1985a, 1985b). As shown in Excerpt 1 below from Varonis & Gass (1985b), where NNS stands for non-native speaker, a negotiation routine or exchange occurs when one interlocutor lets the other know in an overt way (Indicator or Signal) that the other's preceding turn (Trigger) has not been successfully understood. The other interlocutor, then, provides additional information in a subsequent turn (Response). An optional turn (Reaction to Response) may tie up the negotiation routine.

Excerpt 1

NNS1	NNS2
-My father now is retired (Trigger)	-retire? (Signal)
-yes (Response)	-oh yeah (Reaction to Response)

From a theoretical standpoint, it has been claimed that participation in negotiation can provide learners with an effective context for L2 learning as it allows them to: (1) increase input comprehensibility, (2) gain feedback on production, and (3) modify interlanguage output, and test hypotheses about the language being learned. It is widely acknowledged in the SLA field that exposure to the L2 input is a necessary albeit an insufficient condition for acquisition to take place. That is, for the learner to be able to internalise the L2 system, the input must be comprehensible (Krashen, 1980, 1985). However, comprehensible input is not always sufficient given that not all the input that is comprehensible to the learner gets to be processed for acquisition purposes (VanPatten, 1990, 1996). Some researchers have argued (Long, 1983a, 1996; White, 1987) that a failure to comprehend may sometimes be needed if interlanguage development is to proceed. Long, for example, points out that 'Communicative trouble can lead learners to recognize that a linguistic problem exits, switch their attentional focus from message to form, identify the problem, and notice the needed item in the input' (Long, 1996: 425). That is, through negotiation learners are exposed, on the one hand, to modified input that makes L2 data available for learning by segmenting L2 units and highlighting relationships among them. On the other, learners may be exposed to negative input and feedback that calls their attention to possible gaps between their own output and the target input (Gass, 1988, 1989; Long, 1996; Schmidt, 1990).

An additional contribution of negotiation to the learning process is that it provides learners with opportunities to produce modified output. Swain (1985) claims that when communicative demands are placed on the learners to produce comprehensible modified output, learners are given opportunities to test hypotheses about their interlanguage, experiment with new structures and forms, and stretch their interlanguage resources to meet communicative needs.

Communication tasks as a context for negotiated interaction

Communication tasks are seen as the principle means by which learners can be provided opportunities to negotiate meaning (Lee, 2000; Nunan, 1989; Pica *et al.*, 1993). Moreover, Pica *et al.* (1993) see communication tasks as a particularly appropriate tool both to assist language learning and to study the processes of SLA. They propose a framework to characterise and differentiate communication tasks based on four features: interactant relationship, interaction requirement, goal orientation and outcome options. As a result of combining these four features, a continuum of task types emerges that ranges from those tasks that generate the most opportunities for interactants to engage in negotiation, to those that generate the least, as follows: jigsaw, information-gap, problem-solving, decision-making, and opinion exchange.

At one end of the continuum of task types, the jigsaw would generate the most opportunities for negotiation of meaning, because interactants hold different portions of the information needed to complete the task and, therefore, must give and request information as they work toward a convergent single goal. At the opposite end of the continuum, the opinion exchange task would generate the least opportunities for negotiation of meaning because each interactant has access to the same information, and there is no requirement for interactants to converge toward a single goal in order to complete the task.

There is some empirical evidence that shows that different types of tasks produce different amounts of modified interaction. Long (1983a) reports that tasks where the information must flow in two directions, i.e. two-way tasks, resulted in significantly more conversational modifications by the native speaker than tasks where one interactant has the information that the other interactant needs, i.e. one-way tasks. Extending this type of research to communication between learners, Doughty and Pica (1986) observed that a task with an information exchange requirement (i.e. a two-way information gap task) generated more modified interaction than a task without an information exchange requirement (i.e. a decision-making task).

However, results are not always consistent or easy to compare across studies. Gass and Varonis (1985) compared the language produced by non-native speakers (NNSs) interacting with each other while completing a one-way task (i.e. a picture-drawing task) and a two-way task (i.e. discovering who the thief was), and examined only negotiation of meaning, that is, a subset of what Long (1983a) referred to as modified interaction. Their results did not support Long's findings as no significant difference in number of negotiations between the two tasks was found. Gass and Varonis (1985) proposed that a greater shared background in the two-way task had facilitated comprehension between interactants, which had in turn resulted in fewer breakdowns in communication. Furthermore, in their study, the one-way task often elicited a two-way exchange of information, which made their results difficult to compare to Long's. In other words, qualitative differences in task design rendered the one-way and two-way tasks in Gass and Varonis' study very close to each other in the continuum of task types proposed by Pica *et al.* (1993). Such contiguity would in part explain why there was no significant difference in the amount of negotiation between the two.

Gass and Varonis (1985) further note that methodological issues make comparison of results across studies quite difficult. One of these issues is how different studies characterise and differentiate among task types. For example, the task used in the Doughty and Pica study (1986), though characterised as a required information exchange task, is more similar to Gass and Varonis' one-way task than to their two-way task. Another dimension that Gass and Varonis mention differentiates between the task types and further complicate the process of comparison across studies is the type of media that the tasks involve (e.g. linguistic input and output only versus going from linguistic input to paper-and-pencil/drawing output versus going from linguistic input to object manipulation output). Consequently, Gass and Varonis (1985: 159) argue that future research should control for the input/output medium together with the amount and type of information exchange that tasks involve.

Evidence to support Gass and Varonis' claim is found in a study involving NS–NNS interaction (Shortreed, 1993). Shortreed compared two one-way information gap tasks, and found that significantly more negotiation work (measured as use of repair strategies) was needed to complete a drawing task (consisting of 16 squares with pictures that the NNS had to draw) than a picture recognition task (where one interactant had to put 20 pictures in order following the other interactant's instructions). Shortreed argues that less shared background in the picture drawing task explained the need for more negotiation work in this task as compared to the picture recognition task.

Robinson's (2001) construct of cognitively defined task complexity may shed some light on Shortreeds's results. He argues that 'task complexity is the result of the attentional, memory, reasoning, and other information processing demands imposed by the structure of the task on the language learner' (Robinson, 2001: 29). Following Robinson's arguments, we could hypothesise that the drawing task is cognitively more complex than the recognition task, given that reproducing visuals places more demands on the learners' processing system than recognising them. More need for negotiation work would, therefore, emerge, within the context of a cognitively more complex task such as the picture drawing task.

Summarizing, research on NNS–NS and NNS–NNS interaction has shown that the variable task type has an impact on the amount of negotiation required to complete a given task. This research suggests that in order to arrive at a meaningful comparison of task types it is crucial to control for variables such as the amount of shared task background, the amount and type of information exchanged, and the type of media that the tasks involve.

Negotiation as a context for provision of modified input and production of modified output

Studies that examined NNS–NS interactions have revealed that learners are able to adjust and expand their own previous utterances when responding to NSs' signals during negotiation exchanges (Pica, 1987, 1992, 1994; Pica *et al.*, 1989, 1990, 1991). Likewise, studies that examined learner–learner interactions (Gass & Varonis, 1985, 1989; Pica & Doughty, 1985a, 1985b; Porter, 1986; Varonis & Gass, 1985b) show that learners are also able to repair their previous utterances when responding to signals in negotiation exchanges with other learners. That is, learners can take advantage of a range of interactional contexts that offer them opportunities for the production of modified output, a process claimed to be fundamental for the development of learners' interlanguage system (Swain, 1985).

Research on L2 negotiated interaction has also noted differences with regard to learners and NSs as a source of modified input for L2 learning (Pica, 1987, 1992; Pica *et al.*, 1989, 1990, 1991). This research found that learners produced fewer modifications in response to NSs' negotiation signals than NSs produced in response to learners' signals. Pica (1992) and Pica *et al.* (1990) also noted that learners appeared to be more limited than NSs in the type of modifications they produced. Learners' predominant form of modification was through segmentation (Peters, 1985), that is, through the extraction and repetition of a word or phrase from a prior utterance. NSs' modified responses, on the other hand, exhibited more lexical and other structural modifications.

Following these observations, the study of Pica *et al.* (1996) examined learner–learner and learner–NS interactions as a possible source of modified input for learning. In terms of the type of modified input provided for learning, a comparison of learners' responses during learner–learner negotiations and NSs' responses to learners during learners–NS negotiations yielded no significant difference in the use of segmentation across both groups. Moreover, although learners' responses that modified previous utterances through segmentation were infrequent, they conformed to the L2 morphosyntax as often as responses of other modification types. While the study of Pica *et al.* (1996) involved low-intermediate English language learners in a second language context, similar results were obtained by García-Mayo and Pica (2000) with advanced learners of English in a foreign language situation.

Taking together, the results of these studies suggest that learner–learner interaction can serve learners' needs for L2 learning in ways comparable to learner–NS interaction. Through negotiation with each other learners are exposed to modified input that contains L2 structural and semantic information. Likewise, learner–learner interactions offer learners opportunities to adjust and modify their output semantically or structurally and, thus, to test hypotheses about the L2. There is also evidence that suggests that learners at intermediate and advanced stages of acquisition are able to modify their previous utterances not only through segmentation but in a variety of ways, and in conformity to L2 morphosyntax. The implication would be, therefore, that learners at initial stages of acquisition would rely more on segmentation, that is, on a simpler form of modification, and that they would be more accurate when using segmentations as compared to other modification types.

Negotiation as a context for feedback

Of particular interest for the present study is the line of research that examined learner–learner interaction, and found that learners do provide useful feedback to each other in negotiated interactions (e.g. Gass & Varonis, 1985, 1989; Pica & Doughty, 1985a, 1985b; Porter, 1986). Learners are not only able to draw other learners' attention toward the comprehensibility of their messages but to divergences from the L2 norm as well. Furthermore, previous research (García-Mayo & Pica, 2000; Jacobs, 1989; Pica *et al.*, 1996) has also documented that learners are able to provide feedback to each other that is consistent with the L2 norm.

The study by Pica *et al.* (1996) examined learners' signals to each other during negotiation exchanges, and found that low-intermediate learners provided feedback to each other mainly through segmentation of their previous utterances. In most cases learners extracted words or phrases from previous utterances that themselves had already conformed to L2 morphosyntax. Feedback through signals that used other types of modifications also conformed to L2 morphosyntax. Thus, overall, peer feedback conformed to the L2 norm across all types of modification. In contrast to Pica *et al.*'s study (1996), García-Mayo and Pica (2000) found that when signalling for message comprehensibility, the advanced foreign language learners of their study did not use predominantly segmentations but rather a variety of modification types. They attributed this finding to the learners' more developmentally advanced language system. Nevertheless, as in Pica *et al.*'s study (1996), these advanced learners' signals conformed to L2 morphosyntax across all modification types.

The above reviewed studies suggest that through negotiation learners are able to offer feedback to each other while signalling for message comprehensibility. Furthermore, learners are able to offer feedback that conforms to the L2 norm, and that increases in linguistic complexity as learners progress in the language acquisition process.

Research questions and hypotheses

The following research questions guided the present study:

(1) Does the variable shared background have an impact on the amount of negotiation generated by tasks? Specifically, do beginning foreign language learners of Spanish engage in negotiation when completing a one-way task as often as they do when completing a two-way task with a higher amount of shared task background?

When beginning foreign language learners of Spanish respond to each other's signals of non-understanding,

(2) Do they modify their previous utterances mainly through segmentation or do they make use of segmentation as often as they make use of other types of modification?
(3) Do responses that modify previous utterances through segmentation conform to L2 morphosyntax as often as responses with other modification types?

When beginning foreign language learners of Spanish signal non-understanding to each other,

(4) Do they modify each other's previous utterances mainly through segmentation or do they make use of segmentation as often as they make use of other types of modification?
(5) Do signals that modify previous utterances through segmentation conform to L2 morphosyntax as often as signals with other modification types?

The above reviewed studies suggested the following hypotheses:

(1) Beginning foreign language learners of Spanish will engage in negotiation when completing a one-way task as often as they will when completing a two-way task with a higher amount of shared task background.

When beginning foreign language learners of Spanish respond to each other's signals of non-understanding,

(2)   they will modify their previous utterances mainly through segmentation, that is, they will make use of segmentation more often than they will make use of other types of modification;

(3)   responses that modify learners' previous utterances through segmentation will conform to L2 morphosyntax more often than responses with other modification types.

When beginning foreign language learners of Spanish signal non-understanding to each other,

(4)   they will modify each other's previous utterances through segmentation more often than through other types of modification;

(5)   signals that modify previous utterances through segmentation will conform to L2 morphosyntax more often than signals with other modification types.

The study

Participants

The participants of the study were foreign language learners of Spanish enrolled in a second-semester course at Northeastern University (USA). All participants claimed English to be their native language. Four whole sections of this course participated in the study. Sections were randomly assigned to one of the two tasks of the study. The final pool of participants consisted of 42 students (21 dyads).[1] Eleven dyads carried out the two-way task (13 females and nine males), and 10 dyads (14 females and six males) carried out the one-way task. Final composition of dyads according to participants' gender was as follows: five female–male dyads, four female–female dyads, and two male–male dyads in the two-way task; four female–male dyads, five female–female dyads, and one male–male dyad, in the one-way task.

Tasks

The two tasks used in this study were a two-way and a one-way information gap tasks. The two-way information gap task was 'What's missing?' (from Shrum & Glisan, 2000: 196–197); the one-way information gap task was 'The living-room' (from Shrum & Glisan, 2000: 188–189).[2] In the two-way task each participant was given one of two versions of the same drawing of a house that had three floors and seven rooms. The difference between the two versions was that each was missing an object in each room. In order to complete the task each participant had to draw the missing objects in the appropriate places based on the descriptions of her partner. The one-way task consisted of two versions of the floor plan of a living room. One version depicted all the furniture items arranged in the floor plan; the other version depicted the same floor plan but with no furniture. Both versions included drawings that represented the furniture items in a column to the left of the floor plan. Each item in the column was labeled with its name in the version with the complete floor plan; the version with the empty floor plan did not include any labels with names.[3] In order to complete this task the participant with the empty floor plan had to draw each furniture item in its proper position in the living room according to the descriptions provided by her partner, who had the complete floor plan.

The tasks described above were selected for use in the present study for several reasons. Firstly, in the continuum of task types described by Pica *et al.* (1993) both tasks are located toward the left end of the continuum, which means that they are hypothetically among the tasks that generate the most opportunities for negotiation of meaning, and, are, therefore, more facilitative of the acquisition process. They offer, then, an ideal context to investigate specific predictions regarding task type and meaning negotiation. Secondly, both tasks are picture-drawing tasks, which allows to control for the type of media they involve, and facilitates comparison of results across tasks. Thirdly, while one of them is a two-way task and the other a one-way task, we propose here that they are rather close to each other in the continuum of task types due to a difference in shared background. In the two-way task interactants share a good amount of task background; they are missing some objects but the rest of the information is shared (i.e. all the other items in each of the rooms of the house). Conversely, in the one-way task, one interactant has all the items in the floor plan; the other has none. This lack of shared background will place considerable attentional and memory demands on the learner's processing system. Thus, the participant that draws will very likely need to maintain an active role requesting and clarifying information to make up for this lack of task background. It is therefore expected that the one-way task will prompt a two-way exchange of information, placing both tasks rather close to each other in terms of generating opportunities for the negotiation of meaning.

Data collection procedures

The data was collected in the Language Laboratory during participants' regular class periods. Participants were randomly assigned to a particular dyad. Dyads worked in individual booths that were separated from each other by a screen that was high enough for participants not to be able to see each other's drawings for the task but low enough to be able to see each other's faces.

Instructions to complete the tasks were given in written form to participants and were also read aloud to them. Time was given for questions regarding task procedures as necessary. Dyads' conversations were recorded simultaneously in independent cassette tapes. After completing the tasks, participants filled out a background questionnaire about their previous language experience.

Data coding

The oral data was transcribed and then coded[4] following the framework for coding data on negotiated interaction described and used in Pica (1987), Pica (1992), Pica *et al.* (1989) and Pica *et al.* (1991). According to such framework, signals and responses can modify interactants' previous utterances in three different ways: (1) semantically, through the use of synonym and paraphrase, (2) morphologically, through addition, substitution, or deletion of inflectional morphemes, and (3) syntactically, by extracting one or more constituents such as lexical items or phrases from previous utterances, and then producing them in isolation or incorporating them into a longer utterance. We focused the analyses on those signals and responses that were simple segmentations (SSs) of one or more constituents from previous utterances versus those that corresponded to other modification types (OMs), be they lexical, morphological, or syntactic.

To address the research questions of this study, we began by identifying and counting the negotiations in the interactive discourse generated by each dyad. Then, within each negotiation, the signals that modified participant's previous utterances through SS, and those that contained OMs were identified and counted. Also within each negotiation, the responses that were SSs, and those that were of OM types were identified and counted. Signals that conformed to the L2 morphosyntax were identified, and separate counts were made of those that were SSs, and of those that used OM types. Likewise, responses that conformed to the L2 morphosyntax were identified, and separate counts were made of those that were SSs, and of those that used OM types.

Excerpt 2 offers two examples of participants' modified utterances that conformed to the L2 morphosyntax.

Excerpt 2

NNS1	**NNS2**
-y enfrente un alfombra	-¿una una alfombra?
-and in front of it a rug	*-a a rug?*
-sí	-¿qué es una alfombra?
-yes	*-what is a rug?*
-es un rug	-okay yeah
-it's a rug	*-okay yeah*

NNS2 signals non-understanding to NNS1 by repeating a noun phrase in the trigger with rising intonation, and modifying it morphologically with the addition of the feminine morpheme to the determiner 'un', thus, making the phrase conform to the L2 norm. The second indicator incorporates the extracted phrase into a question '¿qué es una alfombra?', and also conforms to the L2 norm.

Excerpt 3 offers examples of modified utterances that did not conform to the L2 norm.

Excerpt 3

NNS1	NNS2

-yeah, enfrente de la sofa
  es la mesita cuadrada
-yeah, in front of the sofa is
  the square table

-¿cuadrada? ¿qué es? ¿cuatro
  mes- cuatro pequeño mesas?
-square? what's that? four
  (incomplete) four small tables

-uhh no um la um. the. um lla
  mmessa joven th
-uhh no um the um. the. um
  the young ttable th

-sí
-yes

-yeah sí [enfrente de la sofá]   -[la mesa más pequeño]
-yeah yes [in front of the sofa]   *-[the smallest table]*
-sí yeah
-yes yeah

In this excerpt, NNS2 tries to find out the meaning of the adjective 'cuadrada' used in her partner's previous utterance. Part of her utterance, the description she ventured '¿cuatro mes- cuatro pequeño mesas?', does not conform to the L2 morphosyntax given that noun-adjective position is reversed and gender-number agreement does not show in the adjective. This portion of the signal, therefore, was classified and counted as not conforming to the L2 norm. NNS1's response utterance attempts another description by using the adjective 'joven' (young), a semantic modification that does not conform to the L2 norm. NNS2 follows up with another semantic/ morphosyntactic modification in the signal 'la mesa más pequeño', which approximates the target norm (i.e. through the segmentation of the noun and adjective in previous utterances and their incorporation into a superlative structure), but is still missing the feminine gender morpheme. In this last signal, the morphosyntactic modification that incorporates words of previous utterances into the superlative structure was counted as conforming to the L2 norm; however, in terms of gender agreement, the modification did not conform morphologically to the target norm.[5]

Results and Discussion

Hypothesis 1 had predicted that beginning foreign language learners of Spanish would engage in negotiation when completing a two-way task as often as they would when completing a one-way task, provided the one-way task was designed in such a way that less task background was shared between dyad members. Table 4.1 shows the results of a Welch two-tailed

Table 4.1 Comparison of number of negotiations in the two-way information gap task and the one-way information gap task

Task type	n	Mean	sd	t	df	p
Two-way info gap	11	10.8	8.96	0.04	13	n.s.
One-way info gap	10	10.7	3.83			

t-test with number of negotiations and task type as the dependent and independent variables, respectively. In the two-way information gap task there were a total of 119 occurrences of negotiation exchanges in the 11 dyads, with an average of 10.8; in the one-way information gap task the total occurrences of negotiation exchanges for the 10 dyads was 107, with an average of 10.7. As Table 4.1 shows, there was no significant difference between the number of negotiations in the two tasks ($t = 0.04, df = 13, p = 0.9687$).

Though cautiously, given the higher standard deviation for the two-way task, these results give support to the first hypothesis of this study. It seems that, as Gass and Varonis (1985: 159) pointed out, 'the amount of information exchange required by a given task is a continuous rather than a dichotomous variable'. There are numerous examples in the transcripts from the one-way task that show that the participant that was in charge of drawing (the receiver) did indeed play an active role, being often on an equal footing with the participant in charge of describing (the sender). Excerpt 4 below illustrates this active role of the receiver who, together with the sender, co-constructs the description by asking specific questions about features that are crucial to distinguish one item from another, as well as questions aimed at determining the exact position of the items she has to draw. Furthermore, in her active role, the receiver contributes by making inferences about what the sender is trying to communicate, and by predicting the location of items based on the information provided so far.

Excerpt 4

NNS1 (Sender)   **NNS2 (Receiver)**
-ti-tiene un uh la mmmmesa grande   -¿la mesa?
-do you have a uh the big table?   *-the table?*
-la mesa   -¿grande eh eh circular?
-the table   *-big eh eh circular?*
-no uh rec-rectangular   -oh sí sí la más grande de el dos
-no uh rec-rectangular   *-oh yes the biggest of the two*
-mhm sí   -¿enfrente la ventana?
-mhm yes   *-in front the window?*
-mhm sí   -okay bueno
-mhm yes   *-okay good*

Hypotheses 2 through 5 made predictions related to the type of modified input, feedback, and modified output that emerges in negotiation exchanges between beginning foreign language learners of Spanish. We advanced four hypotheses: two of them, Hypotheses 2 and 3, concerned the type of modified input and of modified output that emerges within the context of a negotiation exchange. Specifically, Hypothesis 2 had predicted that beginning foreign language learners' negotiation responses would modify their previous utterances mainly through SS.

Table 4.2 shows the results of chi-squared goodness of fit tests on the relative proportions for each task. As the table shows, the percentage of learners' responses modified through modifications other than SS was much higher than the percentage of responses modified through SS, in both tasks (76% versus 24%, in the two-way task; 70% versus 30% in the one-way task). This difference between the use of SSs and OMs in learners' responses was significant for each of the two tasks ($\chi^2 = 36.56$, $df = 1$, $p < 0.05$, for the two-way task; $\chi^2 = 17.28$, $df = 1$, $p < 0.05$, for the one-way task).

These results, therefore, do not give support to Hypothesis 2. The present study does not find evidence to support that beginning foreign language learners' responses modify their previous utterances mainly through SS. It appears that these learners' linguistic resources did not preclude them from attempting to achieve message comprehensibility through modifications that are more complex than SSs. In their study, Pica *et al.* (1996) found that the percentage of SSs used by both learners and NSs was much higher on one of the tasks. They suggested that the use of SSs may respond to a task effect on negotiation rather than to the linguistic resources of the learners. In a similar vein, it is possible that the picture-drawing tasks used in the present study had in part accounted for the high use of OM types in learners' negotiation responses. The need to convey clear specific information about items and their location may have prompted learners to recode their messages in more complex forms to better achieve message comprehensibility.

Table 4.2 Simple segmentations versus other type of modifications in learners' negotiation responses on two communication tasks

Communication task	Response type	n	%	χ^2	df	p
				36.56	1	<0.05
Two-way info gap	S Seg	32	24			
	Oth Mod	102	76			
				17.28	1	<0.05
One-way info gap	S Seg	32	30			
	Oth Mod	75	70			

Note: S Seg = simple segmentations; Oth Mod = other type of modifications.

While this is a plausible explanation, the results of this study suggest a need to further investigate the relative contributions of task type and level of language proficiency on learners' modified responses of negotiation.

Hypothesis 3 had predicted that beginning foreign language learners of Spanish responses that modified previous utterances through SS would conform to L2 morphosyntax more often than responses with OM types. Table 4.3 presents the results of Pearson's chi-squared tests with Yates' continuity correction for each task. As shown in the table, for the two-way task, 47% of the responses modified through SS and 45% of the responses with OM types conformed to the L2 morphosyntax. This difference was not significant ($\chi^2 = 0.0007$, $df = 1$, $p =$ n.s.). In the case of the one-way task, the percentage of responses modified through SSs that conformed to the L2 morphosyntax was much higher than the percentage of responses with OMs that did so, 78% versus 25%. As the table shows, this difference was significant ($\chi^2 = 23.68$, $df = 1$, $p < 0.05$).

The results of these analyses provide partial support to Hypothesis 3. Only in the one-way information gap task was the percentage of responses with SSs that conformed to L2 morphosyntax significantly higher than the percentage of responses with OMs that did so. In contrast, in the two-way task, a segmented response conformed to L2 morphosyntax as frequently as responses with linguistic modifications more complex than SSs. Taken together, these results indicate that both SSs and OMs in learners' responses

Table 4.3 Simple segmentations versus other type of modifications in learners' negotiation responses in conformity with L2 morphosyntax on two communication tasks

Communication task	Response type	S Seg		Oth Mod		χ^2	df	p
		n	%	n	%			
Two-way info gap	Conform	15	47	46	45	0.0007	1	n.s.
	Do not Conform	17	53	56	55			
	Total	32	100	102	100			
						23.68	1	<0.05
One-way info gap	Conform	25	78	19	25			
	Do not Conform	7	22	56	75			
	Total	32	100	75	100			

Note: S Seg = simple segmentations; Oth Mod = other type of modifications.

to each other are an important source of grammatical input for L2 learning. Taking into account the low proficiency level of the learners of this study, these results speak favourably of negotiation as a productive context for learners to obtain modified input and to produce modified output when interacting with each other.

Hypotheses 4 and 5 addressed the contributions of learners as a source of feedback for L2 learning. In particular, they were concerned with the type of feedback provided by signals in negotiation exchanges, attending to the type of modification and to adherence to L2 morphosyntax. Hypothesis 4 had predicted that when beginning foreign language learners signaled non-understanding to each other, they would modify each other's previous utterances through SS more often than through OM types.

Table 4.4 shows the results of chi-squared goodness of fit tests for given probabilities for each task. In the two-way task, 48% of learners' signals modified each other's prior utterances through SS, and 52% through OM types. In the one-way task, 50% of modified signals used SS, and 50% used OM types. No significant difference was found between these percentages of SSs and of OMs for either task ($\chi^2 = 0.15, df = 1, p =$ n.s., for the two-way task; $\chi^2 = 0, df = 1, p =$ n.s., for the one-way task).

Hypothesis 4 was, thus, not supported. Learners' signals modified each other's prior utterances through SS as often as through OM types. Although the participants of the current study were beginning language learners, unlike the ones in Pica *et al.* (1996) and in García-Mayo and Pica (2000), they used a variety of modification types in their signals to each other.

One likely explanation for the findings of the present study may reside in the nature of the tasks used. The current study used picture-drawing tasks and, as noted above, these tasks seemed to have required learners to

Table 4.4 Simple segmentations versus other type of modifications in learners' negotiation signals on two communication tasks

Communication task	Signal type	n	%	χ^2	df	p
				0.15	1	n.s.
Two-way info gap	S Seg	49	48			
	Oth Mod	53	52			
	Total	102	100			
				0	1	n.s.
One-way info gap	S Seg	56	50			
	Oth Mod	56	50			
	Total	112	100			

Note: S Seg = simple segmentations; Oth Mod = other type of modifications.

be rather specific in their responses so that they could convey the information necessary for their partners to be able to draw the targeted items in their precise location. In a similar way, when signalling for message comprehensibility, the need to be specific seemed to have translated into a high use of modifications other than SSs. These results suggest that the variable task type may have an impact on the type of modifications learners use in their negotiation signals and responses to each other. Excerpt 5 below illustrates how the learner in the role of receiver uses multiple signals in her attempt to ascertain the meaning of the word 'lamp'.

Excerpt 5

NNS1 (Sender)	NNS2 (Receiver)
-es un *lampara lampara	-¿qué es eso?
-it's a lamp lamp	*-what's that?*
-uh uh	-¿para recuerdar los uh videos?
-uh uh	*-to record the uh videos?*
-uh es. no es. uh es lampa pa uh	-¿lampara?
-uh it's. it isn't. uh it's lamp	
(incomplete form) uh	-lamp?
-lampara	-¿para luz?
-lamp	*-for light?*
-sí	
-yes	

*All instances of this word with stress placed on the syllable 'pa' throughout the excerpt. The target-like form carries the stress on the syllable 'lam'.

NNS1's utterance (*it's a lamp lamp*) triggers NNS2's first signal in the form of a question that does not reproduce the trigger or any part of it (*what's that?*). When NNS1 hesitates, NNS2 follows up with a second signal that describes a possible function of the object (*to record the uh. videos?*), and thus, modifies semantically the utterance that served as initial trigger. NNS1 begins a second response that seems to repeat, albeit in an incomplete form, the trigger utterance (*uh it's. it isn't. uh it's lamp -incomplete form-uh*). NNS2 completes NNS1's utterance with a third signal that repeats through simple segmentation and rising intonation the word 'lampara'. The second response of NNS1 repeats again the word segmented by NNS2, *lamp*, thus confirming that it was the word she intended to use. Once again NNS2 tries to verify the meaning of the word *lamp* by using a fourth signal that describes another possible function of the object (*for light?*), and thus constitutes a second semantic modification of the trigger. The last response of NNS1 confirms with a simple *yes* that the use of the object was the one described by NNS2's last signal. Throughout this exchange, NNS2 was able to find out and confirm the meaning of the word 'lampara'. For that purpose, she made use of signals with various types of modification that allowed her to obtain the necessary information to identify the item that she needed to draw.

The prediction of Hypothesis 5 was that beginning foreign language learners' signals that modified other learners' previous utterances through SS would conform to L2 morphosyntax more often than signals with OM types. Table 4.5 presents the results of Pearson's chi-squared tests with Yates' continuity correction for each task. As shown in the table, for the two-way task, the percentage of signals modified through SSs that conformed to the L2 morphosyntax was higher than the percentage of signals modified through OMs that did so, 73% versus 53%. Although there was a trend in the direction of support, this difference, however, was not significant ($\chi^2 = 3.79$, $df = 1$, $p =$ n.s.). In the case of the one-way task, 59% of the signals modified through SS and 50% of the signals modified through OM types conformed to the L2 morphosyntax. This difference was not significant ($\chi^2 = 0.57$, $df = 1$, $p =$ n.s.).

The results of these analyses did not support Hypothesis 5. That is, signals that modified previous utterances through SS conformed to L2 morphosyntax as frequently as signals with more complex modifications. This study, therefore, provides evidence that beginning foreign language learners of Spanish can get feedback in the form of grammatical input from a variety of modification types. Considering only those modified signals that

Table 4.5 Simple segmentations versus other type of modifications in learners' negotiation signals in conformity with L2 morphosyntax on two communication tasks

Communication task	Signal type	S Seg		Other Mod		χ^2	df	p
		n	%	n	%			
Two-way info gap	Conform	36	73	28	53	3.79	1	n.s.
	Do not Conform	13	27	25	47			
	Total	49	100	53	100			
						0.57	1	n.s.
One-way info gap	Conform	33	59	28	50			
	Do not Conform	23	41	28	50			
	Total	56	100	56	100			

Note: S Seg = simple segmentations; Oth Mod = other type of modifications.

were accurate in terms of adherence to the L2 norm, 56% (36 out of 64 signals) used SS, and 44% (28 out of 64 signals) OM types, in the two-way task; in the one-way task, 54% (33 out of 61) used SS, and 46% (28 out of 61) OM types. In other words, grammatical feedback was provided and received by these beginning language learners' signals through various forms of modification.

Summary and Conclusions

The present study focused on two issues related to negotiated interaction and language learning in a foreign language setting. The first one was motivated by previous research that examined tasks as devices for generating interaction and, in particular, negotiation of meaning among language learners. Two communication tasks, a two-way information gap task and a one-way information gap task, were compared to this respect. The results of this study indicated that learners engaged in negotiation in the one-way task as often as they did in the two-way task. We proposed that, as Gass and Varonis (1985) had pointed out, the amount of information exchange that is required by given tasks is better described as a continuous variable. In the current study, less shared task background in the one-way task prompted a two-way exchange of information between dyad members. The dyad member in the role of receiver frequently contributed with question, predictions and inferences to make up for lack of task background. Therefore, lack of shared task background in a one-way task appears to propitiate a two-way exchange of information, and opportunities for negotiation in ways similar to a two-way information gap task.

The present study also examined the type of linguistic modifications present in beginning foreign language learners' modified signals and responses in negotiation exchanges with each other. Learners' use of linguistic modifications in negotiation responses was examined to determine in which ways learners were able to provide modified input to each other and to generate output that modified their own previous utterances to achieve greater comprehensibility. The results indicated that learners attempted to make input comprehensible by modifying their previous utterances through a variety of modification types, but more often through modifications that involved more linguistic complexity than SSs. It was proposed that a task effect might account for this finding. The picture-drawing tasks used in this study required interactants to convey clear specific information so as to be able to draw each item in its precise location. This need may explain that learners recoded their messages in more complex forms to achieve message comprehensibility. These results suggest a need to further investigate the relative contributions of task type and level of language proficiency on learners' modified responses of negotiation.

The results of this study also revealed that beginning foreign language learners can be a source of grammatical input for each other. Modified responses through SSs adhered to the L2 norm more frequently than responses with OMs in the one-way task; in the two-way task, modified responses through SSs adhered to the L2 norm as often as responses with other modification types. That is, learners were able to offer L2 models to each other through SS but also through OMs that involved more linguistic complexity. Considering the low level of language proficiency of the learners in this study, this evidence comes to support interaction and negotiation as an effective context for L2 learning at early stages of acquisition.

With respect to learners' provision of feedback to each other, the analyses of learners' modified signals showed that they used a variety of modification types to indicate lack of understanding. Learners attempted to provide feedback not mainly through SSs, as it had been predicted, but through different modifications of varying degrees of linguistic complexity. As noted for learners' responses, the type of modifications that learners used in their negotiation signals seemed to be related to the impact of the task on negotiation. The tasks of this study seemed to have required that learners used modifications that allowed them to be specific enough when asking for and giving the information necessary to visually reproduce the target items. Future research is needed that addresses the impact of task type on learners' linguistic modifications in negotiation signals and responses at different stages of acquisition.

The analyses of learners' modified signals indicated that grammatical feedback was provided through various forms of modification. This finding dismisses possible concerns about beginning language learners' ability to provide each other with feedback that is morphosyntactically accurate. It should be noted that, in both signals and responses, learners' linguistic modifications other than SSs tended to adhere to the L2 morphosyntax when they involved simple morphological modifications (e.g. the addition of one morpheme) or simple syntactic modifications (e.g. the segmentation of a word or noun phrase and its insertion in a simple question or sentence). In need of further research are questions raised by this study concerning the range of linguistic modifications that learners are able to incorporate in modified signals and responses, and the extent to which such modifications adhere to the L2 norm at different stages of acquisition.

To conclude, this study provides evidence that supports the use of tasks that promote learners' interaction and negotiation of meaning with learners at initial stages of acquisition. Furthermore, this evidence corroborates the effectiveness of interaction and negotiation to serve language learners' needs for modified input, feedback and modified output in the foreign language setting. This study, hence, contributes with evidence from the foreign language context to the database on negotiation and interaction. It is expected that this database will grow and help to understand the language learning process as future research in a foreign language setting continues to address the questions and concerns of this area of SLA.

Acknowledgements

This study was supported by a Research Development Program Fund from the Office of the Provost at Northeastern University. I would like to thank Darin McGill (Statistics Department, Harvard University, Cambridge, MA) for his help with the statistical analyses.

Notes

1. Five dyads were eliminated from the pool of participants because it was evident from their data that either they had not understood the directions for the task or had not followed them as it had been specified.
2. Shrum and Glisan cite as the original source for the two-way task: T. Fall, 1991, personal communication; the one-way task appeared originally in B. Freed and B.W. Bauer (1989) *Contextos: Spanish for Communication*. New York: Newbury House.
3. In the original activity, both versions included labels for each furniture item in the column. To make the two-way and the one-way tasks comparable in terms of the linguistic information provided, labels should have been deleted from both versions of the task. However, a pilot test indicated that some of the furniture drawings were ambiguous for some participants. To avoid such ambiguities and still make both tasks as comparable as possible, the labels were kept for the version with the complete floor plan but were deleted from the version with the empty floor plan.
4. A trained research assistant coded 20% of the data. Intercoder agreement for the categories coded ranged from 92% to 98% consistency.
5. Due to the low proficiency level of the participants, it was not always possible to establish a clear-cut distinction among morphosyntactic and semantic modifications within a modified utterance. In those cases, the whole modified utterance was classified and counted as adhering or not adhering to the L2 target norm.

References

Doughty, C. and Pica, T. (1986) 'Information gap tasks'. Do they facilitate second language acquisition? *TESOL Quarterly* 20, 305–325.

Fernández-García, M. and Martínez-Arbelaiz, A. (2002) Negotiation of meaning in nonnative-speaker-nonnative speaker synchronous discussions. *CALICO Journal* 19 (2), 279–294.

Fernández-García, M. and Martínez-Arbelaiz, A. (2003) Learners' interactions and the negotiation of meaning: A comparison of oral and computer-assisted written conversations. *ReCALL* 15 (1), 113–136.

García-Mayo, M.P. and Pica, T. (2000) L2 learner interaction in a foreign language setting: Are learning needs addressed? *International Review of Applied Linguistics* 38, 35–58.

Gass, S.M. (1988) Integrating research areas: A framework for second language studies. *Applied Linguistics* 9, 198–217.

Gass, S.M. (1989) Second and foreign language learning: Same, different or none of the above? In B. VanPatten and J.F. Lee (eds) *Second Language Acquisition – Foreign Language Learning* (pp. 34–44). Clevedon: Multilingual Matters.

Gass, S.M. and Varonis, E.M. (1985) Task variation and nonnative/non-native negotiation of meaning. In S.M. Gass and C.G. Madden (eds) *Input in Second Language Acquisition* (pp. 149–161). Rowley, MA: Newbury House.

Gass, S.M. and Varonis, E.M. (1986) Sex differences in non-native speaker/non-native speaker interactions. In R.R. Day (ed.) *"Talking to Learn": Conversation in second language acquisition* (pp. 327–351). Cambridge, MA: Newbury House.

Gass, S.M. and Varonis, E.M. (1989) Incorporated repairs in NNS discourse. In M. Eisenstein (ed.) *The Dynamic Interlanguage* (pp. 71–86). New York: Plenum.

Hatch, E. (1978) Discourse analysis and second language acquisition. In E. Hatch (ed.) *Second Language Acquisition: A Book of Readings* (pp. 401–435). Rowley, MA: Newbury House.

Jacobs, G. (1989) Miscorrection in peer feedback in writing class. *RELC Journal* 20, 68–76.

Krashen, S.D. (1980) *Second Language Acquisition and Second Language Learning*. Oxford: Pergamon.

Krashen, S.D. (1985) *The Input Hypothesis; Issues and Implications*. London: Longman.

Lee, J.F. (2000) *Tasks and Communicating in Language Classrooms*. New York: McGraw-Hill.

Long, M. (1983a) Linguistic and conversational adjustment to non-native speakers. *Studies in Second Language Acquisition* 5 (2), 177–193.

Long, M. (1983b) Native speaker/non-native speaker conversation and the negotiation of comprehensible input. *Applied Linguistics* 4 (2), 126–141.

Long, M. (1996) The role of the linguistic environment in second language acquisition. In W.C. Ritchie and T.K. Bhatia (eds) *Handbook of Second Language Acquisition* (pp. 413–468). San Diego: Academic Press, Inc.

Nunan, D. (1989). *Designing Tasks for the Communicative Classroom*. Cambridge: Cambridge University Press.

Pellettieri, J. (2000). Negotiation in cyberspace: The role of chatting in the development of grammatical competence. In M. Warschauer and R. Kern (eds) *Network-Based Language Teaching: Concepts and Practice* (pp. 59–86). New York: Cambridge University Press.

Peters, A.M. (1985) Language segmentation: Operating principles for the perception and analysis of language. In D. Slobin (ed.) *The Crosslinguistic Study of Language Acquisition* (pp. 1029–1064). Hillsdale, NJ: Erlbaum.

Pica, T. (1987) Interlanguage adjustments as an outcome of NS-NNS negotiated interaction. *Language Learning* 38 (1), 45–73.

Pica, T. (1992) The textual outcomes of NS-NNS negotiations. In C. Kramsch and S. McConnell-Ginet (eds) *Text and Context: Cross-Disciplinary Perspectives on Language Study* (pp. 198–237). Lexington, MA: D.C. Heath & Co.

Pica, T. (1994) Research on negotiation: What does it reveal about second language learning conditions, processes, and outcomes? *Language Learning*, 44, 493–527.

Pica, T. and Doughty, C. (1985a) Input and interaction in the communicative classroom: A comparison of teacher-fronted and group activities. In S.M. Gass and C.G. Madden (eds) *Input in Second Language Acquisition* (pp. 115–132). Rowley, MA: Newbury House.

Pica, T. and Doughty, C. (1985b) The role of classroom second language acquisition. *Studies in Second Language Acquisition* 7, 233–248.

Pica, T., Holliday, L., Lewis, N. and Morgenthaler, L. (1989) Comprehensible output as an outcome of linguistic demands on the learner. *Studies in Second Language Acquisition* 11, 63–90.

Pica, T., Holliday, L. and Lewis, N. (1990) NS-NNS negotiation: An equal opportunity for speech modification? Paper presented at the 24th Annual TESOL Convention, San Francisco.

Pica, T., Holliday, L., Lewis, N., Berducci, D. and Newman, J. (1991) Language learning through interaction: What role does gender play? *Studies in Second Language Acquisition* 13, 343–376.

Pica, T., Kanagy, R. and Falodun, J. (1993) Choosing and using communication tasks for second language instruction. In G. Crookes and S. Gass (eds) *Tasks and Language Learning* (pp. 9–33). Clevedon: Multilingual Matters.

Pica, T., Lincoln-Porter, F., Paninos, F. and Linnell, J. (1996) Language learners' interaction: How does it address input, output and feedback needs of L2 learners? *TESOL Quarterly* 30 (1), 59–84.

Porter, P. (1986) How learners talk to each other: Input and interaction in task-centered discussions. In R. Day (ed.) *Talking to Learn: Conversation in Second Language Acquisition* (pp. 200–222). Rowley, MA: Newbury House.

Robinson, P. (2001) Task complexity, task difficulty, and task production: Exploring interactions in a componential framework. *Applied Linguistics* 22 (1), 27–57.

Schmidt, R. (1990) The role of consciousness in second language learning. *Applied Linguistics* 11 (1), 17–46.

Shortreed, I. (1993) Variation in foreign language input: The effects of task and proficiency. In G. Crookes and S. Gass (eds) *Tasks and Language Learning* (pp. 96–122). Clevedon: Multilingual Matters.

Shrum, J.L. and Glisan, E.W. (2000) *Teacher's Handbook: Contextualized Language Instruction*. Boston, MA: Heinle Thomson.

Swain, M. (1985) Communicative competence: Some roles of comprehensible input and comprehensible output in its development. In S.M. Gass and C.G. Madden (eds) *Input in Second Language Acquisition* (pp. 236–244). Rowley, MA: Newbury House.

VanPatten, B. (1990) Attending to form and content in the input. *Studies in Second Language Acquisition* 12, 287–301.

VanPatten, B. (1996) *Input Processing and Grammar Instruction: Theory, Research, Challenges and Implications*. Norwood, NJ: Ablex.

Varonis, E.M. and Gass, S.M. (1985a) Miscommunication in native/nonnative conversation. *Language in Society* 14 (3), 327–343.

Varonis, E.M. and Gass, S.M. (1985b) Non-native/non-native conversations: A model for negotiation of meaning. *Applied Linguistics* 6 (1), 71–90.

White, L. (1987) Against comprehensible input: The input hypothesis and the development of L2 competence. *Applied Linguistics* 8, 95–110.

Chapter 5

Attention to Form Across Collaborative Tasks by Low-Proficiency Learners in an EFL Setting

ANA ALEGRÍA DE LA COLINA and
MARÍA DEL PILAR GARCÍA MAYO

Introduction

Recent studies in second language pedagogy advocate the use of tasks which require learners to produce output collaboratively (Kowal & Swain, 1997; Swain, 1995, 1998; Swain & Lapkin, 1995, 1998, 2000, 2001). Collaborative focus-on-form (FonF) tasks are designed to meet the need of integrating attention to language form with a communicative orientation and their study can be approached from two different but complementary perspectives (Ellis, 2000). The psycholinguistic tradition is based on a computational model of acquisition in which tasks are viewed as devices which can influence learners' information processing. Research from this perspective attempts to explore the influence that different task types and task conditions may have on performance (Skehan, 1998). Recently, a new approach has been developed which is derived from the conviction that the processes involved in language learning cannot be completeley explained from the psycholinguistic viewpoint, dominant in the field of second language acquisition (SLA). Some researchers argue for a sociocultural approach (Lantolf & Appel, 1994) which claims that knowledge is constructed through social interaction between individuals and is then internalised (Vygotsky, 1978). This view has led to an increasing interest in collaborative dialogue, where language use and language learning take place simultaneously (Donato, 1994; LaPierre, 1994; Swain, 1998, 2000; Swain & Lapkin, 2000, 2002). From this theoretical perspective, language is viewed as a social activity as well as a cognitive activity and both aspects are considered necessary for its complete understanding.

Within this backdrop, the aim of the present study is to determine the effectiveness of collaborative FonF tasks as a pedagogical tool for low-proficiency learners of English as a foreign language (EFL). This chapter is organised as follows: firstly, we include a review of the literature on attention to form in collaborative tasks and how this is related to the building of knowledge in discourse. Then, we describe the study and its methodological aspects. The results are set forth, and then the discussion of our findings and implications for classroom practice is comprised.

Literature Review

Attention to form in communicative activities

Interest in tasks arose from the need for a pedagogical tool that promoted natural and communicative use of the target language. Interaction which allowed students to negotiate the meaning of some features that caused communication breakdowns was considered facilitative for SLA. It ensured negative input and feedback that drew learners' attention to form-meaning relationships and helped them to notice a gap between their own output and target input they need to access (Pica, 1994).

However, findings from immersion acquisition studies in Canada suggested that emphasis on communicative success is insufficient for the development of targetlike proficiency. Learners in immersion programmes were able to convey meaning in their second language but they normally did so with non-targetlike morphology and syntax (Swain, 1985). Long (1991) proposed a reactive FonF intervention consisting in paying attention to certain language features when they arise incidentally in meaning-oriented activities. Other authors have adopted a wider perspective admitting a proactive FonF, that is, previous manipulation of the task by the teacher in order to focus students' attention on certain features (see Ellis, 2001 for a detailed review).

As pointed out above, some researchers advocate the use of tasks which require learners to produce output collaboratively. Swain (1995) suggests that it is possible to design tasks that get learners to produce language and then reflect upon its form. She has emphasised the importance of output in triggering cognitive processes likely to change the learners' interlanguage. On this view, output forces students to process the L2 synctactically, leading them to notice gaps in their knowledge, and pushes them to formulate and test hypotheses about the L2 and so reflect about language. Swain and her colleagues have searched for tasks which elicit metatalk, that is, the language used to talk about language and about the task itself, in order to demonstrate its relation to SLA. They have found collaborative writing tasks especially adequate for this purpose, as these activities are reported to be effective for drawing the participants' attention to form although they are meaning-oriented.

Research that has investigated collaborative writing tasks has operationalised attention to linguistic aspects as language related episodes (LREs), those segments of the participants' dialogue in which learners talk about or question their own or their intelocutor's language use while trying to complete the task. This kind of attention to form may help participants understand the relationship between meaning, form and function in a given context (Swain, 1998). A positive relationship was found between the number of LREs produced by students performing a collaborative writing task and the post-test scores obtained by those students when working individually (LaPierre, 1994). Furthermore, these episodes may represent language learning in progress (Swain & Lapkin, 2000).

Some collaborative writing tasks that research has found effective to draw the students' attention to form are jigsaw (Swain & Lapkin, 2001), dictogloss (Kowal & Swain, 1997; Lapierre, 1994; Swain, 1998; Swain & Lapkin, 2000, 2001), and text reconstruction (García Mayo, 2001a, 2001b, 2002; Storch, 1998), in which learners must pool together their resources to reconstruct a scene or passage. A number of studies have compared different types of collaborative tasks to determine if they can serve different pedagogical goals and to study the effect of manipulating certain variables and task conditions on performance. These studies conclude that collaborative tasks are effective for drawing attention to form and forcing learners to reflect about language, but report certain differences between task types that need to be confirmed for different settings and levels of proficiency.

Collaborative tasks and the building of knowledge

According to sociocultural theory, human cognitive development is a socially situated activity mediated by language (Vygotsky, 1978), that is, knowledge is socially constructed by interaction and is then internalised. Individuals learn how to carry out a new function with the help of an expert (in an expert/novice pair) and then they can perform it individually. Vygotsky (1978) establishes two levels of development: the developmental level of a novice, that is, the level of what an individual can do without help, and the potential level of development, or what that individual can do with the help of an expert. The distance between the two is known as the zone of proximal development (ZPD) and is considered as a key variable in intellectual development. If the distance between the two levels is so great that it can not be bridged, then no development will occur. The dialogic process by means of which a speaker helps another speaker bridge the gap and perform a new function is known as scaffolding, and includes the social and affective support mutually provided by participants during interaction (Ellis, 2000). Recent studies (Storch, 2002; Swain *et al.*, 2002) demonstrate the impact of peer–peer dialogue on second language learning. Through interaction learners regulate or restructure their knowledge; therefore, learning, cognition and interaction are closely connected (Esteve & Cañada, 2001).

Thus, the sociocultural approach claims that interaction is an opportunity to learn. During interaction learners are given the possibility to develop not only their linguistic skills but their cognitive and problem solving capacities as well. Some authors have studied interaction to discover how dialogue is used as a cognitive tool (Donato & Lantolf, 1990). From this perspective, collaborative dialogue is language learning mediated by language (Swain, 2000). Participants build knowledge through metatalk as they perform the task, and the interaction reveals the mental processes of the interactants, the support they provide to each other, as well as the mechanisms they use to adjust the complexity of the task, facilitating its regulation. Both LaPierre (1994) and Swain and Lapkin (1998) demonstrate that LREs are occasions for learning. A crucial aspect of collaborative dialogue seems to be verbalisation. Swain (2000) concludes that verbalisation is a powerful cognitive tool for mediating the internalisation of meaning created and claims that collaborative dialogue is particularly useful for learning language processes as well as grammatical aspects of language.

Task research within the sociocultural framework has aimed to demonstrate how scaffolding can help students to reach a satisfactory solution when performing a task. Donato (1994) described how a group of students was able to produce jointly a specific grammar structure although none of them was able to do it individually. The knowledge constructed in collaboration was internalised and could be used individually on subsequent occasions.

Scaffolding studies share a qualitative, interpretative case-study perspective on L2 instruction that allows the observation of language development at the moment it is taking place (de Guerrero & Villamil, 2000). A detailed microgenetic analysis of the interaction that occurs when students work collaboratively is essential to understand how psychological processes develop. Empirical studies of peer revision in writing classes suggest that certain students' attitudes and behaviours are more facilitative than others in providing support. Showing affectivity, making effective use of discourse strategies such as advising, eliciting and requesting clarification, and using the L1 to maintain control of the task have been identified as facilitative language learning processes (de Guerrero & Villamil, 2000; Swain & Lapkin, 2001).

In this context it should be pointed out that the use of the L1 can be an essential support to deal effectively with task demands. Brooks and Donato (1994) observed that learners used the L1 to initiate and sustain oral interaction when they attempted to produce the L2, suggesting that L1 use is a normal psycholinguistic process that facilitates L2 production. Anton and DiCamilla (1999: 238) have emphasised the importance of the L1 as a semiotic instrument, especially between students sharing the same L1 and with low proficiency in the L2. During the exchange, 'utterances in L1 mediate the cognitive processes that learners use in problem solving tasks, specifically, to reflect on the content and the form of the text'. The L1 is used both to generate content and to reflect on the material, thus fostering scaffolding. It is important for establishing and maintaining intersubjectivity and serves the purpose of externalising private speech, the speech used when a task is cognitively difficult. Swain and Lapkin (2000) found that, when used within a pedagogical context, different task types may provide greater or lesser needs for different uses of the L1, suggesting interaction between achievement and task with respect to the use of the L1.

Thus the concept of output has been extended to be considered as a socially-constructed cognitive tool. As such, dialogue serves to learn the L2 by mediating its own construction (Swain, 2000: 112). By means of external speech, internalisation of knowledge is facilitated. This position is an additional reason in favour of the use of collaborative work in L2 learning.

The Present Study

Motivation

As seen above, previous studies have supported the effectiveness of collaborative writing tasks for acquisition, claiming that they confront students with their knowledge gaps. However, some researchers (Storch, 1998; Williams, 2001) have cautioned that low-proficiency students may not benefit so much from these tasks. The purpose of this study is, thus, to determine the effectiveness of collaborative FonF tasks as a pedagogical tool for low-proficiency EFL learners. It is of great importance to determine whether these learners are able to discuss linguistic aspects of the L2 and provide mutual support to construct knowledge in their ZPD.

Research questions

In this study, we have compared three task types (jigsaw, dictogloss and text reconstruction) in order to determine which one fosters most FonF and metatalk. The study addresses the following research questions:

(1) Are collaborative production tasks effective for promoting focus-on-form and metatalk when completed by low-proficiency students? If so, are some tasks more effective than others?

In order to answer this question we formulated three hypotheses:

Hypothesis 1: text reconstruction will be the activity that generates the greatest amount of attention to form (García Mayo, 2001a, 2001b).
Hypothesis 2: the jigsaw will generate more attention to lexis because it is a task claimed to be specially suited to the negotiation of meaning (Swain & Lapkin, 2001).

Hypothesis 3: if the task conditions are modified appropriately, the dictogloss task will produce a greater amount of focus on form than evidenced in other studies with foreign language students (García Mayo, 2001a, 2001b, 2002).

(2) Do different tasks focus attention on different linguistic features? If so, what are their differential effects?

(3) What role does metalinguistic knowledge play when students focus on form?

(4) Are low-proficiency students able to reflect on L2 linguistic form and provide each other with scaffolding in order to jointly construct L2 linguistic knowledge in the ZPD?

Participants

The participants in this study were 24 undergraduate (first year) students, 12 females and 12 males. Their mean age was 22 and the mean length of exposure to the English language in a classroom setting was eight years. They were studying an EFL course which is part of a degree programme in Maritime Studies at the University of Cantabria (Spain). The course is content-based and students use English maritime texts as a basis for classroom work. The English language classes (four hours per week during seven months at the time the tasks were carried out) have a reactive and incidental FonF component.

The learners were administered the Oxford Quick Placement Test which classified them as elementary level learners [Level 1 (Waystage) of the Association of Language Testers in Europe (ALTE)]. This level of proficiency is defined by a 'capacity to deal with simple straightforward information and to get by in familiar contexts'. In spite of their years of instruction in English in primary and secondary education, students are still at a low proficiency level, indicating that the classroom environment in which they have received instruction is not successful at promoting genuine oral communication. Due to the technical content of their training, our students master a wide range of specific vocabulary corresponding to more proficient language levels, but they have clear morphosyntactic and discoursal deficiencies. This fact, which has also been pointed out in other contexts (Pica, 2002; Swain, 1985, 1995, among others) is even more serious in foreign language contexts. The opportunities to produce oral language in the classroom are rather scarce and basically limited to answering questions formulated by the teacher.

The participants worked in 12 self-selected pairs (eight male–female dyads, three male–male pairs and one female–female pair). Each task (jigsaw, dictogloss and text reconstruction) was completed by four pairs.

Task description

As mentioned above, we chose three different activities which research has found to be suitable for pushing students to develop their interlanguage by drawing their attention to form while they are trying to create meaning. The tasks selected were a jigsaw, a text reconstruction and a dictogloss, which we will now describe briefly.

Jigsaw: this is an information gap task in which each participant has part of the necessary information and must exchange it in order to perform the task. It is a task intended to promote negotiation of meaning. In our case the information provided was visual, not linguistic. According to Pica *et al.* (1993), the jigsaw is a type of task where opportunities for negotiation of meaning are likely to be generated. The members of the pairs work to create a text based on a series of pictures. Each student looks only at the pictures that s/he holds. Then they exchange the information to form a coherent whole and write the text in collaboration.

Text reconstruction: in this task a text is deprived of function words and inflections which students have to insert in order to come up with an accurate product. This task has been claimed to be an effective form-focused task as learners work collaboratively and peer feedback is available (García Mayo, 2001a, 2001b, 2002; Kowal & Swain, 1997; Storch, 1998).

Dictogloss: This procedure (described in Wajnryb, 1990) encourages students to reflect on their own output. A short text is read twice at normal speed: the first time the learners just listen, and the second time they jot down some words which can help them recall the text. Then, the two members of the dyad pool their resources together to reconstruct the text and write a final version. This task has proved to be suitable to make students process synctactically and notice the gaps in their interlanguage (Swain, 1998), to notice the mismatch between their own language use and the target language (Doughty & Williams, 1998), and to trigger metatalk on the connections between form and meaning in relation with the writing process (Kowal & Swain, 1997). Although some researchers have reported dictogloss to be effective, other studies have not obtained such positive findings. These less favourable results may be attributed to the oral nature of the stimulus, lack of familiarity with the task, and students' attempts to produce complex structures influenced by the text (García Mayo, 2001a, 2001b, 2002). Another factor could be the choice of the text. The texts by Wajnryb (1990), used in some of the studies cited, are rather difficult to retain because they are of an episodic nature. Unless quite detailed information is jotted down, it is very difficult for foreign language students to reconstruct the passage, since their comprehension skills are not as good as those of immersion students. Therefore, it was hypothesised that better results would be obtained if a passage with a clear structure was chosen and if students were acquainted with the task procedure and the topic.

Task conditions

In order to compare the impact of the three activities on the amount and nature of FonF they generate, the three activities were designed with a common content (Swain & Lapkin, 2001). Other studies (García Mayo, 2001a, 2001b; Storch, 1998) have compared various activities using texts dealing with different topics, which seems to reduce comparability. Therefore, we decided to use the same passage to design the three tasks. We chose a passage from Blakey (1985) on a topic our participants are familiar with (*containerisation* – see Appendix 5.A), with a clear structure that low-proficiency students could comprehend and remember. First, a passage was selected for the dictogloss. Then, the same passage was deprived of all inflections, prepositions, determiners and connectors to elaborate the text reconstruction task. Finally, the jigsaw was created: the content of the text was transferred to six pictures or ideograms which were designed to elicit the same content as the other two activities.

Obviously, the learners would not focus on all the features in the text, but the variety of linguistic features introduced must be considered when comparing data. All the language features in the passage had been presented in the classroom but they frequently cause problems to our learners for a variety of reasons. They may be difficult to master through mere input exposure (zero articles), or because they differ from the L1 (some uses of passive voice); they may not be salient enough, or not essential for communication (inflectional markers).

Students had previously performed all three task types in class to get acquainted with them, and were also familiar with the topic so that the lexical difficulties would be kept to a minimum and their attention could be focused on form (Swain & Lapkin, 2001). Instructions were given in their L1 to avoid any possibility of misunderstanding the task procedure (Fotos & Ellis, 1991). Similarly, students were allowed to use their L1 during task performance because of their extremely limited ability to carry out metatalk in the L2. No time restriction was imposed, as long as the task was completed in a 50-minute class period.

Data collection procedures

The study was carried out in a laboratory setting. Participants were distributed in three groups of four pairs each. One of the groups performed the dictogloss task, the second group did the jigsaw task and the third group completed the text reconstruction task. The groups worked in self-selected pairs and their dialogues were recorded while completing the task. A total of 84 hours and 16 minutes of data were recorded and transcribed for this study.

The unit of analysis used to code the data was the language related episode (LRE) defined as a segment of the students' dialogue in which they talk about language, question and/or correct (explicitly or implicitly) their interlocutor's language use while trying to complete the task (Swain, 1998: 70). LREs have been widely used in FonF research as they are signs of the learners' paying attention to form. The verbalisation of their ideas about the L2 helps them

deepen their understanding of the language and facilitates the necessary connections between form, meaning and function. LREs also provide insights into the mental processes of the students while they are working and may represent learning in progress (Donato, 1994; Swain, 1998; Swain & Lapkin, 1998).

Each LRE dealt with one linguistic item. If students referred to more than one linguistic feature in the same segment, they were counted separately. LREs were subdivided into lexis-based and form-based episodes. Lexis-based LREs included a lexical search or the selection of synonyms or nearly equivalent terms, as illustrated in example (1):[2]

(1) Pair 1 (Jigsaw)
A: *Do you know how to say "grúa"?*
B: eh ... crane ... cranes, we can use cranes

Form-based LREs included those occasions on which students discussed spelling, phonetic, morphological, syntactic, or discourse features, and were subclassified into linguistic categories following the taxonomy used by Storch (1998) which was also adopted by García Mayo (2002). Example (2) features a form-based LRE:

(2) Pair 2 (Jigsaw)
A: We will talk about the main advantages of the containerization
B: *Aha*
A: In general terms, containerization ... *I think we should omit the "the"*
B: *Yes, I was going to say that too*

We have considered the term form in its widest sense, that is, all levels and components of the linguistic system (Doughty & Williams, 1998). In order to determine the effectiveness of collaboration, LREs were also coded as either solved correctly or incorrectly (including those left unsolved).

A further subclassification of form-based LREs was made. We coded as metalinguistic episodes those occasions where students used technical or semitechnical grammar terms to discuss linguistic form. These episodes indicate specific knowledge which can serve to talk about language and justify choices. They were accounted for separately from form-based LREs to determine to what extent students made use of this type of knowledge. Explicit knowledge is not exactly the same thing as metalinguistic knowledge, but the latter can help verbalise the former (Fotos & Ellis, 1991). The example in (3) illustrates a metalinguistic episode:

(3) Pair 10 (Text reconstruction)
A: *Instead of 'easier' it should be 'easily' ... It's an adverb ... isn't it?*
B: *But this is the ... easier stowage ... It's that comparative, but not the superlative*

Those instances of the dialogue where students talked about the task, its aims, the best way to complete it, or the organisation of the information, etc.,

were coded as metacognitive episodes and were accounted for separately. These episodes illustrate the mental management of cognitive processes – planning, evaluating, organising information . . ., etc – (see Esteve & Cañada, 2001) and are good indicators of the collaboration established between the members of the pair. In (4) we include an example of a metacognitive episode:

(4)   Pair 8 (Dictogloss)

A: *Ah, but we also have to talk about the work force before this because this was the last thing, I mean, first is time, then the work force and after that the part about* 'loading and unloading')

B: *wouldn't it be* 'handling'?

Data Analysis and Results

Classification of LREs

The first research question addressed whether some tasks would be more effective than others in drawing low proficiency learners' attention to form. Table 5.1 features the total number of LREs, the number of turns and the time taken to complete the activity across the three tasks. The data show that students did focus on form as all tasks generated many LREs. The task with the largest number of LREs was the text reconstruction, which also generated the greatest number of turns. This confirms Hypothesis 1, which predicted that text reconstruction would be the activity that promotes the most attention to form. A statistical analysis using the Mann–Whitney–Wilcoxon test revealed significant differences between the dictogloss and the text reconstruction relative to the total number of LREs (<0.02), and the number of form-based LREs (<0.021).

Table 5.1 Number of LREs, turns and time taken to complete tasks

	Jigsaw	*Dictogloss*	*Text reconstruction*
Total LREs	165[*a]	92[*a,b]	206[*b]
Mean	41.25	23	51.5
Standard deviation	7.41	9.76	11.82
Time (minutes)	46.32	31.55	45.26
No turns	324	232	397
No turns/minute	7.01	7.52	8.91
No LREs/minute	0.90[*a]	0.72[*a,b]	1.15[*b]
No LREs/turn	0.14	0.98	0.13

[*]Statistically significant difference between tasks types (Mann–Whitney–Wilcoxon test).
[a]Statistically significant difference between jigsaw and dictogloss.
[b]Statistically significant difference between dictogloss and text reconstruction.

Table 5.2 LREs (form-based and lexis-based) produced in the three tasks

	Number of LREs	Lexis-based LREs				Form-based LREs			
		n	*Mean*	*SD*	*(%)*	*n*	*Mean*	*SD*	*(%)*
Jigsaw	165*[a]	47/165	11.75	9.22	28%	118/165	29.5	6.56	72%
Dictogloss	92*[a,b]	14/92	3.5	4.04	12.7%	78/92*	19.5	6.45	85%
Text reconstruction	206*[b]	28/206	7	1.15	14%	178/206*	44.5	11.59	86%

*Statistically significant difference between tasks types (Mann–Whitney–Wilcoxon test).
[a]Statistically significant difference between jigsaw and dictogloss.
[b]Statistically significant difference between dictogloss and text reconstruction.

Table 5.2 features the total, average and percentage of lexis-based and form-based LREs generated across the three tasks. The data confirm Hypothesis 2, which postulated that the jigsaw task would trigger a larger number of lexical LREs, given its claimed effectiveness for eliciting meaning negotiation (Swain & Lapkin, 2001). However, the percentages of form-based LREs were greater than those of lexis-based LREs in all tasks.

Hypothesis 3 conjectured that better results could be obtained with dictoglosss if care was taken to select a passage with a clear structure to facilitate memory of content, and to ensure that students were acquainted with the task procedure and the topic of the text. The results do not support the hypothesis as to the number of LREs produced.

In summary, the data above seem to show that the three tasks under study are effective at drawing low-proficiency students' attention to form, given the large number of LREs generated and the higher percentage of form-based LREs across the three task types.

Classification of form-based LREs

The second research question asked whether the different activities under study would focus attention on different linguistic features. Tables 5.3 and 5.4 show the grammatical features which students focused on across the three tasks and their frequency.

The findings suggest that there are differences attributable to task type, derived in turn from the task demands caused by the input. The categories with the highest incidence for the jigsaw task include spelling, connecting words, noun and verb morphology, prepositions and determiners. Students had to consider a wide range of linguistic features to create the text from scratch using only the picture cues. Regarding the dictogloss task, students focused mainly on connecting words, spelling and subject-verb agreement. As the discourse was ready-made for them in the input, their main concern focused on the spelling of words they had jotted down and the connectors

Table 5.3 Classification of form-based LREs

	Jigsaw			Dictogloss			Text reconstruction			Total
	n	*Mean*	*SD*	*n*	*Mean*	*SD*	*n*	*Mean*	*SD*	
Determiners	9*c	2.25	2.06	7*b	1.75	0.5	40*b,c	10	4.08	56
Connectors	20	5	4	21	5.25	4.27	11	2.75	2.06	52
Spelling	22	5.5	7	13	3.25	2.5	6	1.5	1.91	41
Noun form	15	3.75	3.22	7	1.75	1.71	11	2.75	1.71	33
S-V agreement	3*c	0.75	0.96	10*b	2.5	1.25	20*b,c	5	0.82	33
Prepositions	10*a	2.5	1.73	—*a,b			21*b	5.25	2.65	31
Verb form	11	2.75	3.59	3	0.75	0.5	17	4.25	3.30	31
Passive voice	3*c	0.75	0.96	5*b	1.25	0.96	22*b,c	5.5	0.58	30
Punctuation	6	1	1.29	2	0.5	1	9	2.25	1.8	17
Sentence structure	5	1.25	0.96	5	1.25	0.5	6	1.5	1	16
Pro-drop	2	0.5	0.58	—*			6*	1.5	1.29	8
Noun modifiers	4	1.5	2	1	0.25	0.5	3	0.75	0.96	8
Plurals	2	0.5	1	3	0.75	1.5	2	0.5	1	7
Phonetics	4*	1	0.52	—*			1	0.25	0.75	5
Word order	—			—			3	0.75	0.96	3
Verb aspect	1	0.25	0.58	1	0.25	0.5	—			2
Verb time	1	0.25	0.58	—			—			1

*Statistically significant difference between task types (Mann–Whitney–Wilcoxon test).
[a]Statistically significant difference between jigsaw and dictogloss.
[b]Statistically significant difference between dictogloss and text reconstruction.
[c]Statistically significant difference between jigsaw and text reconstruction.

needed to link them up and recreate the discourse they had heard while listening to the passage. The collaboration may have been effective for checking grammatical features such as subject-verb agreement.

The most structured of the three tasks, text reconstruction, forced students to consider inflections, prepositions, and connecting words. Among the LREs generated by this task the most frequent category by far was article usage, followed by passive voice, prepositions, subject-verb agreement and verb form. The Mann–Whitney–Wilcoxon test found significant differences between the text reconstruction and the other two activities regarding the number of LREs dealing with determiners (<0.017 dictogloss, <0.019 jigsaw), passive voice (<0.019), and subject-verb agreement (<0.028 dictogloss, <0.019 jigsaw). Significant differences were also found between

Table 5.4 Grammatical categories most frequently focused on across tasks

Jigsaw			Dictogloss			Text reconstruction		
Spelling	22/118	18.6%	Connectors	21/78	26.9%	Determiners	40/178	22.4%
Connectors	20/118	16.9%	Spelling	13/78	16.6%	Passive voice	22/178	12.3%
Noun form	15/118	12.7%	S-V agreement	10/78	12.8%	Prepositions	21/178	11.7%
Verb form	11/118	9.3%	Determiners	7/78	8.9%	S-V agreement	20/178	11.2%
Prepositions	10/118	8.4%	Noun form	7/78	8.9%	Verb form	17/178	9.5%
Determiners	9/118	7.6%						

dictogloss and the other activities regarding the number of LREs dealing with prepositions (<0.013 jigsaw, <0.014 text reconstruction) and between dictogloss and text reconstruction as to the number of LREs concerning the possibility of dropping subject pronouns in main clauses (*pro*-drop) (<0.049). These results will be considered in more detail in the discussion section.

Metalinguistic episodes

Research question 3 addressed the role played by metalinguistic knowledge when students focus on form. Table 5.5 compares the number and type of metalinguistic episodes generated across the three activities.

The data reveal that the text reconstruction was the activity with the largest number of metalinguistic episodes. A total of 47 episodes were identified which accounted for 22.8% of the total number of LREs and 26.4% of the form-based LREs generated by this task. A possible explanation for this finding is that text reconstruction is a problem solving task which forces students to deal with certain linguistic problems and the use of metalinguistic terms may help them justify their choices by verbalising and

Table 5.5 Metalinguistic episodes

	Jigsaw		*Dictogloss*		*Text reconstruction*	
	n	%	*n*	%	*n*	%
Absence verb/subject	2	(18%)	1	(14%)	13	(28%)
Passive voice	2	(18%)	1	(14%)	11	(23%)
Verb form/time	2	(18%)	3	(43%)	2	(4%)
Comparat/superlat	2	(18%)	—		3	(6%)
S-V agreement	—		1	(14%)	3	(6%)
Plural	1	(9%)	—		3	(6%)
Grammar category	—	—			3	(6%)
Noun form	1	(9%)	—		2	(4%)
Word order	—		—		3	(6%)
Articles	—		—		2	(4%)
Possessive case	—		1	(14%)	1	(2%)
Prepositions	1	(9%)	—		—	
Punctuation	—		—		1	(2%)
Total	**11**		**7***		**47***	
Standard deviation	2.22		1.71		11.75	

*Statistically significant difference between task types (Mann–Whitney–Wilcoxon).

resorting to grammar rules. The most frequent categories are those referring to the absence of subject or verb and the passive voice. These are categories widely used by teachers and which students may have internalised. In some segments of the dialogue students, in a clear example of inner speech, even verbalise the passive formation rule, as seen in excerpt (5) below:

(5)   Pair 12 (Text reconstruction)
A: *And the verb here?*
B: *'Check' ..., well, actually it's* 'are not checked', *passive, and* 'remain' *the other one*
A: *And if it is* '-ed', *isn't it* 'has'? *Or is it* 'are'?
B: *Let's see, the verb* 'to be' *in the same form as it is and then the participle*
A: *OK. OK* ... are not checking ... checked.

For between-group comparisons of the total number of metalinguistic episodes, the Mann–Whitney–Wilcoxon test found significant differences between the dictogloss task and text reconstruction (<0.029) and a nearly significant difference between jigsaw and text reconstruction (<0.059). The frequent use of metalinguistic terms in the text reconstruction task, which induces the most FonF, suggests that overt metalinguistic instruction may provide students with a useful tool for thinking about and discussing language form.

Correctly solved LREs

In order to answer research question 4, which asked about whether low-proficiency foreign language students would be able to engage in language discussions and construct L2 knowledge in their ZPD, we have quantified the number of LREs correctly solved across the three tasks under study. As illustrated in Table 5.6, there is a high percentage of LREs correctly solved for all three activities, which suggests that collaboration has been effective in finding solutions for the linguistic problems encountered. The fact that students raise language-related questions indicates that they have noticed the gaps between their own production and the L2 they were trying to produce. Since the participants were also able to provide correct solutions, it seems reasonable to conclude that collaboration was effective in creating knowledge.

A comparison of the percentages of LREs correctly solved across task types provides greater insight into the different tasks under study. As Table 5.6 shows, there seems to be an inverse relationship between the number of LREs generated and the percentage of LREs correctly solved. Although text reconstruction was the task type that generated the greatest amount of attention to form (operationalised by the number of LREs produced), it yielded the lowest percentage of correct solutions. A Mann–Whitney–Wilcoxon test revealed significant differences between the text reconstruction

Table 5.6 Number and percentage of LREs correctly solved across the three tasks

	LREs correctly solved			Lexis-based LREs correctly solved			Form-based LREs correctly solved		
	n	*SD*	*%*	*n*	*SD*	*%*	*n*	*SD*	*%*
Jigsaw	117/165*[*a]	6.02	(71%)	24/47	5.60	(51%)	93/118	6.34	(79%)
Dictogloss	70/92*[*a,b]	7.19	(76%)	9/14	2.63	(64%)	61/78	5.74	(78%)*
Text reconstruction	136/206*[b]	7.79	(66%)	19/28	1.71	(67%)	117/178	7.23	(65.7%)*
Total	**323/463**		**(70%)**	**52/89**		**(57%)**	**271/374**		**(72%)**

*Statistically significant difference between task types (Mann–Whitney–Wilcoxon).
[a]Statistically significant difference between jigsaw and dictogloss.
[b]Statistically significant difference between dictogloss and text reconstruction.

and the dictogloss (<0.029) as to the percentage of correct LREs. Significant differences were also found between the jigsaw and the dictogloss (<0.043) and a nearly significant difference between the text reconstruction and the jigsaw (<0.083). These results indicate that while text-reconstruction activities may be suitable for raising questions, they may force students to focus on features beyond their control. On the other two activities, students' attention to form seems to have been driven by their own needs, so the solutions were more likely to be within their linguistic possibilities.

The high percentage of LREs correctly solved across the three activities suggests that collaboration was effective and that the students provided each other with scaffolding in their ZPD. Moreover, the linguistic forms that led to the largest number of LREs were those that resulted in the highest proportion of correct solutions. Thus, it seems that low proficiency learners are able to reflect on L2 linguistic form and provide each other with scaffolding to jointly reconstruct L2 linguistic knowledge.

Metacognitive episodes

Analysing metacognitive episodes may provide greater insights into the processes involved in interaction. These episodes are generated to regulate task demands and establish intersubjectivity (a shared perspective on the task, the establishment of goals and a collaborative attitude), which is considered to be a basic requirement for the existence of progress in the ZPD. Table 5.7 shows the frequency of different types of metacognitive episodes across tasks.

All three task types generated many metacognitive episodes, with the categories accounting for the largest number of episodes being those involving negotiation of content, organisation of information and discussion of procedure. The prevalence of metacognitive episodes further confirms the collaboration between participants, allowing them to control the task and support each other in the pursuit of a common goal. Nevertheless, there appears to be a clear difference between the number of metacognitive episodes generated by the text reconstruction and by the other two activities (although the differences are not statistically significant). The fact that the text reconstruction generated a smaller number of metacognitive episodes than the other two activities suggests that the most structured task requires less task regulation. Students did not need to discuss the content of the passage and the requirements of the task so much as in the other activities, and focused their attention on form, perceiving the grammatical goal of the task. This interpretation is consistent with the fact that the text reconstruction was the activity which produced the largest number of metalinguistic episodes.

Discussion and Implications for Classroom Practice

This study aimed to explore three different task types in order to ascertain whether they were effective at focusing low-proficiency students'

Table 5.7 Metacognitive episodes

	Jigsaw			Dictogloss			Text reconstruction		
	n	*SD*	*(%)*	*n*	*SD*	*(%)*	*n*	*SD*	*(%)*
Organisation of information	**10**	2.08	**(19%)**	**12**	2.16	**(21%)**	9	2.06	**(26%)**
Procedure	**12**	2.45	**(23%)**	**10**	2.08	**(18%)**	6	1.73	**(18%)**
Negotiation of content (in L1)	**13**	3.40	**(25%)**	**11**	3.10	**(19%)**	1	0.50	**(3%)**
Style or discourse	**4**	0.82	**(8%)**	**8**	2.83	**(14%)**	7	2.36	**(21%)**
Encoding of meaning	**1**	0.50	**(2%)**	**7**	0.5	**(12%)**	5	2.50	**(5%)**
Evaluation	**5**	2.50	**(10%)**	**7**	1.71	**(12%)**	—		
Focus on task	**6**	1	**(12%)**	**2**	1	**(4%)**	3	0.50	**(9%)**
Role agreement/ scribe	**1**	0.5	**(2%)**	—			3	0.5	**(9%)**
Total	**52**			**57**			**34**		
Standard deviation	2.04			6.18			1.04		

attention on language form, and if so, to examine the potential facilitating effects of the different task types.

The first research question addressed the suitability of the three task types under study for drawing low-proficiency students' attention to form. Based on previous research, three hypotheses were formulated. Our results confirmed Hypothesis 1, which posited that the text reconstruction would be the activity generating the greatest attention to form. These results are consistent with the findings of García Mayo (2001a, 2001b, 2002). Hypothesis 2, which formulated that the jigsaw would generate more attention to lexis than the other tasks (since it has been traditionally considered a more meaning oriented activity), was confirmed. Nevertheless, we must point out that the jigsaw task generated more form-based than lexis-based LREs, suggesting its value for focusing students' attention on form as well. This finding is consistent with previous research (Swain & Lapkin, 2001) and confirms the possibility of manipulating the task (using a topic and vocabulary known by the students) in order to free up attention for focusing on form (Swain & Lapkin, 2001; VanPatten, 1996). Finally, the results of this study did not support Hypothesis 3, which conjectured that the dictogloss task could produce a greater amount of focus on form than evidenced in other EFL studies (García Mayo, 2001a, 2001b, 2002) if task conditions were manipulated to solve some difficulties this task type may pose for low-proficiency foreign language students.

The results indicate that the three activities have generated a great amount of attention to form and reflection on language features, given the large number of LREs produced. Interestingly, a higher percentage of form-based LREs than lexis-based LREs were recorded, a result which is consistent with that reported by Swain and Lapkin (2001), who found no significant differences between the attention to form generated by a jigsaw and a dictogloss. They attributed this finding to the fact that both tasks required participants to produce a written text in collaboration, paying attention to grammatical accuracy.

As for the second research question, which addressed the nature of the attention elicited by each one of the three task types under study, the results suggest that the task type seems to condition the nature of the attention. Thus, the jigsaw forces students to focus on a wide range of language features, since the absence of linguistic input pushes the students to organise content and process the L2 morphosynctactically to encode the meaning. Unlike the study by Swain and Lapkin (2001), our students focused on connectors, trying to organise the ideas represented by the pictures into an elaborated discourse. This may be because the students in the present study were older and, therefore, more mature than those in the study by Swain and Lapkin (grade 8 students), or it may be due to the instructions provided to complete the task.

The dictogloss focused attention on connectors and spelling. The use of connectors was crucial to structure the discourse, and concern for spelling was due to the absence of written input (as was true for the jigsaw). Students produced a smaller number of LREs than in the other task types because the linguistic input solved many questions they might have raised.

The text reconstruction focused attention specially on determiners, passive voice, verb form, prepositions and subject-verb agreement. This is a consequence of the task type which forces learners to complete all the features absent from the text and is directly influenced by the forms present in the original text.

The focus of the third research question was the role played by the students' metalinguistic knowledge. Our findings indicate that it is a resource of considerable importance for students when they are carrying out metatalk. Metalinguistic knowledge is specially important in the context of foreign language learning, where students often lack sufficient exposure to the L2. This, together with the fact that our students are adults with some metalinguistic knowledge about their L1, makes such knowledge a useful tool for discussing language. This is specially evident in the text reconstruction task, an activity which required students to solve language problems to complete the text, forcing them to resort to grammatical knowledge to guide their decisions. The statistically significant differences found between the number of metalinguistic episodes produced on the text reconstruction and the dictogloss tasks indicate the importance of meta-linguistic knowledge when attention has been drawn to form. This in turn supports the usefulness of providing feedback which incorporates meta-linguistic explanations once attention has been drawn to a given aspect in order to establish the crucial connections between form, meaning and function. This finding supports previous studies emphasising the importance of explicit knowledge of grammatical rules (Fotos & Ellis, 1991) as long it is provided within a communicative context.

Finally, the fourth research question considered the issue of whether low-proficiency students would be able to carry out metatalk and provide mutual support to construct knowledge in their ZPD. The data reveal a high percentage of correctly solved LREs, which confirms the effectiveness of collaboration. In addition, the analysis of metacognitive episodes provides deeper insight into the collaboration established between students. Although we did not intend to make an extensive analysis of the interaction features from a microgenetic viewpoint, the data corroborate the existence of mutual scaffolding, shown to be effective in the construction of knowledge (Donato, 1994). The dialogues uncover the mutual support provided by students to control and regulate the task and make it manageable (Anton & DiCamilla, 1999). Students were successful at organising the content to improve comprehension and elaborating strategies to jointly solve the problems they faced. The numerous signs of supportive behaviour evidence the establishment of intersubjectivity, considered crucial for mutual scaffolding (de Guerrero & Villamil, 2000). This leads us to conclude that the use of their L1 was a key factor which made it possible for the members of the pair to engage in metatalk and collaborate on the tasks (see also Storch & Wigglesworth, 2003). If these low-proficiency students had not been allowed to use their L1 they would not have been able to deploy their cognitive resources to reflect verbally about the L2.

We can conclude that the tasks under study proved to be beneficial for low-proficiency level adults studying a foreign language as they draw attention to form, allow students to solve linguistic problems suited to their needs and make them receptive to feedback. No great differences have been found as to the potential of these three tasks for promoting FonF although they differ in the amount and type of linguistic discussions they generate. These differences depend on the cognitive demands set by each task, which in turn are derived from the nature of the input, and can be used pedagogically according to the purposes targeted by the teacher.

It is obvious that a single task does not have immediate effects but, rather, triggers a process, so repeated exposure is needed to consolidate gains. Swain and Lapkin (2002) attributed the successful results of the post-tests used in their study to the repeated opportunities for collaborative dialogue offered through the three stages of their task, which made participants revise their production in different ways.

Since the three tasks considered in the present study promote the production of different language features, they could be used sequentially. Students would be forced to consider the same content in different ways, thus favouring repetition without the activity becoming too tedious. The jigsaw task could be used first to make students reorganise content, activate vocabulary, and encode the intended meaning. This would lead them to notice the holes and gaps in their knowledge. After that, the original text in the jigsaw could be used in a dictogloss task. The input would consist of an elaborated model of organisation based on the same ideas and therefore it would not be difficult to remember because the content would be familiar. This activity fosters a cognitive comparison between the solutions attempted by students on the jigsaw and the target language presented in the dictogloss. Finally, learners would perform a text reconstruction task which would force them to face the language problems they had not considered on the two previous tasks and so resort to the feedback received. The work performed in the different stages, combined with adequate feedback, could be useful in the L2 classroom, as it is a good way of integrating the necessary repetition with a combination of the different characteristics that each task incorporates.

Conclusion

The goal of this study has been to determine the efficiency of three different collaborative FonF tasks as pedagogical tools for low-proficiency EFL students. The findings provide some evidence that all three task types under study were effective at drawing students attention to form and engaging them in metatalk. Inevitably, however, the study has a number of limitations. Further research is needed with tailor-made post-tests (Swain, 1998) and delayed post-tests to confirm that the knowledge constructed in collaboration can be used individually on subsequent occasions.

Some differences have emerged between the different tasks as to the number of LREs produced, suggesting that highly structured tasks focus students' attention on form more effectively. But the inverse relationship between the number of LREs produced and the number of LREs correctly solved in the most structured task suggests that this task type may force students to consider forms beyond their capacities. It may be possible to overcome this drawback with adequate feedback once attention has been drawn to a given feature, but this should be investigated further. Otherwise, the wrong solutions students arrive at could be perpetuated.

It would also be desirable to provide students with feedback after task completion and compare the effect of such feedback with that of discussion generated during the LRE. This would help us refine our understanding of the process and improve classroom implementation of tasks.

The data seem to lend support to the notion that different task types focus students' attention on different features. This result can help teachers make informed decisions when implementing tasks in the classroom depending on their pedagogical goals. It also suggests the usefulness of combining different task types so as to integrate the different aspects on which they focus students' attention. This can help provide repetition and at the same time motivate students to consider different features.

Finally, the analysis of the dialogues has been extremely useful. The three tasks have proved to be highly communicative. Students engaged actively in creating the meaning they were trying to convey, collaborating in a common pursuit, an essential condition for cognitive development in the ZPD. The resulting collaboration allowed them to solve a high percentage of problems, and numerous instances of scaffolding have been found. Through the interaction, students have been shown to cooperate to complete the task, reflect about form, formulate and test hypotheses, use their metalinguistic knowledge and resort to strategies when they did not have any other resource. This also highlights the reported value of collaborative tasks for teachers, who have the opportunity to monitor the students' mental processes, and consequently to offer feedback suitable to the students' needs.

Acknowledgements

A preliminary version of this paper was presented at SLRF 2005 (Second Language Research Forum), held in New York (7–9 October). We would like to thank Patsy Lightbown and the audience for interesting comments. We would also like to thank the students who participated in the tasks used in this research and Ken Friedman and Ian Williams (Department of Philology at the University of Cantabria) for their help with the statistical analyses. Thanks are also due to Edward Dalley for his assistance in proofreading the manuscript. All errors remain our responsibility.

Notes

1. The instructions for the three tasks appear in English in Appendix 5.A but were provided in Spanish to the participants.
2. In the different examples italics have been used to indicate that those utterances were uttered in Spanish, the participants' L1.

References

Anton, M. and DiCamilla, F. (1999) Socio-cognitive functions of L1 collaborative interaction in the L2 classroom. *The Modern Language Journal* 83 (2), 233–247.
Blakey, T.N. (1985) *English for Maritime Studies*, Oxford: Pergamon Press.
Brooks, F.B. and Donato, R. (1994) Vygotskian approaches to understanding foreign language learner discourse during communicative tasks. *Hispania* 77, 262–274.
de Guerrero, M.C.M. and Villamil, O.S. (2000) Activating the ZPD: Mutual scaffolding in L2 peer revision. *The Modern Language Journal* 84 (1), 51–68.
Donato, R. (1994) Collective scaffolding in second language learning. In J.P. Lantolf and G. Appel (eds) *Vygotskian Approaches to Second Language Research* (pp. 33–56). Westport, CT: Ablex Publishing.

Donato, R. and Lantolf, J.P. (1990) The dialogic origins of L2 monitoring. *Pragmatics and Language Learning* 1, 83–97.

Doughty, C. and Williams, J. (eds) (1998) *Focus on Form in Classroom Second Language Acquisition*. Cambridge: Cambridge University Press.

Ellis, R. (2000) Task-based research and language pedagogy. *Language Teaching Research* 4 (3), 193–220.

Ellis, R. (2001) Investigating form-focused instruction. *Language Learning* 51, 1–46.

Esteve, O. and Cañada, M.D. (2001) La interacción en el aula desde el punto de vista de la co-construcción de conocimiento entre iguales. In C. Muñoz (Coord.) *Perspectivas Recientes en la Adquisición de Lenguas* (pp. 73–84). Barcelona: Universitat de Barcelona.

Fotos, S. and Ellis, R. (1991). Communicating about grammar: A task-based approach. *TESOL Quarterly* 25, 605–628.

García Mayo, M.P. (2001a) Are collaborative focus-on-form tasks worthwhile among advanced EFL learners? Some insights from an empirical study. In A.I. Moreno and V. Colwell (eds) *Perspectivas Recientes sobre el Discurso/Recent Perspectives on Discourse*. León: Universidad de León. Documento CD-ROM document.

García Mayo, M.P. (2001b) The effectiveness of two focus-on-form tasks in advanced EFL pedagogy. *International Journal of Applied Linguistics* 12 (2), 156–175.

García Mayo, M.P. (2002) Interaction in advanced EFL pedagogy: A comparison of form-focused activities. *International Journal of Educational Research* 37 (3–4), 323–341. Special issue on 'The role of interaction in instructed language learning'. Guest editors: M.P. García Mayo and E. Alcón Soler.

Kowal, M. and Swain, M. (1997) From semantic to syntactic processing. How can we promote it in the immersion classroom? In R.K. Johnson and M. Swain (eds) *Immersion Education: International Perspectives* (pp. 284–309). Cambridge: Cambridge University Press.

Lantolf, J.P. and Appel, G. (1994) Theoretical framework: An introduction to Vygotskian perspectives on second language research. In J.P. Lantolf and G. Appel (eds) *Vygotskian Approaches to Second Language Research* (pp. 1–32). Westport, CT: Ablex Publishing.

LaPierre, D. (1994) Language output in a cooperative learning setting: Determining its effects on second language learning. MA thesis, University of Toronto, Canada.

Long, M.H. (1991) Focus on form: A design feature in laguage teaching methodology. In K. de Bot, D. Coste, R. Ginsberg and C. Kramsch (eds) *Foreign Language Research in Cross-Cultural Perspectives* (pp. 39–52). Amsterdam: John Benjamins.

Pica, T. (1994) Research on negotiation: What does it reveal about second-language learning conditions, processes, and outcomes? *Language Learning* 44 (3), 493–527.

Pica, T. (2002) Subject-matter content: How does it assist the interactional and linguistic needs of classroom language learners? *The Modern Language Journal* 86 (i), 1–19.

Pica, R., Kanagy, R. and Falodun, J. (1993) Choosing and using communication tasks for second language instruction and research. In G. Crookes and S. Gass (eds) *Tasks and Language Learning: Integrating Theory and Practice* (pp. 9–34). Clevedon: Multilingual Matters.

Skehan, P. (1998) Task-based Instruction. *Annual Review of Applied Linguistics* 18, 268–286.

Storch, N. (1998) A classroom-based study: Insights from a collaborative text reconstruction task. *ELT Journal* 52 (4), 291–300.

Storch, N. (2002) Patterns of interaction in ESL pair work. *Language Learning* 52 (1), 119–158.

Storch, N. and Wigglesworth, G. (2003) Is there a role for the use of the L1 in an L2 setting? *TESOL Quarterly* 37 (4), 760–770.

Swain, M. (1985) Communicative competence: Some roles of comprehensible input and comprehensible output in its development. In S. Gass and C. Madden (eds) *Input in Second Language Acquisition* (pp. 235–253). Rowley, MA: Newbury House.

Swain, M. (1995) Three functions of output in second language learning. In G. Cook and B. Seidlhofer (eds) *Principle and Practice in Applied Linguistics: Studies in Honour of H. G. Widdowson* (pp. 125–144). Oxford: Oxford University Press.

Swain, M. (1998) Focus on form through conscious reflection. In C. Doughty, and J. Williams (eds) *Focus on Form in Classroom Second Language Acquisition* (pp. 64–84). Cambridge: Cambridge University Press.

Swain, M. (2000) The output hypothesis and beyond: Mediating acquisition through collaborative dialogue. In J.P. Lantolf (ed.) *Sociocultural Theory and Second Language Learning* (pp. 97–114). Oxford: Oxford University Press.

Swain, M. and Lapkin, S. (1995) Problems in output and the cognitive processes they generate: A step towards second language learning. *Applied Linguistics* 16 (3), 371–391.

Swain, M. and Lapkin, S. (1998) Interaction and second language learning: Two adolescent French immersion students working together. *The Modern Language Journal* 83, 320–338.

Swain, M. and Lapkin, S. (2000) Task-based second language learning: The uses of the first language. *Language Teaching Research* 4 (3), 251–274.

Swain, M. and Lapkin, S. (2001) Focus on form through collaborative dialogue: Exploring task effects. In M. Bygate, P. Skehan and M. Swain (eds) *Researching Pedagogic Tasks. Second Language Learning, Teaching and Testing* (pp. 99–118). Harlow: Longman.

Swain, M. and Lapkin, S. (2002) Talking it through: Two French immersion learners' response to reformulation. *International Journal of Educational Research* 37 (3–4), 3305–322. Special issue on 'The role of interaction in instructed language learning'. Guest editors: M.P. García Mayo and E. Alcón Soler.

Swain, M., Brooks, L. and Tocalli-Beller, A. (2002) Peer-dialogue as a means of second language learning. *Annual Review of Applied Linguistics* 22, 171–185.

VanPatten, B. (1996) *Input Processing and Grammar Instruction*. New York: Ablex.

Vygotsky, L.S. (1978) *Mind in Society: The Development of Higher Psychological Processes*. Cambridge, MA: Harvard University Press.

Wajnryb, R. (1990) *Grammar Dictation*. Oxford: Oxford University Press.

Williams, J. (2001) Learner-generated attention to form. *Language Learning* 51, 303–346.

Appendix 5.A

Dictogloss

Instructions

Try to reconstruct the text you are going to listen to with the help of your partner. You must reproduce the original text as faithfully as possible and in a grammatically accurate form. The text will be read twice at normal speed. The first time you listen to the text try to understand the meaning and do not write anything down. The second time you may take notes, writing down either key words or expressions that will help to reconstruct the text. Working together you will have to write a final version that is as correct as possible grammatically speaking. Revise carefully what you have written attempting to correct anything that does not look right.

Input

Containerisation has many advantages as a method of transporting general cargo. Time is an important factor and is directly related to cost, because in any service time costs money. Containerisation reduces handling and less handling means less time is necessary for transporting the goods. Time is further reduced by the easier stowage of containers compared with non-containerised general cargo. Containers are of a standard shape and dimensions, therefore they are easily stowed. In addition to easier stowage, containers are more easily loaded and unloaded. This is done quickly by special cranes. Time is also reduced by the fact that less handling means less paperwork. Because the goods remain in the container they do not have to be checked when loaded and unloaded into and off the ship.

Text reconstruction

Instructions

Try to reconstruct the text with the help of your partner. You will have to add the words that are missing so that the text is meaningful. Linkers (i.e. prepositions, conjunctions, etc.) have been omitted. Verb endings and articles have also been eliminated. Discuss with your partner the most accurate way of completing the text. You can also make changes if you consider them necessary. You may wish to add some words to connect the different sentences to improve cohesion. Write a grammatically correct final version of the text.

Input

Containerisation several advantages as method transport cargo. Time important factor and directly relate cost, in any service time cost money. Containerisation reduce handling and less handling mean less time necessary transport goods. Time further reduce by easier stowage containers compare non-containerised general cargo. Containers standard shape and dimensions, easily stow. Easier stowage, containers more easily load and unload. This do quickly special cranes. Time also reduce less handling mean less paperwork. Goods remain container not check when load and unload ship.

Jigsaw

Instructions

Try to convey to your partner in English the meaning of the pictures you are holding. Study them carefully so that you know exactly what they mean. One of you will have pictures 1, 3 and 5; and the other, pictures 2, 4 and 6. You cannot look at each other's pictures. Beginning with picture number 1 you will have to convey the information contained in your respective pictures (in order). Once the information is complete, you should write the information in a coherent and grammatically correct paragraph. Please, revise your text carefully.

Sample visual stimulus

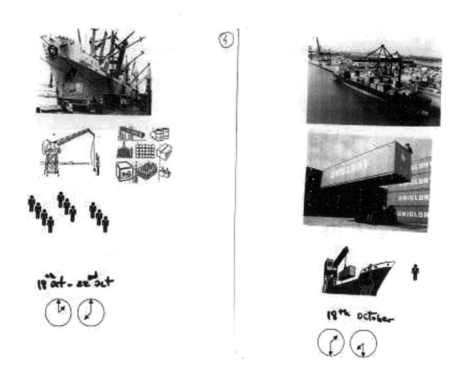

Chapter 6

Cognitive Task Complexity and Linguistic Performance in French L2 Writing

FOLKERT KUIKEN and INEKE VEDDER

Introduction

Lately more and more weight has been attributed to the role of attention in various theories about second language acquisition (Schmidt, 2001). Skehan (1998) and Skehan and Foster (1999, 2001) for example adhere in their Limited Attentional Capacity Model to the idea that language tasks which are cognitively demanding are likely to draw attentional resources away from language forms, which will affect accuracy negatively. A different position is taken by Robinson (2001a, 2001b, 2005) who advocates with his Cognition Hypothesis that a complex task may result in greater linguistic complexity and promote accuracy.

As the evidence for none of these two assumptions is decisive we set up a series of experiments in which L2 learners were asked to write two argumentative texts. These texts concerned letters in which the writers had to convince a friend regarding the choice of a holiday destination out of five possibilities, taking into account a varying number of criteria like the opportunity to swim, a quiet location and the proximity of the historical centre. The study focused on the relation between the cognitive complexity of the task and the complexity of the linguistic output: does the quality of the text decrease when L2 writers have to take into account a considerable amount of criteria, corresponding to what Skehan and Foster assume, or will it result in a syntactically and lexically better text as supposed by Robinson?

In what follows the design and the results of the study will be described in detail, but let us first take a look at two of the texts that were produced in the experiment by Dutch university students who took French as their second language: text A addressed to Valéry and text B to Simone.

Cher Valéry,

Souvent il faut qu'on faire des choix, c'était facile cette fois! A mon avis, nous allons au Vallée du Haut Bréda! Pourquoi? Ecoute! L'endroit est très tranquille, il âgit que l'environ est très suave et riant, avec beaucoup de possibilités de faire des activités.

Pour moi, maison Lory Bretagne est un autre option, avec son petit-dejeuner et son aventures culinaires, mais je crois que la proximté d'un village avec des petite shops et un boulanger est indispensable. De ce fait nous avons la possibilité d'aller retour à la maison à pied dans un état pris de vin. Baffelan B&B se trouve à 800 mètres d'un village! Le seul, vrai manque est l'absence d'un lac ou une piscine. Allez, nous ne pouvons pas avoir tout!
Bon, à mon opinion Baffelan est notre destination!

Salut!

A.

Text A: text addressed to Valéry

Chère Simone,

Oh la la, c'était dure! Tel choix! Il y a beaucoup de possibilités, et les destinations sont tous les plus belle possible.
A mon avis, le service maternelle et le service medical sont les conditions principales, de sorte qu'ils nous, les adultes, rendent un condition pour nous jouions optimalement pendant la vacation. Tes enfants sont encore raisonnable jeunes. Pour cette raison je crois qu'ils n'ont pas besoin des 'grande choses', comme faire le planche à voile, snorkling et plonger. Ils sont heureux avec la plage, ses petits jeus et le contat avec des autres enfants. C'est pour ces raisons que je crois que les Maledives est la destination plus appropriée et agreable pour tous!

Une baise,

B.

Text B: text addressed to Simone

In both texts one destination is recommended to the addressee, so the writers have accomplished the task they were asked to carry out. However, as may be expected from intermediate learners, the texts contain some awkward sentences, badly chosen words and many more errors of all kinds.

In order to have an idea about teachers' opinions on the quality of these texts four groups, each consisting of four teachers of French, were asked to judge the texts with regard to accuracy, syntactic complexity and lexical variation, and to give them an overall judgement on a scale from one to ten. On all aspects text A received higher marks (on average six) than text B (on average five). In the Dutch educational system, where six is sufficient and five is insufficient, this would mean the difference between pass and fail.

At the end of this chapter we will come back to the teacher judgements and see if they corresponded with a more detailed analysis of the texts. First we will start with an account of the background of the study and a description of the two competing views of Skehan and Foster, on the one hand, and Robinson, on the other. The research questions are formulated and the design of the study is explained. Then the results of the experiment are presented and finally the conclusions with regard to our research question will be drawn. In the last section we will also come back to the examples given in A and B; based on our results we will make some suggestions with regard to the assignment of tasks in language teaching.

Background of the Study

In the study we test two models proposed to explain the influence of cognitive task complexity on linguistic performance in L2: Skehan and Foster's Limited Attentional Capacity Model and Robinson's Cognition Hypothesis.

The basic assumption of Skehan and Foster's Limited Attentional Capacity Model is that attentional resources are limited and that to attend to one aspect of performance (complexity of language, accuracy, fluency) may well mean that other dimensions suffer. Therefore a balance needs to be established between these different performance dimensions and since a learner's processing capacity is limited, a prioritisation of one aspect will hinder development in the other areas (Skehan, 1998, 2001, 2003; Skehan & Foster, 1999, 2001, 2005).

This notion of limited processing capacity on which the Limited Capacity Model is based, is founded both on theories on working memory (Carter, 1998; Gathercole & Baddeley, 1993) and on a study by VanPatten (1990) among L2 learners of Spanish. In the VanPatten study learners had to focus either on content, on form or on both, while they were listening to a text in Spanish under different conditions. The main finding of the study was that learners cannot pay attention to language forms without a loss of attention to language content.

With regard to the relationship between task content and performance Skehan and Foster argue, based on VanPatten's results, that if a task requires significant attention to be given to its content and a high level of cognitive processing, there will be less attention avalaible to be given to the linguistic output. As a consequence, tasks which are cognitively demanding are likely to draw attentional resources away from language forms. This may result in learners paying insufficient attention to forms and structures which still require controlled processing. The major claim of the Limited Attentional Capacity Model, in summary, is that an increase in cognitive task complexity will cause learners to pay attention first of all to the content of the task. As a consequence, the complexity and accuracy of the linguistic output will decrease.

A different view on the effect of cognitive task complexity on linguistic output is held by Robinson (2001a, 2001b, 2005). Integrating information-processing theories (Schmidt, 2001) and interactionist explanations of L2 task effects (Long, 1996), Robinson proposes in the Cognition Hypothesis that, contrary to Skehan and Foster's predictions, learners can access multiple and non-competitional attentional resources. This claim is based on Givón (1985, 1989) and Talmy (2000) among others, who argue that structural complexity and functional complexity are associated with each other. According to Robinson, cognitively more demanding tasks are thought to elicit a greater amount of negotiation of meaning and to promote noticing. As a result increasing task complexity will trigger greater linguistic complexity and higher accuracy.

In the Cognition Hypothesis Robinson provides a framework for describing task complexity by means of which sequencing decisions may be operationalised. The framework distinguishes three groups of factors which interact to influence task performance and learning: cognitive variables, interactive variables and learner variables (see Table 6.1).

The first group of factors concerns *task complexity*. With task complexity Robinson refers to cognitive task features which can be manipulated to increase or lessen the cognitive demands made by a task. Task complexity needs to be distinguished from *task difficulty*. Task difficulty refers to the learners' perceptions of the demands made by certain tasks and is determined by the abilities (intelligence, working memory, language aptitude) and affective responses (e.g. anxiety, motivation, confidence) the learners bring to the task. Interactive factors refer to *task conditions*, comprising

Table 6.1 A triad of task complexity, task conditions and task difficulty factors (Robinson, 2005: 5)

Tasks complexity (cognitive factors)	Task conditions (interactive factors)	Task difficulty (learner factors)
(a) Resource directing e.g. +/− few elements +/− here-and-now +/− no reasoning demands	(a) Participation variables e.g. open/closed one-way/two-way convergent/divergent	(a) Affective variables e.g. motivation anxiety confidence
(b) Resource-dispersing e.g. +/− planning +/− single task +/− prior knowledge	(b) Participant variables e.g. gender familiarity power/solidarity	(b) Ability variables e.g. aptitude working memory intelligence

participation variables such as the nature of the task (open/closed, one-way/two-way, convergent/divergent) and participant variables (same/different gender, extent of familiarity, power and status, etc.).

With regard to the cognitive variables a further distinction has to be made between the so-called resource-directing and resource-dispersing variables (Robinson, 2005). Resource-directing variables are inherent design factors of tasks, such as the number of elements and relationships to be distinguished and described ([+/− few elements]), the temporal and spatial references of the task ([+/− Here-and-Now]), and the necessity to give reasons to support statements made ([+/− no reasoning demands]). The resource-directing variables are related to particular features of the language code, such as using present or past tense, attributive clauses, conjunctions, etc. Increasing cognitive task complexity on these developmental dimensions will push learners to greater accuracy and complexity of L2 production.

Task complexity can also increase along resource-dispersing dimensions, which are not related to any particular linguistic features. Examples of resource-dispersing variables are the amount of planning time allowed ([+/− planning]), the increase of the number of tasks that have to be performed simultaneously ([+/− single task]) and the existing linguistic and extra-linguistic knowledge of the learners ([+/− prior knowledge]). Tasks which are cognitively more complex on these resource-dispersing dimensions make extra attentional demands compared to cognitively simpler tasks. Increasing complexity along these dimensions has therefore the effect of depleting the attention available for the task over many non-specific linguistic aspects of production. As a result performance will be poorer.

Robinson's Cognition Hypothesis constitutes a complete agenda for research into the effect of task complexity on L2 learning. Although research in some areas has started (Ellis & Yuan, 2004; Gilabert, 2005, this volume; Peters, 2004, this volume; Robinson *et al.*, 1995) the results of these studies have not always been clear and are often only discussed in relation to either the Limited Capacity Model or the Cognition Hypothesis. Particularly with regard to the effect of resource-directing variables on task performance more research is needed (Robinson, 2001a, 2001b, 2005). In our study both the Limited Capacity Model and the Cognition Hypothesis are put to the test. The study presented in this chapter investigates the effect of increasing cognitive complexity in an L2 writing task through manipulation of two closely linked factors of the resource-directing dimension, +/− few elements and +/− no reasoning demands (Kuiken & Vedder, 2004a, 2004b, in preparation; Kuiken *et al.*, 2005).

Design

The present study aims to investigate the effects of cognitive task complexity on various aspects of written performance in L2 at different levels of proficiency. The focus is on the question of whether cognitively more demanding tasks do lead to greater syntactic complexity and lexical variation, and to higher accuracy. Based on the results of a pilot study (Kuiken & Vedder, 2004a, 2004b) we chose to include in the experiment L2 learners with a low language proficiency level as well as more advanced learners. One of the outcomes of this pilot study was that cognitive complexity seemed to be affected by the level of language proficiency, as could be expected on the basis of the Threshold Hypothesis (Cummins, 1979), in which it is postulated that learners first have to achieve a certain level of L2 proficiency before they can do a specific task (e.g. reading in L2). The participants of the study are Dutch university students who take Italian or French as a second language. In this article we report on the results of the students of French L2. The results of a subset of the students of Italian L2 are discussed in Kuiken *et al.* (2005).

Research questions

Our main research question regards the influence of task complexity on different aspects of linguistic performance, at different levels of L2 proficiency. With regard to this influence the following two questions were formulated:

(1) Is the influence of manipulating cognitive task complexity the same for syntactic complexity, lexical variation and accuracy and, if not, in what ways does the influence differ?
(2) Is this influence the same for learners at different levels of proficiency and, if not, in what ways does the influence differ?

With respect to the first question the Limited Capacity Model predicts a better performance on the less complex task, because L2 learners have to direct a larger part of their attentional capacity towards the content of the task. The Cognition Hypothesis, however, predicts that an increase in cognitive complexity will lead to greater syntactic complexity and more lexical variation and to higher accuracy on the complex task. With regard to our second question, following Cummins' Threshold Hypothesis (Cummins, 1979), no or smaller effects of task complexity for low proficiency students can be expected. It seems likely that for low proficiency students, who still have to deal with basic formulation processes, the less complex task is already extending their interlanguage to its maximum. As a consequence, in the case of increased task complexity, no attention will be left to be paid to both task content and linguistic form.

Participants and tasks

In the experiment, 91 students of Italian and 76 university students of French were involved. In this chapter the results of the learners of French in their first year and third year of study are discussed. The first-year

Table 6.2 Participants and tasks

Language: French	Year group	Task			
		Time 1		Time 2	
		+complex	−complex	+complex	−complex
	1	n = 48	n = 48	n = 33	n = 33
	3			n = 12	n = 12

n = number of observations.

students were tested at two different moments of the curriculum, in the autumn (number of observations = 48) and the spring (number of observations = 33) with an interval of five months. The group of participants tested at Time 1 does not completely coincide with those tested at Time 2, since some students only followed the autumn classes, and others, who already had previous knowledge of French, came in in the spring. The third-year students were tested once (number of observations = 12). Table 6.2 features this information.

Two writing tasks were assigned to the learners in which cognitive complexity was manipulated. In both experimental conditions participants were presented with a prompt in L1 (Dutch) explaining that they had to write a letter to a friend regarding the choice of a holiday destination from five options. In the letter a varying number of requirements had to be taken into account, six in the complex and three in the non-complex condition. In the complex condition a choice of a Bed & Breakfast in France had to be made (Bretagne, Ile de France, Alpes Maritimes, Aquitaine, Isère), while in the non-complex condition the writers had to choose a holiday resort in an exotic country (Brazil, Cuba, Kenya, Egypt or the Maldives; see Appendix 6.A). The letter had to consist of a minimum of 150 words; there was a time limit of 40 minutes per task and use of a dictionary was allowed (see for an example the two letters shown previously). A cloze test was constructed, consisting of a shortened version of an article from l'Express (30-10-2003), in order to obtain a separate measure of language proficiency. In this cloze test every eleventh word was deleted, leaving 33 gaps.

Data analysis and measures of performance

Linguistic performance in French was operationalised as accuracy, syntactic complexity and lexical variation. Specific measures were chosen following the considerations and recommendations of Wolfe-Quintero et al. (1998). In determining accuracy we first counted the total number of errors per T-unit (EtotperT). Then a division was made into three degrees of errors. First-degree errors (E1perT) include minor deviations in spelling, meaning or grammatical form that do not interfere with the comprehensibility of the text, second-degree errors (E2perT) contain more serious deviations in spelling, meaning, grammatical form or word order. Third-degree errors (E3perT) make the text nearly incomprehensible. Accuracy was scored by two raters, both native speakers of French, who had received training in order to reach interrater reliability. Specific criteria for each error type were developed. See for an illustration the following examples taken from the two letters shown earlier. The number between brackets refers to the type of error that was made and the correction suggested by the rater has also been added.

(1) *Pour moi* (1; à mon avis) *maison* (1; la maison) Lory Bretagne (2; en Bretagne) est *un* (1; une) autre option.
(2) *Le seul, vraie manque* (2; la seule chose qui manque vraiment) est l'absence d'un lac ou *une* (1; d'une) piscine.
(3) L'endroit est très tranquille, *il âgit que l'environ est très suave et riant* (3; les environs ont l'air très agréable).
(4) C'est pour ces raisons que je crois que les *Maledives* (1; Maldives) est la destination *plus* (1; la plus) appropriée.

Syntactic complexity was operationalised as the number of clauses per T-unit (CperT). Apart from this T-unit ratio a dependent clause ratio was used examining the degree of syntactic embedding per clause (DCperC). Lexical variation was established by means of the type-token ratio, the number of word types divided by the total numer of word tokens (TTR1). Also an alternative ratio was computed, which corrects for text length [the number of word types divided by the square root of two times the total number of word tokens (TTR2)].

Proficiency level was defined on the basis of the cloze scores (maximum score 33) and not in terms of study year, since within group variance turned out to be very large. Instead, scores were split into two groups (number of observations low proficiency group 84; high proficiency group 100), with the low proficiency group consisting of learners with a score of 16 or less (mean 10.54; s.d. 3.02) and the high proficiency group containing scores higher than 16 (mean 18.31; s.d. 2.16).

Results

Before answering the main research questions we will compare the performance of the first-year students with the output of the third-year students. As stated above, there were more first-year students ($n = 48$ at Time 1 and $n = 33$ at Time 2) than third-year students ($n = 12$). Although the latter demonstrated on the whole a better accuracy, a higher syntactic complexity and a larger lexical variation, the results of two-samples

Table 6.3 Performance comparisons between first and third year students (two-samples *t*-tests)

Measure type	Measure*	Year 1 Mean	SD	Year 3 Mean	SD	t	df	p
Accuracy	EtotperT	2.17	0.84	2.02	1.33	0.717	184	0.4745
	E1perT	1.50	0.59	1.50	0.92	0.003	184	0.9976
	E2perT	0.57	0.32	0.48	0.44	1.223	184	0.2229
	E3perT	0.10	0.11	0.05	0.06	1.975	184	0.0498*
Syntactic complexity	CperT	1.71	0.37	1.82	0.31	−1.443	184	0.1508
	DCperC	0.36	0.10	0.40	0.08	−1.597	184	0.1120
Lexical variation	TTR1	0.52	0.08	0.53	0.06	−0.520	178	0.6036
	TTR2	4.75	0.45	4.95	0.48	−1.935	178	0.0546

*EtotperT = total errors per T-unit, E1perT = 1st degree errors per T-unit, E2perT = 2nd degree errors per T-unit, E3perT = 3rd degree errors per T-unit, CperT = clauses per T-unit, DCperC = dependent clauses per clause, TTR1 = type-token ratio, TTR2 = ratio of word types to the square root of two times the word tokens.

t-tests only yielded a significant difference with respect to the third degree errors (see Table 6.3, $p < 0.05$).

The finding that the third-year students did not differ that much from the first-year students might be explained by the fact that in the Dutch situation language students form a rather heterogeneous group. This holds especially for the first-year students. French is a main subject for some of them, whereas it is subsidiary for others; some have a French background or have spent a considerable amount of time in a French-speaking country, others have not. The rather large standard deviations reflect this heterogeneity. What is clear, however, is that the third-year students make significantly fewer serious errors (third degree errors) than the first-year students. This was the reason why we decided to split the group into low and high proficient performers, as has been pointed out in the preceding section.

Our second comparison concerns the results of the first-year students on the first and second occasion they were measured: first in autumn (Time 1) and then, about five months later, in spring (Time 2). What we can observe (see Table 6.4) is that accuracy has significantly improved on the second occasion (two-samples *t*-tests yield significant differences on *all* accuracy measures) and that the texts contain more lexical variation (as demonstrated by a significantly higher score for TTR2). No differences with regard to the syntactic complexity of the texts are found. This means that in the course of the first year a progress in performance can be observed with regard to accuracy and lexical variation.

Our main research question concerned the influence of task complexity on linguistic performance. We will first examine if this influence is the same

Table 6.4 Performance comparisons of first year students on Time 1 (autumn) and 2 (spring) (two-samples *t*-tests)

Measure type	Measure*	Time 1 Mean	SD	Time 3 Mean	SD	t	df	p
Accuracy	EtotperT	2.41	0.89	1.81	0.60	5.144	160	0.0000***
	E1perT	1.66	0.61	1.25	0.44	4.942	160	0.0000***
	E2perT	0.62	0.35	0.49	0.24	2.892	160	0.0044**
	E3perT	0.11	0.11	0.07	0.09	2.807	160	0.0056**
Syntactic complexity	CperT	1.70	0.37	1.71	0.38	−0.097	160	0.9226
	DCperC	0.36	0.09	0.37	0.10	−0.802	160	0.4235
Lexical variation	TTR1	0.52	0.09	0.52	0.07	0.143	154	0.8864
	TTR2	4.67	0.42	4.86	0.48	−2.541	154	0.0121*

*EtotperT = total errors per T-unit, E1perT = 1st degree errors per T-unit, E2perT = 2nd degree errors per T-unit, E3perT = 3rd degree errors per T-unit, CperT = clauses per T-unit, DCperC = dependent clauses per clause, TTR1 = type-token ratio, TTR2 = ratio of word types to the square root of two times the word tokens.

for different aspects of linguistic performance. What we find is that cognitive task complexity affects various aspects of linguistic output to a different degree. With regard to accuracy we observe that the students make fewer mistakes in the complex task than in the less complex one. For the total number of errors per T-unit as well as for the first and second degree errors these differences are significant, but not for the third degree errors (see Table 6.5, paired samples *t*-tests). No significant differences in the output

Table 6.5 Performance comparisons between tasks (paired samples *t*-tests)

Measure type	Measure*	+Complex Mean	SD	−Complex Mean	SD	t	df	p
Accuracy	EtotperT	1.97	0.71	2.33	1.06	−3.917	92	0.0001***
	E1perT	1.40	0.51	1.59	0.73	−2.794	92	0.0063**
	E2perT	0.48	0.27	0.64	0.38	−4.392	92	0.0000***
	E3perT	0.08	0.10	0.10	0.11	−1.495	92	0.1385
Syntactic complexity	CperT	1.73	0.37	1.71	0.36	0.238	92	0.8127
	DCperC	0.36	0.10	0.37	0.09	−1.198	92	0.2341
Lexical variation	TTR1	0.53	0.08	0.51	0.07	2.470	89	0.0154*
	TTR2	4.81	0.47	4.74	0.45	1.524	89	0.1310

*EtotperT = total errors per T-unit, E1perT = 1st degree errors per T-unit, E2perT = 2nd degree errors per T-unit, E3perT = 3rd degree errors per T-unit, CperT = clauses per T-unit, DCperC = dependent clauses per clause, TTR1 = type-token ratio, TTR2 = ratio of word types to the square root of two times the word tokens.

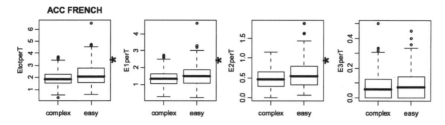

Figure 6.1 Performance comparisons between tasks: Accuracy

on the complex and less complex task are found with respect to syntactic complexity. Lexical variation in the texts based on the complex task as measured by the type-token ratio is significantly larger than in those based on the less complex task; however, this finding is not confirmed by the alternative type-token ratio (TTR2).

The findings of Table 6.5 are visualised in Figures 6.1 and 6.2, in which the boxes with the thick black line represent 50% of the participants with the black line indicating the mean score. Figure 6.1 displays the results with regard to accuracy, Figure 6.2 those of syntactic complexity and lexical variation. As can be seen in Figure 6.1 the means for accuracy are lower in the complex task than in the less complex one.

Having established different effects of cognitive task complexity on the written performance of students with regard to accuracy, syntactic complexity and lexical variation, we will now consider the second research question: whether this influence is the same for learners at different levels of proficiency. Although ANOVA results (see Table 6.6) show a significant effect of proficiency level on accuracy (total number of errors and second and third degree errors) and lexical variation (TTR2), as well as a significant effect of task complexity on accuracy (total number of errors and first

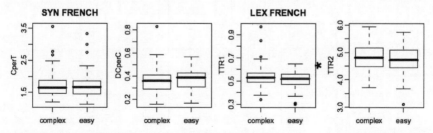

Figure 6.2 Performance comparisons between tasks: Syntactic complexity and lexical variation

Table 6.6 Effects of proficiency level, task complexity and their interaction (ANOVA)

Measure type	Measure	Level			Task			Level*Task		
		F	df	p	F	df	p	F	df	p
Accuracy	EtotperT	9.8414	1, 90	0.0023**	15.0807	1, 90	0.0002***	0.3574	1, 90	0.5514
	E1perT	2.6326	1, 90	0.1082	7.7406	1, 90	0.0066**	0.7262	1, 90	0.3964
	E2perT	21.321	1, 90	0.0000***	18.8902	1, 90	0.0000***	0.4944	1, 90	0.4838
	E3perT	18.265	1, 90	0.0000***	2.2268	1, 90	0.1391	1.8603	1, 90	0.1760
Syntactic complexity	CperT	1.7416	1, 90	0.1903	0.1028	1, 90	0.7492	2.0571	1, 90	0.1550
	DCperC	0.692	1, 90	0.4077	5.8762	1, 90	0.1753	2.2842	1, 90	0.1342
Lexical variation	TTR1	1.2807	1, 90	0.2609	5.8762	1, 90	0.01742*	0.1903	1, 90	0.6638
	TTR2	8.7612	1, 90	0.0040**	1.8636	1, 90	0.1757	0.4544	1, 90	0.5020

*EtotperT = total errors per T-unit, E1perT = 1st degree errors per T-unit, E2perT = 2nd degree errors per T-unit, E3perT = 3rd degree errors per T-unit, CperT = clauses per T-unit, DCperC = dependent clauses per clause, TTR1 = type-token ratio, TTR2 = ratio of word types to the square root of two times the word tokens

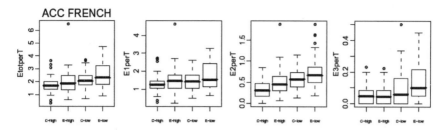

Figure 6.3 The relation between task complexity and proficiency level (accuracy)

and second degree errors) and lexical variation (TTR1), no significant interaction of task and proficiency level on any of the measures scored can be established.

This means that the effects of cognitive complexity are not related to language proficiency. Again we have visualised the results of Table 6.6 (Figure 6.3 for accuracy and Figure 6.4 with regard to syntactic complexity and lexical variation). In these figures the two left columns represent the scores of the high proficient students (high), the two on the right of the low proficient ones (low); the first and third columns concern the results of the complex (C) task, the second and fourth those of the less complex (E) task (respectively C-high, E-high, C-low, E-low). Figure 6.3 clearly demonstrates the general tendency that students make fewer errors in the complex tasks (first and third columns) than in the less complex ones (second and fourth columns) and that the more proficient students (first and second columns) do better than the less proficient ones (third and fourth column). The diagram of the alternative type-token ration (TTR2) in Figure 6.4 shows that the students display a greater lexical variation in the complex tasks (first and third columns) and that the texts of the more proficient students (first and second columns) are more varied than those of the less proficient students (third and fourth columns).

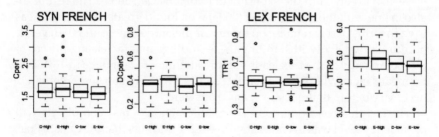

Figure 6.4 The relation between task complexity and proficiency level (syntactic complexity and lexical variation)

Conclusion and Discussion

Our study was based on two competing theories: Skehan and Foster's Limited Attentional Capacity Model and Robinson's Cognition Hypothesis. The former predicted a better performance on the less complex task, the latter on the complex task. Drawing up the balances of our results we have to conclude that we did not find support for Skehan and Foster's model as the students involved in our study did not perform significantly better on the less complex task on any of the measures scored. We did, however, find (partial) evidence in support of Robinson, as the texts based on the complex task contained significantly fewer errors than those based on the less complex task. The complex task also resulted in a higher lexical variation, but since we only found a significant difference for the classic type-token ratio (TTR1) and not for TTR2 which takes text length into account, we feel that we should not attribute too much importance to that. So with regard to our first research question we can conclude that task complexity does have an effect on linguistic performance, in the sense that an increase in cognitive task complexity along resource-directing variables results in a more accurate text, suggesting that the students pay more attention to language form.

In answer to the second question whether this influence is the same for learners at different levels of proficiency, we expected to find – based on Cummins' Threshold Hypothesis – no or smaller effects of task complexity for low proficiency students. However, on the basis of our data we could not establish such an effect and therefore we had to reject this assumption.

Although our findings point mostly in the direction of Robinson one may wonder why our data do not fully confirm the Cognition Hypothesis as we were not able to show an effect of task complexity concerning syntactic complexity and only partially with regard to lexical variation. However, in earlier studies we could not establish such an effect either (Kuiken & Vedder, 2004a, 2004b; Kuiken *et al.*, 2005).

Regarding the effect of task complexity on accuracy, a more or less stable picture seems to emerge, as these findings corroborate those of our pilot study (Kuiken & Vedder, 2004a, 2004b) and of the students of Italian who were also involved in the experiment (Kuiken *et al.*, 2005). The results are also in line with those of Gilabert (2005) who found greater accuracy (measured in terms of self-repairs) on more complex tasks (there and then versus here and now). Notwithstanding these findings that increasing the cognitive complexity of the task leads to more attention to language form, it is by no means clear where this attention comes from. Further research will be necessary before that question can be answered.

The fact that we did not observe an interaction of task complexity with proficiency level was in contrast with earlier findings that the effect of task complexity on accuracy measures was stronger for high-proficiency learners (Kuiken *et al.*, 2005). In the latter study however, not all the students of Italian participating in our experiment were involved. Therefore, it may be that the selection of participants in our earlier paper was biased in the sense that the differences between the high and low performers were bigger than in the present study. But it may also be the case that these different results have to do with the distinction between the students of French and the students of Italian. Students of Italian start from scratch in their first year, as no basic knowledge of Italian is assumed when they begin their study. Students of French, on the other hand, have studied French at high school for several years and therefore start their university study at a higher level than the students of Italian. In other words, first year students of Italian may be hindered by their insufficient command of the target language (threshold), whereas the students of French are not. We will try to unravel if this is really what is happening in further research (Kuiken & Vedder, in preparation).

What are the implications of our results for the practice of language teaching? In order to answer that question we now come back to the two texts addressed to Valéry and Simone that were presented in the introduction. These texts were not written by two students, but by one and the same writer! Text A (Cher Valéry) is an example of the complex task, whereas text B (Chère Simone) is the result of the less complex task. The results of the analysis for both texts are displayed in Table 6.7.

A comparison of the scores on both texts reveals that they are rather similar to the results that are described earlier. The accuracy of the complex text is far better than that of the less complex text. The scores on the syntactic measures and the type-token ratio are very similar for both texts, whereas the lexical variation as measured by TTR2 is better in the complex text. Remember that the teachers also judged Text A better than B, so their judgements are confirmed by our detailed analysis. A pedagogical implication

Table 6.7 Results of measures scored on Text A and B

Measure type	Measure*	Text A (+complex)	Text B (−complex)
Accuracy	EtotperT	2.14	4.11
	E1perT	1.43	2.44
	E2perT	0.57	1.33
	E3perT	0.14	0.33
Syntactic complexity	CperT	1.29	1.33
	DCperC	0.28	0.33
Lexical variation	TTR1	0.63	0.64
	TTR2	5.22	4.97

*EtotperT = total errors per T-unit, E1perT = 1st degree errors per T-unit, E2perT = 2nd degree errors per T-unit, E3perT = 3rd degree errors per T-unit, CperT = clauses per T-unit, DCperC = dependent clauses per clause, TTR1 = type-token ratio, TTR2 = ratio of word types to the square root of two times the word tokens.

then might be that increasing the complexity of a task does not necessarily mean that the number of errors increases. In fact, rather the opposite seems to be true, as our data show that – all other things being equal – errors drop when task complexity increases.

References

Carter, R. (1998) *Mapping the Mind*. London: Weidenfeld and Nicolson.

Cummins, J. (1979) Cognitive academic language proficiency, linguistic interdependence, the optimum age question and some other matters. *Working Papers in Bilingualism* 19, 197–205.

Ellis, R. and Yuan, F. (2004) The effects of planning on fluency, complexity, and accuracy in second language narrative writing. *Studies in Second Language Acquisition* 26, 59–84.

Gathercole, S.E. and Baddeley, A.D. (1993) *Working Memory and Language*. Hove: Lawrence Erlbaum.

Gilabert, R. (2005) Tasks complexity and task sequences. Effects of their manipulation on L2 oral narrative production. PhD dissertation, University of Barcelona.

Givón, T. (1985) Function, structure, and language acquisition. In D. Slobin (ed.) *The Cross-Linguistic Study of Language Acquisition* (Vol. 1) (pp. 1008–1025). Hillsdale, NJ: Lawrence Erlbaum.

Givón, T. (1989) *Mind, Code and Context: Essays in Pragmatics*. Hillsdale, NJ: Lawrence Erlbaum.

Kuiken, F. and Vedder, I. (2004a) Il Bed & Breakfast più bello d'Italia. Cognitieve taakcomplexiteit en tekstkwaliteit in Italiaans T2. [Il Bed & Breakfast più bello d'Italia. Cognitive task complexity and text quality in Italian L2.] *Incontri* 19 (1), 31–39.

Kuiken, F. and Vedder, I. (2004b) De relatie tussen cognitieve taakcomplexiteit en linguïstische performance bij het schrijven in T1 en T2. [The relationship between cognitive task complexity and linguistic performance in L2 and L2 writing.] *Toegepaste Taalwetenschap in Artikelen* 72, 23–32.

Kuiken, F. and Vedder, I. (forthcoming) Cognitive task complexity and written output in Italian and French as a second language. *Journal of Second Language Writing*.

Kuiken, F., Mos, M. and Vedder, I. (2005) Cognitive task complexity and second language writing performance. In S. Foster-Cohen, M.P. García-Mayo and J. Cenoz (eds) *Eurosla Yearbook* (Vol. 5) (pp. 195–222). Amsterdam: John Benjamins.

Long, M.H. (1996) The role of the linguistic environment in second language acquisition. In W. Ritchie and T. Bhatia (eds) *Handbook of Second Language Acquisition* (pp. 413–468). San Diego: Academic Press.

Peters, E. (2004) Vocabulary acquisition and reading comprehension by intermediate foreign language learners. The influence of task complexity. Paper presented at Eurosla 14, San Sebastián, Spain.

Robinson, P. (2001a) Task complexity, cognitive resources, and syllabus design: A triadic framework for examining task influences on SLA. In P. Robinson (ed.) *Cognition and Second Language Instruction* (pp. 287–318). Cambridge: Cambridge University Press.

Robinson, P. (2001b) Task complexity, task difficulty, and task production: Exploring interactions in a componential framework. *Applied Linguistics* 22, 27–57.

Robinson, P. (2005) Cognitive complexity and task sequencing: Studies in a componential framework for second language task design. *International Review of Applied Linguistics* 43 (1), 1–32.

Robinson, P., Ting, S.C.-C. and Urwin, J. (1995) Investigating second language task complexity. *RELC Journal: A Journal of English Language Teaching in Southeast Asia* 26, 62–79.

Schmidt, R. (2001) Attention. In P. Robinson (ed.) *Cognition and Second Language Instruction* (pp. 3–32). Cambridge: Cambridge University Press.

Skehan, P. (1998) *A Cognitive Approach to Language Learning*. Oxford: Oxford University Press.

Skehan, P. (2001) Tasks and language performance assessment. In M. Bygate, P. Skehan and M. Swain (eds) *Researching Pedagogic Tasks: Second language Learning, Teaching and Testing* (pp. 167–185). Harlow: Longman.

Skehan, P. (2003) Task-based instruction. *Language Teaching* 36, 1–14.

Skehan, P. and Foster, P. (1999) The influence of task structure and processing conditions on narrative retellings. *Language Learning* 49, 93–100.

Skehan, P. and Foster, P. (2001) Cognition and tasks. In P. Robinson (ed.) *Cognition and Second Language Instruction* (pp. 183–205). Cambridge: Cambridge University Press.

Skehan, P. and Foster, P. (2005) Strategic and on-line planning: The influence of surprise information and task time on second language performance. In R. Ellis (ed.) *Planning and Task Performance in a Second Language* (pp. 193–218). Amsterdam/Philadelphia: John Benjamins Publishing Company.

Talmy, L. (2000) *Toward a Cognitive Semantics. Volume 1: Concept Structuring Systems*. Cambridge, MA: MIT Press.

VanPatten, B. (1990) Attending to form and content in the input: An experiment in consciousness. *Studies in Second Language Acquisition* 12, 287–301.

Wolfe-Quintero, K., Inagaki, S. and Kim, H.Y. (1998) *Second Language Development in Writing: Measures of Fluency, Accuracy and Complexity*. Honolulu, HI: Second Language Teaching and Curriculum Center, University of Hawaii at Mañoa.

Appendix 6.A: Instructions for the Complex Task and Description of Destinations

(Translation into English from the original prompt in Dutch.)

Bed and breakfast in France

You are planning to go on holiday in France with a French friend, and want to spend two weeks together in May or June. You have decided to go to a bed and breakfast. Your friend has already surfed the internet and made a first selection. He/she picked five addresses, in Bretagne, Paris, Beaulieu-sur-Mer, Aquitaine and in the Isère, and is now asking for your advice. The guesthouse or apartment you choose, however, has to satisfy a number of conditions. These criteria are:

- presence of a garden;
- a quiet location;
- located in (the proximity of) the centre;
- the possibility of doing physical exercise;
- swimming facilities;
- includes breakfast.

None of the five addresses your friend sent you meets all of the criteria. A carefully considered choice has to be made, however. Read the five descriptions and then write a letter of at least 150 words in which you explain which bed and breakfast you think is most suitable and fits the conditions best. Keep in mind that your text does not have to reflect your personal preferences. Write a letter in which you try to convince your friend that your choice is right and support it with arguments. You have 40 minutes to write the text. Use of a dictionary is permitted.

(1) Maison Lory
Location: Morbihan (Bretagne). Situated 15km from Vannes.
Description: Quiet location, in rural setting. Bedroom in classical style, large terrace with view, garden. Grand old house, completely restored in 1998. Swimming pool 2km away.
Breakfast: Extensive breakfast included in the price: home-made pies, fresh eggs, a variety of local cheeses and assorted cold meats.

(2) Europe B and B
Location: Ile de France, Paris. Situated in the old centre of the city.
Description: In the dynamic heart of the Ile de la Cité, 10 minutes distance from the Gare du Nord. Apartment, four rooms, two bathrooms, fitness room, private garden, garage. Special discounts for theatre and concert tickets. Cable television, safe, air conditioning.
Breakfast: No breakfasts served.

(3) Bed and Breakfast Hotel Migani Plage
Location: Alpes Maritimes, Beaulieu-sur-Mer, at a considerable distance from the city centre, but situated directly next to the boulevard and sea front, with a lot of activity, even at night.
Description: Attractively priced, young and dynamic, open day and night, free parking, fitness, beach activities, bicycles available for guests, reduced entrance fees and shuttle bus to and from the clubs, special discounts for young guests and groups.
Breakfast: Comprehensive breakfast buffet, American style, between 8.30 and 11.00.

(4) Auberge Charles III de Bourbon
Location: Arcachon, Gironde (department of Aquitaine), Bay of Biscay.
Description: Situated on the boardwalk, in the old city centre, apartment in historical block (18th century). Ideally located for those seeking to spend a quiet holiday on the beach, or to go hiking in the mountains, but with shops, bars and restaurants conveniently located in close proximity.
Breakfast: Breakfast service: during high season, between mid July and mid August.

(5)   Baffelan B and B
      Location: Isère, Vallée du Haut Breda, Massif d'Allevard, 800 metres
      from the village, situated at the foot of Le Pleynet.
      Description: For those looking for peace, and mountain aficionados.
      Fully restored farmhouse with garden in tranquil region not yet dis-
      covered by mass-tourism. We have two rooms for our guests on the
      top floor, with a total of 4/5 beds. The bathroom is shared between
      both bedrooms. Mountain bikes available upon request, mountain
      walks, horse-riding.
      Breakfast: Guests can prepare their own breakfast; not included.

Chapter 7

The Effect of Manipulating Task Complexity Along the (±Here-and-Now) Dimension on L2 Written Narrative Discourse

TOMOHITO ISHIKAWA

Background

The past two decades have witnessed increasing interest in the use of tasks in second language pedagogy and second language acquisition (SLA) research. This has culminated in a number of publications on task-oriented research and pedagogy (e.g. Brown et al., 1984; Bygate et al., 2001a; Crookes & Gass, 1993a, 1993b; Ellis, 2003; Long, 1989; Long & Crookes, 1992, 1993; Nunan, 2004; Prabhu, 1987; Robinson, 2001a, 2001b, 2005; Skehan, 1996, 1998, 2003). As reviewed by Bygate *et al.* (2001b), the advent of the use of tasks as a unit of planning for language classroom activities was primed by several ideas influenced by Communicative Language Teaching, among them the role of authentic language in the classroom.

The 1980s fostered three major approaches to task-based syllabus design (Long & Crookes, 1992): the procedural syllabus (e.g. Prabhu, 1987), the process syllabus (e.g. Breen, 1987), and task-based language teaching (TBLT) (e.g. Long, 1985, 1989; Long & Crookes, 1992, 1993; Long & Robinson, 1998). Long and Crookes's (1992) influential paper emphasised several strengths of TBLT over the other syllabi with regard to the compatibility with decades of SLA and classroom research findings, notably its methodological principle of focus on form (see Doughty & Williams, 1998; Long & Robinson, 1998). After advocating the use of tasks as a potentially effective means for language pedagogy, Long and Crookes voiced the concern of TBLT with grading and sequencing criteria for pedagogic tasks. They state that it 'remains one of the oldest unsolved problems in language teaching of all kinds' (Long & Crookes, 1992: 46).

In order to contribute to the issue of grading and sequencing pedagogic tasks, the current study examines the validity of two hypotheses. The first, Skehan's *Single-Resource, Limited-Capacity Hypothesis* (Skehan, 1996, 1998, 2003), assumes that there is only a single attentional resource and that second language (L2) learners' attentional capacity is limited. Skehan and Foster (1997, 2001) claim that because L2 learners' attentional capacity is limited, there are tradeoff effects of accuracy versus complexity even when attentional resources are available to L2 learners (e.g. when planning time is available). Thus, learners are hypothesised to prioritise either accuracy or complexity depending on task demands. In other words, Skehan predicts that when there are available cognitive resources, increasing task complexity will lead to competitions between accuracy and complexity due to the limited capacity of attention.

The other partially contrasting approach to Skehan's has been put forward by Robinson (2001a, 2001b, 2004, 2005). His *Cognition Hypothesis* assumes that there are multiple attentional resources (e.g. verbal-visual/verbal-auditory resources) and that explaining the effects of task demands on L2 learning and performance by invoking a critical limit on a finite pool of attention, as Skehan does, is theoretically questionable (see also Neumann, 1996). Robinson's predictions for the effects of task demands on learning and performance differ from those of Skehan. The essential claim of the Cognition Hypothesis is that more cognitively demanding tasks increasingly direct cognitive resources to learning mechanisms (e.g. instance learning and cue strengthening), which results in observable performance effects (e.g. more incorporation of input and modification of output). Robinson predicts that increasing task complexity along what he calls 'resource-directing dimensions' (e.g. the [±Here-and-Now] feature) will lead to gains in accuracy and complexity simultaneously, without trade-off effects.

The importance of the (±Here-and-Now) dimension

The present study attempts to examine the effects of manipulating task complexity along the [±Here-and-Now] dimension on L2 written narrative discourse. To my knowledge, there have been only studies of spoken narrative performance that have explicitly examined the effects of manipulating task complexity along the [±Here-and-Now] dimension. Therefore, I first briefly review spoken narrative studies and characterise the task demands of the present study by pointing out differences and similarities between previous research and the research presented in this chapter.

Several studies have examined the effect of manipulating the [±Here-and-Now] dimension on L2 spoken narrative discourse. Robinson (1995) found positive effects of increasing task complexity (i.e. from

[+Here-and-Now] to [−Here-and-Now]) on lexical complexity (i.e. lexical density), and on accuracy as measured in target-like use (TLU) of articles, and a negative effect on fluency as reflected in words per pause. Rahimpour (1999) also found positive effects of increasing task complexity on accuracy, error-free T-unit (EFT) and TLU of articles, and a negative effect on fluency. Iwashita *et al.* (2001) found that tasks with the [−Here-and-Now] feature triggered a higher level of accuracy. Finally, Gilabert (2005) reported positive effects of increasing task complexity on accuracy (percentage of self-repairs and ratio of repaired to unrepaired errors) and negative effects on fluency.

The available empirical evidence seems to run counter to Skehan's Single-Resource, Limited-Capacity Hypothesis, and to support some of the predictions of the *Cognition Hypothesis* (Ellis, 2003: 119); i.e. increasing task complexity, and so the attentional and memory demands of tasks, along the [±Here-and-Now] dimension seems to bring about positive changes in accuracy (rather than decrements, as Skehan predicts) though at the cost of fluency.

The current study's operationalization of the [±Here-and-Now] dimension is similar to the one in previous studies in (1) the removal/ non-removal of a strip cartoon, and (2) the use of present tense in the [+Here-and-Now] condition and the use of past tense in the [−Here-and-Now] condition, with the exception that the study's focus is on written discourse. In what follows, the cognitive demands of the present study's task as well as their potential effects on L2 written discourse will be considered in three realms: absence of shared contexts, memory demands, and attentional demands.

(i) Absence of shared contexts. Unlike previous studies, the current research does not feature a shared context in the [±Here-and-Now] conditions. In the [+Here-and-Now] conditions of the preceding studies, the listener was present at the time of the experiment; therefore, the context was shared between the speaker and the listener. In the [±Here-and-Now] conditions of the present study, and due to the nature of the writing task, the reader is physically absent and the context is not shared. It is therefore assumed that the communicative demands of the [±Here-and-Now] conditions of the current study are more demanding than those of the preceding studies.

The absence of shared contexts may direct learner's attention to accuracy of article use (Robinson, 1995). In narratives, a canonical use of articles is introducing a participant and subsequent mentions to the same participant (Celce-Murcia & Larsen-Freeman, 1999: 283). Once a participant is introduced, the reference to the same participant needs to be established so that the reader can retrieve the entity mentioned in previous discourse from working memory (Ariel, 1990).

(ii) Memory demands. Another way to characterise cognitive task demands of the current study is in memory terms. The [±Here-and-Now] conditions in the current study seem to impose differential memory demands, which may in turn affect the nature of information processing. Because learners in the [−Here-and-Now] condition need to memorise and retrieve the storyline and details, and subsequently produce a coherent narrative, they may be pushed to ruminate on the storyline, to infer the relationships between events, and to create larger informational chunks to facilitate memory encoding, storage and retrieval (Robinson, 1995). This is similar to Bartlett's (1932) conception of 'effort after meaning', which helps establish elaborated semantic representations prior to task performance (i.e. planning). Thus, task demands in the [−Here-and-Now] condition may encourage deeper semantic processing than those in the [+Here-and-Now] condition, which may establish more elaborated output plans, out of which more complex language can be unpacked.

Such effects of elaborative conceptualisation may be captured by the use of various production measures. For instance, syntactic complexity measures (e.g. S-nodes per T-unit, clauses per T-unit) may capture the assumed deeper semantic processing in terms of subordinating and embedding clauses, which are associated with the discourse structure of narratives (e.g. Berman & Slobin, 1994; Labov, 1972) and more directly associated with 'the construction of higher-order events in which event phases are subordinated and interrelated' (Berman & Slobin, 1994: 13). Another type of production measures that may capture some aspect of 'effort after meaning' is lexical variation measures. Deeper semantic elaboration may motivate the learner to explain, assess, predict, or interpret events in a narrative in addition to describing the main storyline. If this is the case, deeper semantic processing may increase the chance to use a wider range of linguistic items. Finally, lexical density measures may be able to capture the effect of elaborative output planning because 'function words provide the mortar which binds the text together' (Biber *et al.*, 1999: 55).

Whether such deeper conceptual planning can be done successfully is claimed to hinge on plannability of discourse (e.g. written vs. spoken discourse, Ochs, 1979), including availability of time for planning (Crookes, 1989), which is a resource-dispersing dimension in Robinson's terminology (see Robinson, 2001a, 2003, 2005). Although macro-planning imposes attentional demands on the language user (Levelt, 1989), given the nature of writing as opposed to speaking and the permission of planning time (i.e. five minutes), the current study's processing conditions may offer sufficient opportunities to make the discourse more plannable. However, whether or not such conceptual plans and their associated linguistic codes can be *accessed* during task performance depends on another processing condition: namely, available attentional resources.

(iii) Attentional demands and resource availability. As suggested above, the realisation of production plans as a result of semantic elaboration may be affected by attentional demands during task performance. For example, in the [+Here-and-Now] condition of the present study, the learner needs to produce written output (i.e. verbal output requiring manual and therefore visual-based operation) as he or she monitors the written output (i.e. verbal-visual) and the visually presented material (i.e. spatial-visual; see Wickens & Hollands, 2000, for the proposed structure of attentional resources). Under such conditions, the learner is likely to be required to shift attention from the written output to the strip cartoon then to writing and so forth. Furthermore, this type of attention shifting requires overt eye movements from the writing sheet to the cartoon and vice versa. Hence, it can be expected that attentional resources available to learners are more difficult to co-ordinate in the [+Here-and-Now] condition. On the other hand, learners in the [−Here-and-Now] condition may be better able co-ordinate attention resources; hence, fluency may be greater.

Based on the characteristics of the current study's task demands, the absence of the non-verbal scaffolding (i.e. cartoon strip) in the [−Here-and-Now] condition may entail: (1) absence of shared context, which directs attention to accuracy; (2) greater memory demands, which encourages 'effort after meaning', and therefore facilitates greater use of complex language, various linguistic items, and function words; and (3) differences in the co-ordination of available attentional resources.

Research questions and hypotheses

The following research question was advanced: What effects on accuracy, complexity and fluency does manipulating task complexity produce in the written modality? According to the Cognition Hypothesis, (1) greater conceptual/communicative demands in the [−Here-and-Now] condition will direct learner's attention to accuracy and complexity (i.e. resource-directing effects) and (2) greater coordination of resources in the [−Here-and-Now] condition will lead to greater fluency *and* serve to promote the above-mentioned resource-directing effects. Based on these assumptions, three hypotheses are formulated:

Hypothesis 1: Accuracy will be statistically significantly higher in the [−Here-and-Now] condition than in the [+Here-and-Now] condition.
Hypothesis 2: Complexity will be statistically significantly greater in the [−Here-and-Now] condition than in the [+Here-and-Now] condition.
Hypothesis 3: Fluency will be statistically significantly greater in the [−Here-and-Now] condition than in the [+Here-and-Now] condition.

The Present Study

Participants

The participants of the present study were 54 Japanese third-year high school students aged 17 to 18. At the beginning of the second semester of the third year and two weeks prior to the experiment, the participants took the Michigan English Placement Test (MEPT). The participants' scores ranged from 50 to 88 on the test. They were randomly assigned to two task conditions. The [+Here-and-Now] condition had 16 females and 11 males, and the [−Here-and-Now] condition 17 females and 10 males. The mean and the standard deviation on the MEPT were 64.5 and 10.9 in the [+Here-and-Now] condition and 64.4 and 10.9 in the [−Here-and-Now] condition (KR21 = 0.81). A one-way ANOVA was applied to the data set and the result showed that there was no main effect for Condition, $F(1, 52) = 0.106$ ($p > 0.05$).

Data collection procedures

In conducting the current study, the participants were informed that the writing task would not be considered as part of their school grades and that they would be given extra points for completing the task. They were also informed that the writing samples would be used for research purposes.

During the experiment, the participants were first given a paper on which instructions for the task were written in their L1. The content of the directions was as follows:

(a) you are allowed to view a strip cartoon for five minutes;
(b) you may take notes (words and/or phrases) during the cartoon-viewing session but the notes will be removed before writing (see also Crookes, 1989);
(c) you are not allowed to name the characters in the strip cartoon (see S. Ishikawa, 1995, for a similar treatment to elicit articles);
(d) you will be required to write a narrative.

Furthermore, the participants in the [+Here-and-Now] condition were told that the strip cartoon would be available for them to view while writing, whereas those in the [−Here-and-Now] condition were told that the strip cartoon would be removed.

After reading the directions, the participants received a prompt (Appendix 7.A) and a strip cartoon taken from Yule (1997) (Appendix 7.B). They viewed the strip cartoon for five minutes before writing. In addition, the participants in both conditions were given four words paired with their Japanese translations to avoid basic vocabulary problems; however, they were not required to use the words. Those words were simply presented as options. They were *shopping cart, bottle, checkout counter*, and *shelf*. After the cartoon-viewing session, the directions sheet and notes were removed in both groups and the participants were given new writing sheets.

There were two differences between the [+Here-and-Now] and the [−Here-and-Now] conditions: (1) the prompt for the first group was written in the present tense whereas that of the second group was written in the past tense (Appendix 7.A); (2) only the participants in the [−Here-and-Now] condition had to return the strip cartoon to the researcher after viewing it for five minutes. In both conditions, the participants were given 30 minutes for writing.

The data coding was conducted by two native speakers of English with master's degrees in TESOL and applied linguistics. The inter-rater reliability reached above 0.90.

Production measures

The current study adopted 14 production measures of four categories: accuracy, structural complexity, lexical complexity and fluency.

Accuracy measures

Three production measures of accuracy were used, two were general measures – percentage of error-free clauses (EFC) and error-free T-units (EFT) – and the other a specific measure of accuracy – percentage of TLU of English articles. With respect to the two global measures of accuracy, Polio's (1997) error guidelines, except for her treatment of spelling errors (i.e. punctuation and capitalisation), were used as criteria. With respect to TLU articles, spelling mistakes concerning the distinction between *a* and *an* were ignored.

Structural complexity measures

Regarding structural complexity, four production measures were used: (1) S-nodes/T; (2) clauses per T-unit (C/T); (3) dependent clauses divided by total number of clause (DC/C); and (4) S-nodes per clause (S-nodes/C). With respect to T-unit related measures, a T-unit was defined as a main clause plus any subordinating clauses (Hunt, 1965). A T-unit could occur across periods although there were only a few such instances. In addition, sentence fragments were not counted as T-units (e.g. Hirano, 1991; S. Ishikawa, 1995). Concerning the definition of clauses, the current study treated only those with finite verbs as clauses (e.g. Hunt, 1965; Polio, 1997).

Lexical complexity measures

The current study employed four lexical complexity measures. The first two were measures of lexical density: (1) percentage of lexical to function words (L/F) and (2) percentage of lexical words to total number of words (L/W). As in Gilabert (2005), hyphenated words were counted as one word, and adverbs ending with –*ly* were counted as lexical words. The third and forth measures were: (3) WT/$\sqrt{2W}$, which is the total number of different word types divided by the square root of two times the total number of words (Arthur, 1979), and (4) WT^2/W (Wolfe-Quintero *et al.*, 1998), which is word types squared divided by the total number of words. The latter two measures are type-token measures. Such measures have been criticised because they are sensitive to text length (i.e. their score decreases as texts become longer, Wolfe-Quintero *et al.*, 1998). The two measures used in the present study 'may not be perfect' (Wolfe-Quintero *et al.*, 1998: 108), but do take into account the effect of text length. Word types and the total number of words were computed by the CHILDES System (MacWhinney, 2000).

Fluency measures

Regarding fluency, three length measures were employed: (1) words per T-unit (WPT); (2) words per clause (WPC); and (3) the length of text (TXL). As in Gilabert (2005), hyphenated words were counted as one word.

Results

Descriptive statistics for the production measures

Table 7.1 presents the descriptive statistics for the 14 production measures. As the table shows, the [−Here-and-Now] condition consistently elicited more accurate, complex, and fluent productions (note that the lower ratios of the two lexical density measures indicate higher proportions of function words in the [−Here-and-Now] condition).

Hypothesis 1

Hypothesis 1 stated that accuracy would be statistically significantly higher in the [−Here-and-Now] condition than in the [+Here-and-Now] condition. Overall, the effects of task complexity on the specific and general measures largely coincided with the predictions of Hypothesis 1.

As Table 7.1 shows, an ANCOVA revealed a statistically significant main effect for task complexity in TLU of articles ($p = 0.0465$). Thus, the learners in the [−Here-and-Now] condition were more accurate in the use of English articles than those in the [+Here-and-Now] condition. The result therefore supported Hypothesis 1.

Regarding the global accuracy measures of percentage of error-free T-unit (i.e. EFT) and error-free clause (i.e. ETC), there were significant interactions between proficiency and task complexity. Closer examinations revealed that there were no significant differences between the two conditions.[1] However, the [−Here-and-Now] condition elicited higher means of accuracy than the [+Here-and-Now] condition: 25% vs. 28% on EFT and 32% vs. 37% on EFC. Those patterns were attributable to higher accuracy

Table 7.1 Summary of descriptive statistics for, results of analyses of covariance (ANCOVAs) of, and analyses of variance (ANOVAs) of, and the effect sizes of the 14 dependent variables

Source	TLU M/SD	EFT M/SD	EFC M/SD	S-nodes/T M/SD	C/T M/SD	S-nodes/C M/SD	DC/C M/SD	W/T M/SD	W/C M/SD	TXL M/SD	L/F M/SD	L/W M/SD	WT/$\sqrt{2}$W M/SD	WT^2/W M/SD
HN	56.95/ 16.39	25.10/ 14.81	31.54/ 15.59	1.58/ 0.31	1.27/ 0.15	1.24/ 0.16	0.20/ 0.09	8.90/ 1.72	6.98/ 0.96	147.59/ 47.33	85.76/ 12.35	45.95/ 3.51	4.58/ 0.61	42.69/ 11.25
TT	65.28/ 16.78	28.13/ 12.10	36.90/ 11.33	1.82/ 0.33	1.37/ 0.15	1.32/ 0.16	0.26/ 0.08	9.96/ 1.94	7.25/ 1.12	170.26/ 46.12	82.05/ 10.56	44.90/ 3.09	4.80/ 0.50	46.51/ 9.50
F (1, 51)	4.17*	n.a.[1]	n.a.[1]	11.20**	8.15**	4.49*	8.69**	7.75**	1.42	4.08*	1.34[2]	1.29[2]	n.a.[1]	n.a.[1]
d	0.50	n.a.[1]	na.[1]	0.75	0.67	0.50*	0.70	0.58	0.29	0.49	0.32	0.32	n.a.[1]	n.a.[1]

Note: *$p < 0.05$; **$p < 0.01$. TLU = target-like use of English articles, EFT = percentage of error-free T-units, EFC = percentage of error-free clauses, S-nodes/T = number of S-nodes per T-unit, C/T = number of clauses per T-unit, S-nodes/C = number of S-nodes per clause, DC/C = ratio of the number of dependent clauses to the total number of clauses, W/T = number of words per T-unit, W/C = number of words per clause, TXL = length of the text produced, L/F = ratio of lexical words to function words, L/W = ratio of lexical words to the total words, WT/$\sqrt{2}$W = total number of different word types divided by the square root of two times the total number of words, WT^2/W = word types squared divided by the total words.

[1]There were significant interactions between the covariate (i.e. EPT scores) and the independent variable.

[2]One-way ANOVAs rather than ANCOVAs were applied to the data sets with task complexity as the independent variable because the EPT scores were not significant as covariate; consequently, the degree of freedom was F (1, 52) in these cases.

scores on the part of relatively low-to-intermediate-proficiency learners in the [−Here-and-Now] condition. This pattern was particularly evident in the case of the error-free clause measure, which indicated that the low-to-intermediate-proficiency learners in the [−Here-and-Now] condition received more benefits when accuracy was examined in terms of the error-free clause measure. For this reason, I consider this result to partially support Hypothesis 1.

In contrast, examinations of the error-free T-unit measure revealed two tendencies: (1) the more proficient the learners were, the less accurate their production was in the [−Here-and-Now] condition and (2) the more proficient the learners were, the more accurate their production was in the [+Here-and-Now] condition. Thus, what became evident was an X-like proficiency-condition interaction. I consider these patterns to be attributable to inherent problems of the measurement. This issue is addressed in the discussion section. With respect to the global accuracy measures, Hypothesis 1 was partially supported.

Hypothesis 2

Hypothesis 2 predicted that complexity would be statistically significantly greater in the [−Here-and-Now] condition than in the [+Here-and-Now] condition. The hypothesis was tested in terms of structural complexity and lexical complexity.

Task complexity effects on the structural complexity measures

As Table 7.1 shows, ANCOVAs produced significant main effects for task complexity on all the structural complexity measures: S-nodes/T ($p = 0.0015$), C/T ($p = 0.0062$), S-nodes/C ($p = 0.0391$), and DC/C ($p = 0.0048$). Thus, the learners in the [−Here-and-Now] condition produced structurally more complex language. These results gave strong support to Hypothesis 2.

Task complexity effects on the lexical complexity measures

Regarding lexical complexity, the present study used four production measures of lexical complexity. Two were lexical density measures, and the other two were measures of lexical variation.

Regarding the two lexical density measures (i.e. L/F and L/W), because proficiency was not significant as covariate, one-way ANOVAs instead of ANCOVAs were used. Although the means of the two measures pointed toward the predicted directions (i.e. lower in the [−Here-and-Now] condition: L/F 86% vs. 82%; L/W 46% vs. 45%), there were no significant main effects for task complexity ($p > 0.10$ in both cases). Hypothesis 2 was therefore disconfirmed.

With respect to the two lexical variation measures of WT/$\sqrt{2}$W and WT^2/W, there were statistically significant interactions between proficiency (i.e. covariate) and task complexity ($p = 0.04$). Further examinations of the data showed that the two conditions did not differ from each other on both of the lexical complexity measures.[2] However, the means of the two measures pointed toward the predicted directions (i.e. higher in the [−Here-and-Now] conditions: WT/$\sqrt{2W}$ 4.6 vs. 4.8; WT^2/W 42.7 vs. 46.5).

The mean differences were accountable for by greater lexical variation on the part of relatively low-to-intermediate-proficiency learners of the [−Here-and-Now] condition. This became more meaningful when one of the results of fluency (see the next section) was taken into consideration; namely, the result showing that the learners in the [−Here-and-Now] condition produced longer narratives (148 vs. 170 words per narrative on average). The above interpretation was also supported by the non-significant correlation between the narrative length and proficiency ($r = 0.13, p > 0.05$), which suggested that low- to intermediate-proficiency learners in the [−Here-and-Now] condition produced approximately equivalent number of words per narrative. Thus, the low- to intermediate-proficiency learners of the [−Here-and-Now] condition were able to *maintain* higher lexical variation in spite of the production of greater number of words than the counterparts of the [+Here-and-Now] condition. In other words, they received more benefits from the [−Here-and-Now] condition. Therefore, although statistically not significant, I consider the results to partially support Hypothesis 2.

Hypothesis 3

Hypothesis 3 predicted that fluency would be statistically significantly greater in the [−Here-and-Now] condition than in the [+Here-and-Now] condition. As Table 7.1 shows, ANCOVAs revealed that there were significant main effects for task complexity in T-unit length (i.e. WPT)($p = 0.0075$) and in narrative length (i.e. TXL)($p = 0.0481$), but no significant effect for task complexity in clause length (i.e. WPC)($p > 0.10$). Thus, the learners in the [−Here-and-Now] condition produced longer narratives and more words within a T-unit, but not within a clause. The results therefore largely supported Hypothesis 3.

Overall, as we can see in Table 7.2, Hypotheses 1, 2 and 3 received relatively strong empirical support. The accuracy results pointed largely toward the directions of Hypothesis 1; notably, target-like use of English articles. The learners produced more structurally complex language in the [−Here-and-Now] condition, which provided strong empirical support for Hypothesis 2. The effects for lexical complexity were mixed. There were no significant effects of manipulating task complexity on lexical density, but some promising trends were found on the measures of lexical variation that relatively low- to intermediate-proficiency learners received benefits from the [−Here-and-Now] condition. Finally, regarding fluency, two among three measures showed that writing greater fluency was achieved in the

Table 7.2 Summary of the effects of task complexity on accuracy and complexity measures

Production measures	Results
Accuracy	
TLU article (target-like use of articles)	Hypothesis 1 confirmed
EFT (percentage of error-free T-units)	Hypothesis 1 disconfirmed
EFC (percentage of error-free clauses)	Hypothesis 1 partially confirmed
Structural complexity	
S-nodes/T (S-nodes per T-unit)	Hypothesis 2 confirmed
C/T (clauses per T-unit)	Hypothesis 2 confirmed
S-nodes/C (S-nodes per T-unit)	Hypothesis 2 confirmed
DC/C (dependent clauses per clause)	Hypothesis 2 confirmed
Lexical complexity	
L/F (ratio of lexical to function words)	Hypothesis 2 disconfirmed
L/W (ratio of lexical to total words)	Hypothesis 2 disconfirmed
WT/$\sqrt{2W}$ (lexical variation)	Hypothesis 2 partially confirmed
WT^2/W (lexical variation)	Hypothesis 2 partially confirmed
Fluency	
WPC (words per clause)	Hypothesis 3 disconfirmed
WPT (words per T-unit)	Hypothesis 3 confirmed
TXL (length of text)	Hypothesis 3 confirmed

[−Here-and-Now] condition. These results are discussed in the following sections.

Summary and Discussion

The present study attempted to answer the research question: What effects does manipulating task complexity produce on accuracy, complexity and fluency in written modality? The results are summarised and discussed below.

Hypothesis 1

Hypothesis 1 stated that accuracy would be statistically significantly higher in the [−Here-and-Now] condition than in the [+Here-and-Now] condition. In order to test this hypothesis, three accuracy measures were examined, which concerned accurate use of English articles, on the one hand, and error-free clauses and T-units, on the other. Of the three measures, target-like use of article was significantly higher in the [−Here-and-Now] condition.

With respect to the error-free measures of clauses and T-units, there were statistically significant interactions between proficiency and task complexity. Those interactions were probably due to the production measures employed. Polio (1997) points out the importance of the definition of 'error'. Unfortunately, even when a clear definition is given, its validity seems to remain questionable. As Crookes (1989) states, if the learner is pushed to produce longer and more complex output, the chance of committing an error is likely to increase. This seems particularly true for an error-free T-unit measure, where a T-unit can contain multiple clauses. The employment of the error-free clause measure may partially improve the situation although this measure itself is not free of problems (e.g. compare a short clause, *she thought* with a longer clause with coordinated VPs). On the other hand, there seem to be some cases where error-free measures are useful when learners' proficiency levels are low (S. Ishikawa, 1995) or when task demands are relatively low. This is because in both cases learners are not expected to produce structurally less complex language (i.e. clauses without subordinated and/or embedded clauses); therefore, the error-free clause measure is expected to capture the quality of learner language. The validity of this claim clearly requires further empirical support.

Hypothesis 2

Hypothesis 2 stated that complexity be statistically significantly greater in the [−Here-and-Now] condition than in the [+Here-and-Now] condition. The hypothesis was tested in terms of structural and lexical complexity.

Structural complexity

With respect to the structural complexity measures (i.e. S-nodes/T, C/T, DC/C, and S-nodes/C), the participants in the [−Here-and-Now] condition produced more complex language. Thus learners in the [−Here-and-Now] condition demonstrated greater use of subordinating and embedding means as well as VPs within the specified production units (i.e. clause and T-unit).

The evidence for the greater degrees of information packaging can be ascribed to the greater memory demands in the [−Here-and-Now] condition. Compared with producing output simply to describe individual events in isolation, relating events accompanies the use of embedded and subordinating means. Thus, such information packaging or 'narrative connectivity' (Berman, 1988) may have been brought about by deeper semantic processing as a result of 'effort after meaning'. Furthermore, the results of the greater use of subordinating and embedded clauses in the [−Here-and-Now] condition are indicative of a functioning of what Berman and Slobin (1994) call 'event packaging', where events in narratives are hierarchically constructed and interrelated. Berman and Slobin (1994) also state that, generally speaking, only adults as opposed to children have access to highly hierarchical event constructions. Thus, manipulating task complexity may have motivated a shift from a less to a more advanced mode of planning, where complex semantic representations were formed.

Lexical complexity

The current study also examined the effect of task complexity on the two lexical density measures and the two lexical variation measures. With respect to the measures of lexical density (i.e. L/F and L/W), it was predicted that learners would use a relatively higher number of function words than lexical ones as a result of more elaborative planning in the [−Here-and-Now] condition. However, the results did not reach a significant level although they pointed toward the predictions of Hypothesis 2.

Regarding the lexical variation measures (i.e. WT/$\sqrt{2W}$ and WT^2/W), there was evidence that low- to intermediate-proficiency learners in the [−Here-and-Now] condition received more benefits from manipulating task complexity. Thus, those learners were able to maintain higher lexical variation in spite of the production of greater number of words than the counterparts of the [+Here-and-Now] condition.

Hypothesis 3

Finally, Hypothesis 3 predicted that fluency would be statistically significantly greater in the [−Here-and-Now] condition than in the [+Here-and-Now] condition. Regarding the fluency measures (i.e. WPT, WPT, and TXL), the results of the current study showed that the participants in the [−Here-and-Now] condition produced longer T-units (i.e. WPT) and longer narratives (i.e. TXL), but this was not the case in words per clause (i.e. WPC).

Regarding the non-significant result of the number of words per clause, one point needs to be mentioned: clause length can be short (e.g. *she thought*). When this is the case, it unfairly reduces the number of words per clause, which causes a measurement problem. However, the words-per-clause measure may be a suitable one for low-proficiency learners, but probably not for learners of intermediate or advanced levels because the latter groups may be ready to produce relatively complex sentences. As a *post hoc* reflection, it seems like the measurement may not have been suitable for the participants of the present study.

Regarding the result of the longer T-unit production in the [−Here-and-Now] condition, the significant result emerged because a T-unit contained multiple clauses in the [−Here-and-Now] condition as presented above; therefore, the above-mentioned problem of the words-per-clause measure was alleviated. Consequently, the words-per-T-unit measure was able to reflect the predicted greater writing fluency in the [−Here-and-Now] condition, a finding that were in line with the significant result of longer narrative.

Implications and Suggestions for Future Studies

Does limited capacity cause trade-offs?

The overall results seemed to suggest that manipulating task features was able to direct learner's attention to accuracy, complexity and fluency without causing trade-off effects between accuracy and complexity. The simultaneous improvement seems to conflict with the proposal by Skehan (1996) that trade-off phenomena between accuracy and complexity become evident when a task becomes more cognitively demanding and especially when there are cognitive resources to be allocated (e.g. Skehan, 1998; Skehan & Foster, 1997). In the present study, memory demands were high in the [−Here-and-Now] condition (i.e. cognitively more complex), and in this condition greater resource co-ordination was also assumed to be possible due to the lesser degree of attention shifting the task required. In fact, Skehan's claim is that when resources are available in performing cognitively demanding tasks, learners prioritise either accuracy or complexity, but not both. What are the implications of the findings presented here?

As the title of their paper clarifies, Skehan and Foster (1997) was an attempt to compare the effects of planning time (i.e. resource availability) on *different task types* (i.e. personal, narrative, and decision-making tasks). To be more precise, they considered the different task types to represent a continuum of availability of prior knowledge, where the personal task was considered to be the least demanding, the decision-making task to be the most demanding, and the narrative task to stand in the middle. In addition, 10 minutes of planning time were given to the planning group and none was given to the control group. Thus, there were two factors: (1) prior knowledge as an operationalisation of 'cognitive demands' and (2) planning time as an operationalisation of resource availability. The results were that 10 minutes of planning time gave positive effects on fluency of all task types. However, complex relationships emerged regarding accuracy and complexity. Thus, effects on accuracy were evident only in personal and narrative tasks whereas those of complexity were evident only in personal and decision-making tasks. The interpretation given by Skehan and Foster (1997) was that learners were able to allocate attention resources to the three aspects of accuracy, complexity and fluency on the least cognitively demanding personal task, but when performing the narrative tasks, learners prioritised accuracy over complexity (i.e. 'safety first approach', Skehan & Foster, 2001: 189), and when performing the most cognitively demanding decision-making task, learners prioritised complexity over accuracy (i.e. 'accuracy last approach', Skehan & Foster, 2001: 189). The underlying assumption that led Skehan and Foster to postulate the necessary competition between accuracy and complexity was the existence of the limited capacity of attention of L2 learners (e.g. Skehan, 1998; Skehan & Foster, 2001).

In contrast to Skehan and Foster (1997), the present study attempted to demonstrate the effects of manipulating the resource-directing variable using the *same task type* (i.e. written narrative). The results seemed to indicate that the learner's attention could be directed to fluency, accuracy and complexity without trade-off effects, and the results seemed more compatible with the predictions of the Cognition Hypothesis, which does not assume L2 learner's attentional capacity limits to be a necessary cause of decrements in performance on complex tasks.

In my opinion, the results of Skehan and Foster (1997) were attributable to differences in task demands between the task types: task demands that serve to *direct* learners' attention to different aspects of L2 production. The results of the present study seem to suggest that if task demands of narrative and decision-making tasks are manipulated in ways that require learners to pay more attention to accuracy and complexity, then this will have beneficial consequences for both. Thus, an important issue is that of the *directability of attention*, or Ortega's distinction between facilitating versus debilitating modes of attention (Ortega, 2005: 106). Such a distinction is drawn and systematically developed in the Cognition Hypothesis, but not in the Single-Resource, Limited-Capacity Hypothesis. In contrast, some preliminary supporting evidence for some of the claims of the Cognition Hypothesis has been emerging (e.g. Gilabert, 2005; Iwashita *et al.*, 2001; Niwa, 2000; Ortega, 2005; Rahimpour, 1999; Robinson, 1995, 2001b). Clearly, whether capacity limits (as Skehan argues) cause decrements in learning and performance needs to be tested by manipulating the same task types (unlike Skehan & Foster, 1997) rather than different task types.

Task-based strategy

Another issue that needs to be considered is task-based strategies. Although the present study did not take what Ortega (2005) calls 'a process-product approach', an approach to probe what learners actually do during pre-task planning and to connect the gained insights with performance outcomes to reach firm conclusions, what is indeed needed is a developmental study of L2 task-based strategies and the choice of strategies when the learner faces various types of task demands (personal communication with Fujiko Sano at Surugadai University; see also Ikeda & Takeuchi, 2000; Ortega, 2005; Oxford *et al.*, 2004). Ortega's (2005) research was originally done within the context of pre-task planning, and the approach seems particularly relevant and appropriate to many aspects of task-based language learning because it enables us to investigate 'the view from the learner' (Ortega, 2005: 78). The marriage of quantitative and qualitative research seems extremely valuable.

Conclusion

The current study investigated the effect of manipulating the [±Here-and-Now] dimension of task complexity on L2 written narrative discourse. The results showed multiple significant effects of increasing task complexity on accuracy, complexity, and fluency respectively. The overall results seemed more compatible with the Cognition Hypothesis that increases in the cognitive and conceptual demands of tasks can have positive effects on the quality of learner production, if these take place on what Robinson calls 'resource-directing' dimensions.

There are, however, some limitations in this study. First of all, the participants were from a single L1 background, and the findings were based on a single task. Whether the results obtained are particular to the population and the task used, or can be generalised to other populations and other tasks must be empirically demonstrated. Secondly, the level of proficiency of the participants of the current study was from low to high intermediate. Whether task complexity will similarly affect learners of other proficiency levels needs to be further investigated as in Kawauchi (2005), who examined the interaction between proficiency and planning type in oral interaction, and T. Ishikawa (in preparation), who is investigating this issue with a special focus on low-proficiency learners.

Acknowledgements

I thank Dr Peter Robinson, my mentor and professor at Aoyama Gakuin University, for the considerable academic support he has given me. Thanks are also due to Dr Tomoko Takahashi, my former MA advisor at Soka University of America, for her highest encouragement. I am also thankful to Professor Maria del Pilar García Mayo at Universidad del País Vasco for her encouragement, useful comments and advice. All errors remain my responsibility.

Notes

1. The results were based on the application to the data of the Johnson–Neyman technique (Potthoff, 1964). This is a procedure 'for establishing regions of significance associated with a test of the difference between two treatments at any specific point on the X continuum' (Pedhazur, 1997: 593). In the present study, 'X' is equivalent to the proficiency scores (i.e. the MEPT). For the formula, see Pedhazur (1997: 593).
2. Same as note 1 above.

References

Ariel, M. (1990) *Accessing Noun-phrase Antecedents*. London: Routledge.
Arthur, B. (1979) Short-term changes in EFL composition skills. In C. Yorio, K. Perkins and J. Schachter (eds) On TESOL '79: *The Learner in Focus* (pp. 330–342). Washington, DC: TESOL.

Bartlett, F.C. (1932) *Remembering: An Experimental and Social Study*. Cambridge: Cambridge University Press.

Berman, R. (1988) On the ability to relate events in narrative. *Discourse Processes* 11 (4), 469–497.

Berman, R. and Slobin, D. (1994) *Relating Events in Narrative: A Crosslinguistic Developmental Study*. Hillsdale, NJ: Lawrence Erlbaum Associates Inc.

Biber, D., Johansson, S., Leech, G., Conrad, S. and Finegan, E. (1999) *Longman Grammar of Spoken and Written English*. Harlow, England: Pearson Education.

Breen, M. (1987) Lerner contribution to task design. In C. Candline and D. Murphy (eds) *Language Learning Tasks* (pp. 23–46). Englewood Cliff, NJ: Prentice Hall.

Brown, G., Anderson, A., Shillcock, R. and Yule, G. (1984) *Teaching Talk: Strategies for Production and Assessment*. Cambridge: Cambridge University Press.

Bygate, M., Skehan, P. and Swain, M. (eds) (2001a) *Researching Pedagogic Tasks: Second Language Learning, Teaching and Testing*. Harlow, Essex: Pearson.

Bygate, M., Skehan, P. and Swain, M. (2001b) Introduction. In M. Bygate, P. Skehan and M. Swain (eds) *Researching Pedagogic Tasks: Second Language Learning, Teaching and Testing* (pp. 1–20). Harlow, Essex: Pearson.

Celce-Murcia, M. and Larsen-Freeman, D. (1999) *The Grammar Book: An ESL/EFL Teacher' Course* (2nd ed). Boston: Heinle & Heinle.

Crookes, G. (1989) Planning and interlanguage variation. *Studies in Second Language Acquisition* 11 (4), 367–383.

Crookes, G. and Gass, S. (1993a) *Tasks and Language Learning*. Clevedon: Multilingual Matters.

Crookes, G. and Gass, S. (1993b) *Tasks in a Pedagogical Context*. Clevedon: Multilingual Matters.

Doughty, C. and Williams, J. (eds) (1998) *Focus on Form in Classroom Second Language Acquisition*. Cambridge: Cambridge University Press.

Ellis, R. (2003) *Task-Based Language Learning and Teaching*. Oxford: Oxford University Press.

Gilabert, R. (2005) Task complexity and L2 narrative oral production. PhD dissertation, Universitat de Barcelona, Spain.

Hirano, K. (1991) The effect of audience on the efficacy of objective measures of EFL proficiency in Japanese university students. *Annual Review of English Language Education in Japan* 2 (1), 21–30.

Hunt, W. (1965) *Grammatical Structures Written at Three Grade Levels*. Urbana, IL: The National Council of Teachers of English.

Ikeda, M. and Takeuchi, O. (2000) Tasks and strategy use: Empirical implications for questionnaire studies. *JACET Bulletin* 31, 21–32.

Ishikawa, S. (1995) Objective measures of low-proficiency EFL narrative writing. *Journal of Second Language Writing* 4 (1), 51–70.

Ishikawa, T. (in preparation) *The Effect of Manipulating Task Complexity on Low Proficiency Learners' Written Narrative Discourse*.

Iwashita, N., McNamara, T. and Elder, C. (2001) Can we predict task difficulty in an oral proficiency test?: Exploring the potential of an information processing approach to task design. *Language Learning* 51 (3), 401–436.

Kawauchi, C. (2005) The effects of strategic planning on the oral narratives of learners with low and high intermediate L2 proficiency. In R. Ellis (ed.) *Planning and Task Performance in a Second Language* (pp. 143–164). Amsterdam: Benjamins.

Labov, W. (1972) The transformation of experience in narrative syntax. In. W. Labov (ed.) *Language in the Inner City* (pp. 355–399). Philadelphia: University of Philadelphia Press.

Levelt, W. (1989) *Speaking: From Intention to Articulation*. Cambridge, MA: MIT Press.

Long, M. (1985) A role for instruction in second language acquisition. In K. Hyltenstam and M. Pienemann (eds) *Modeling and Assessing Second Language Acquisition* (pp. 77–99). Clevedon: Multilingual Matters.

Long, M. (1989) Task, group and task-group interactions. *University of Hawaii Working Papers in ESL* 8 (2), 1–26.

Long, M. and Crookes, G. (1992) Three approaches to task-based syllabus design. *TESOL Quarterly* 26 (1), 27–47.

Long, M. and Crookes, G. (1993) Units of analysis in syllabus design: The case for task. In G. Crookes and S. Gass (eds) *Tasks in a Pedagogical Context: Integrating Theory and Practice* (pp. 9–54). Clevedon: Multilingual Matters.

Long, M. and Robinson, P. (1998) Focus on form: Theory, research, and practice. In C. Doughty and J. Williams (eds) *Focus on Form in Classroom Second Language Acquisition* (pp. 15–41). Cambridge: Cambridge University Press.

MacWhinney, B. (2000) *The CHILDES System: Tools for Analyzing Talk* (3rd edn). Hillsdale, NJ: Lawrence Erlbaum Associates Inc.

Neumann, O. (1996) Theories of attention. In O. Neumann and A.F. Sanders (eds) *Handbook of Perception and Action*. Vol. 3. (pp. 389–446). San Diego, CA: Academic Press.

Niwa, Y. (2000) Reasoning demands of L2 tasks and L2 narrative production: Effects of individual differences in working memory, intelligence and aptitude. Unpublished MA dissertation, Aoyama Gakuin University, Tokyo.

Nunan, D. (2004) *Task-Based Language Teaching*. Cambridge: Cambridge University Press.

Ochs, E. (1979) Planned and unplanned discourse. In T. Givon (ed.) *Syntax and Semantics 12: Discourse and Syntax* (pp. 51–80). New York: Academic Press.

Ortega, L. (2005) What do learners do?: Learner-driven attention to form during pre-task planning. In R. Ellis (ed.) *Planning and Task Performance in a Second Language* (pp. 77–109). Amsterdam: Benjamins.

Oxford, R., Cho, Y., Leung, S. and Kim, H. (2004) Effect of the presence and difficulty of task on strategy use: An exploratory study. *International Review of Applied Linguistics* 42 (1), 1–47.

Pedhazur, E.J. (1997) *Multiple Regression in Behavioral Research: Explanation and Prediction* (3rd edn). Bermont, CA: Wadsworth.

Potthoff, R.F. (1964) On the Johnson-Neyman technique and some extensions thereof. *Psychometrika* 29 (3), 241–256.

Polio, C. (1997) Measures of linguistic accuracy in second language writing research. *Language Learning* 47 (1), 101–143.

Prabhu, N.S. (1987) *Second Language Pedagogy*. Oxford: Oxford University Press.

Rahimpour, M. (1999) Task complexity and variation in interlanguage. In N. Jungheim and P. Robinson (eds) *Pragmatics and Pedagogy: Proceedings of the third Pacific Second Research Forum, Vol. 2* (pp. 115–134). Tokyo: PacSLRF.

Robinson, P. (1995) Task complexity and second language narrative discourse. *Language Learning* 45 (1), 99–140.

Robinson, P. (2001a) Task complexity, cognitive resources, and syllabus design: A triadic framework for examining task influences on SLA. In P. Robinson (ed.) *Cognition and Second Language Instruction* (pp. 287–318). Cambridge: Cambridge University Press.

Robinson, P. (2001b) Task complexity, task difficulty, and task production: Exploring interactions in a componential framework. *Applied Linguistics* 22 (1), 27–57.

Robinson, P. (2003) Attention and memory during SLA. In C. Doughty and M. Long (eds) *The Handbook of Second Language Acquisition* (pp. 631–678). Malden, MA: Blackwell.

Robinson, P. (2004) Comprehension, cognitive complexity, and task-based language production and acquisition. In D. Smith, S. Nobe, P. Robinson, G. Strong, M. Tani and H. Yoshiba (eds) *Language Comprehension: Perspectives from Linguistics and Language Education* (pp. 187–240). Tokyo: Kuroshio Publishers.

Robinson, P. (2005) Cognitive complexity and task sequencing: Studies in a componential framework for second language task design. *International Review of Applied Linguistics* 43 (1), 1–32.

Skehan, P. (1996) A framework for the implementation of task-based instruction. *Applied Linguistics* 17 (1), 38–62.

Skehan, P. (1998) *A Cognitive Approach to Language Learning.* Oxford: Oxford University Press.

Skehan, P. (2003) Task-based instruction. *Language Teaching* 36 (1), 1–14.

Skehan, P. and Foster, P. (1997) Task type and task processing conditions as influences on foreign language performance. *Language Teaching Research* 1 (3), 185–211.

Skehan, P. and Foster, P. (2001) Cognition and tasks. In P. Robinson (ed.) *Cognition and Second Language Instruction* (pp. 183–205). Cambridge: Cambridge University Press.

Wickens, C. and Hollans, J. (2000) *Engineering Psychology and Human Performance* (3rd edn). Upper Saddle River, NJ: Prentice Hall.

Wolfe-Quintero, K., Inagaki, S. and Kim, H. (1998) *Second Language Development in Writing: Measures of Fluency, Accuracy and Complexity.* Second Language Teaching & Curriculum Center, University of Hawaii.

Yule, G. (1997) *Referential Communication Tasks.* Hillsdale, NJ: Lawrence Erlbaum Associates Inc.

Appendix 7.A: Prompts for the (±Here-and-Now) Conditions

Prompt for the [+Here-and-Now] condition

Today a woman goes to a supermarket. She enters the supermarket through a door. She is wearing a black shirt. She puts her bag in the shopping cart. She is pushing the cart slowly. Maybe she is planning to buy many things for dinner.

Prompt for the [−Here-and-Now] condition

Yesterday a woman went to a supermarket. She entered the supermarket through a door. She was wearing a black shirt. She put her bag in the shopping cart. She was pushing the cart slowly. Maybe she was planning to buy many things for dinner.

Appendix 7.B: Strip Cartoon for the Current Study Taken from Yule (1997)

Note. From *Referential Communication Tasks* (p. 67), by George Yule, 1997, Hillsdale, NJ: Lawrence Erlbaum Associates Inc. Copyright 1997 Lawrence Erlbaum Associates Inc. Adapted with permission.

Chapter 8

Writing Tasks: The Effects of Collaboration

NEOMY STORCH and GILLIAN WIGGLESWORTH

Introduction

The use of small group and pair work activities in classrooms, particularly in second language (L2) writing classrooms, rests on strong theoretical and pedagogical bases. From a psycholinguistic theoretical perspective, second language learners need the opportunity to notice gaps in their interlanguage, test hypotheses about language, receive feedback, confirming or disconfirming their hypotheses, and restructure their hypotheses (Ellis, 1994; Long, 1983, 1996; Schmidt, 1990, 1994). In group and pair work, students have the opportunity to engage in such cognitive processes in a non-threatening environment. From a broader theoretical perspective, the use of small groups or pairs accords with a social constructivist view of learning. Social constructivism, based largely on the work of Vygotsky (1978), sees human development as inherently a socially situated activity. From this perspective, group and pair work provide learners with the opportunity to participate in activities which foster interaction and knowledge co-construction. Research from this sociocultural theoretical perspective (e.g. Donato, 1994; Storch, 2002; Swain, 2000) has shown that collaboration with peers affords students the opportunity to pool their knowledge about language, a process Donato (1994) refers to as collective scaffolding.

A number of tasks have been developed and used in small group/pair work activities. These include information gap and jigsaw tasks for oral activities, or dictogloss and text reconstruction for writing activities. Collaborative writing, as in co-authoring tasks, has rarely been used. When collaborative activities are introduced into writing classes it is generally for the purposes of brainstorming ideas prior to the writing activity itself, or for the purposes of obtaining feedback on the drafted or completed written piece from teacher or peers. While peer reviews have been noted for their benefits by some researchers (e.g. Ferris, 2003; Leki, 1993) it has also been noted that the focus of such activity is on the product rather than the process (e.g. Lockhart & Ng, 1995; Nelson & Carson, 1998; Villamil & de Guerrero, 1996). Most of this research has focussed on learners providing feedback to each other on the finished product, which means that the actual process of the writing itself remains a private one, with learners engaging in individual activity and making decisions about their texts without discussion with others (Hirvela, 1999).

Where collaborative writing has been investigated, the findings have been encouraging. Higgins *et al.* (1992) and Keys (1994), examining the effects of collaborative writing in L1 settings, found that collaborative writing put students in the position of having to explain and defend their ideas to their peers, and thus fostered reflective thinking about their writing. A number of studies (e.g. Donato, 1988; DiCamilla & Anton, 1997; Storch, 2002; Swain & Lapkin, 1998) carried out in L2 classrooms, particularly in the sociocultural framework where the collaborative interactions are closely scrutinised, have shown that collaborative writing processes focus learners not only on grammatical accuracy, but also on discourse. However, only very limited research has been undertaken to investigate these processes, and none of it has been comparative in the sense of controlling other variables, and thus allowing a comparison between what individuals achieve and pairs achieve. Silva and Brice (2004), in their review of the teaching of writing, raise peer interaction as an issue which is under-researched. In this study, therefore, we were concerned with comparing the product from individuals and pairs working on the same writing tasks, and with investigating the process of how pairs approached the tasks and how they interacted as they were completing the activity.

This study was designed to investigate the product of the writing activity in terms of whether individuals and pairs produced notably different texts under otherwise similar conditions. It was also designed to explore the processes taking place in the completion of the writing activities by the pairs. Theoretically, the study is underpinned by sociocultural principles which suggest that collaboration and scaffolding activities may allow learners to work at a higher level of activity than is the case where they are working alone. Pedagogically, the study is designed to provide insights into alternative methods of structuring classroom writing activities.

The Study

This study forms part of a larger study into the writing and revision processes of L2 learners. In the larger study, students participate in writing tasks, either individually or in pairs and complete two writing tasks, a report, and an essay. Five days later they return and are given one of two types of feedback (editing and reformulation) and they rewrite the reports and essays again under the same conditions as previously (i.e. with or without their partner). In this paper, we are not concerned with the responses to feedback, rather the data are taken from the first session. Thus we compared the writing produced by learners working in pairs with that of learners working individually on a number of measures to identify whether there were any differences in terms of the accuracy, fluency or complexity of the scripts produced. Following this, we analysed the talk of the pairs to investigate the approach to the writing task they adopted and the nature of the focus on language they engaged in to try and illuminate the differences identified in the quantitative script analysis.

Participants

The study was conducted in a large research university in Australia. Participants were recruited from advertisements displayed on university notice boards, and were therefore volunteers. All participants had achieved the university entrance requirements for language [IELTS score of 6.5 or above or TOEFL score above 240 with a Test of Written English (TWE) of 4.5 or above]. Two thirds were female, one third male. Most had learnt English as a foreign language in their home countries, on average for eight years at secondary school and university, and were enrolled in postgraduate courses. They ranged in age from 18 to 41, with an average age of 26. The majority came from Asian language backgrounds and were predominantly Chinese. On average, the students had been in Australia approximately eight months. Twenty-four students completed the two writing tasks individually, and 48 students (24 pairs), who self-selected their partners, completed the two tasks in pairs. The interactions for each task for the pairs were audio-recorded.

Tasks

Two tasks were developed. Task 1 was a report task (a data commentary) based on a visual prompt, whilst Task 2 was an argumentative essay. For the report, students were given a graphic prompt showing rainfall in different cities in the world during 2000. The argumentative essay required the participants to write about the advantages and disadvantages of exams. The tasks are given in Appendix 8.A. The tasks were developed to reflect the kind of writing activities students would be familiar with as current and prospective applicants to Australian universities, and represent authentic, real-world tasks.

Individuals were given 20 minutes to complete the report and 40 minutes to complete the essay. Pairs were given 30 minutes to complete the report and 60 minutes to complete the essay. The longer time given to the pairs was based on previous studies which have shown that pairs take longer to complete tasks than individuals (e.g. Storch, 1999, 2005).

Data analysis

The data used in this study included the written reports and assignments of the 24 individuals and pairs, and the transcripts of 12 pairs which were randomly selected from the larger data set. These sources of data are summarised in Table 8.1.

Analysis of written output data

The written reports and essays were analysed quantitatively for fluency, accuracy and complexity. In order to undertake this analysis, all written work was coded in the first instance for T-units and clauses. A T-unit is defined by Hunt (1966: 735) as 'one main clause plus whatever subordinate clauses happen to be attached to or embedded within it'. This measure was originally designed for the analysis of written scripts, but has been widely used for the analysis of both written and oral discourse, despite its limitations with respect to oral data (Foster *et al.*, 2000). However, in this case, with written data, it was considered an appropriate analytic tool. In order to measure for complexity and accuracy, the compositions had to be analysed for clauses, distinguishing between independent and dependent clauses. An independent clause is one which can be used on its own (Richards *et al.*, 1992); a dependent clause must be used with another clause in order to form a grammatical sentence in English. There is some disagreement among researchers as to how to code for clauses, particularly dependent clauses. In this study, following Foster *et al.* (2000), a dependent clause was one which contained a finite or a non-finite verb and at least one additional clause element of the following: subject, object, complement or adverbial (see Appendix 8.B). Subordinate clauses were distinguished from the larger group of dependent clauses, and were identified as adverbial clauses, relative clauses and included reduced relative clauses.

To measure accuracy, global units expressed in terms of the proportion of error-free clauses of all clauses (EFC/C) were used. The choice of global units, as opposed to local units (e.g. subject/verb agreement; use of third person 's', etc.) was based on previous research which suggests that these are a more realistic measure of accuracy (see e.g. Skehan & Foster 1999). As Ellis and Barkhuizen (2005) show, both global and local measures of accuracy tend to correlate closely. Bardovi-Harlig and Bofman (1989) point out that such measures do not distinguish between type or severity of errors,

Table 8.1 Summary of data

	Individuals	*Pairs*
No of essays	24	24
No of reports	24	24
Transcripts	—	12

or number of errors in a single clause. In this study, errors identified included syntactical errors (e.g. errors in word order, missing elements) and morphology (e.g. verb tense, subject-verb agreement, errors in use of articles and prepositions, errors in word forms). Errors in lexis (word choice) were included only when the word used obscured meaning. All errors in spelling and punctuation were ignored (see Appendix 8.B).

In analysing texts it is important to consider not only grammatical accuracy but also complexity. This is because accuracy may be achieved as a result of a learner not taking any risks in their writing and relying on simple, well-controlled forms. At the same time a trade off may exist between complexity and accuracy (Skehan, 1998). The more complex the sentences produced, the more likely they are to contain errors (Foster & Skehan, 1996). Complexity reflects the writer's willingness to engage and experiment with a range of syntactic structures, moving beyond coordination to more complex structures which include subordination and embedding. One measure of complexity is the proportion of clauses to T-units. Foster and Skehan (1996), based on their previous research, conclude that this is a reliable measure, correlating well with other measures of complexity. Another measure of complexity is the proportion of subordinate clauses to clauses, which examines the degree of embedding in a text (Wolfe-Quintero *et al.*, 1998).

In summary, the quantitative measures shown in Table 8.2 were used to analyse the writing produced by the participants.

In order to check for inter-rater reliability in coding, and following the advice of Polio (1997), guidelines were formulated stating clearly what constitutes a T-unit, a clause and an error (see Appendix 8.B). Then, a random sample of six texts (forming approximately 12.5% of the entire data set) were coded by a second rater. Inter-rater reliability for T-unit and clause identification was 98% and 88% respectively; inter-rater reliability for error-free clause identification was lower (84%). Discussion between the raters resolved all disagreements and led to a refining of the protocols used for

Table 8.2 Measures used in analysis of written scripts

Fluency	*Complexity*	*Accuracy*
No of words per text	Percentage of clauses per T-unit	Error-free clauses per clause
No of T-units per text	Proportion of subordinate clauses to dependent clauses	Error-free T-units per T-unit
No of clauses per text	Subordinate clauses per T-unit	
No of words per T-unit	Subordinate clauses per total clauses	

the error-free clauses identification. Multivariate ANOVA was used to check for the statistical significance of the results.

Analysis of pair dialogues

There were three levels of analysis. In the first stage, three distinct phases of the writing process were identified, and the time spent on each phase was noted:

- planning (occurred before the students began to write their texts);
- composing (the actual writing of the texts);
- revision (where the entire text was revised after composing was complete).

For the second level of analysis, all language related episodes (LREs) were identified. This follows the work of Swain and Lapkin (1998), who define LREs as any segment of pair talk where was an explicit focus on an aspect of language. That is, these were segments where learners talked about the language they were producing, self or other corrected. These LREs could be composed of one turn (e.g. a student deliberates over a word choice, shown by pauses and rephrases) or a number of turns. LREs were categorised for focus, distinguishing between Form-focus (F-LRE), Lexis-focus (L-LRE) and Mechanics-focus (M-LRE). F-LREs were episodes in which learners deliberated over morphology (e.g. word forms) or syntax (e.g. length of sentence). L-LREs included episodes in which learners searched for words (in L1 or L2), considered alternative expressions, or explained meaning of words or phrases. M-LREs included episodes in which learners focused on spelling of words or the use of punctuations.

The following extracts from the same pair dialogue on the report task illustrate the three different types of LREs. The bold type shows the aspect of language the learners focused on.

Extract 1:   F-LRE (form focus: word form)
Sam[1]: Beijing has the biggest difference rainfall.
Dan: The biggest difference...
Sam: Is it **differential or difference**.
Dan: I think **difference**.
Sam: yeah yeah yeah, it's noun. **Has the biggest difference among of rainfall. Biggest difference**.

Extract 2:   L-LRE (lexis focus)
Dan: As seen on the graph.
Sam: has the most average, **most** average.
Dan: you mean the **highest**.
Sam: Yes the highest average. The highest average rainfall during the... throughout the year.

Extract 3: M-LRE (mechanics: spelling)

Sam: Lagos has the highest average rainfall throughout the year, that's it. **Through out, that's one word, throughout**. Okay which one is, Bucharest or Mexico. I think Bucharest and Mexico city has nearly the same rate.

The third level of analysis involved segmenting all the talk into (non-language related) episodes. An episode was a single turn, or a number of turns, which constituted a focus on a particular aspect of writing. Five focus areas were identified as indicated below:

- task clarification;
- idea generation;
- structure (organisation and ordering of ideas);
- revision activities;
- other.

Examples of each focus area, taken from the transcripts, are given in Figure 8.1 below.

Results and Discussion

Comparing individual and jointly written texts

In this section we present the results of the quantitative analysis, comparing the results on the measures for fluency, complexity and accuracy for pairs and individual writers.

Fluency

There were no differences on any of the measures of fluency for either the report or the essay task in relation to whether the tasks had been completed by individuals or pairs. The results are presented in Table 8.3.

As the table shows, the essay task is considerably longer than the report task on all measures of length and elicits double the number of T-units over the whole task. The number of clauses elicited is more than double in the essay task, but note that these clauses are shorter in length, averaging seven words per clause as compared with 10 words per clause for the report task. On all these measures of fluency, however, both individuals and pairs perform in a very similar fashion. The similarity of these measures across the individuals and pairs is notable, and provides independent verification of the appropriateness of the different timings allowed for the two groups.

Complexity

Similarly, the measures for complexity revealed no significant differences in the way in which the individuals performed the tasks compared to the pairs. The results for the complexity measures are given in Table 8.4.

Focus area		Example
Task clarification	Episodes where learners read or discuss the given instructions or clarify what the task requires them to do.	**Dan:** So don't we put them as conclusion? **Sam:** Well I think ahh . . . Because I think its only 150words, we don't need to describe this very detail we just jump up to the conclusion because its only 150 words, that's only about 10, 11 lines.
Generating ideas (GI)	Episodes where learners generate and reformulate ideas	**Lilian:** So now comes the fourth point for advantage. **Larry:** Ah . . . it's um . . . **Lilian:** I think that's a kind of measurement of study performance **Larry:** yeah it's a . . . **Lilian:** benchmark or something **Larry:** yeah . . . it's a good way to measure the students of ability **Lilian:** of the . . . yeah academ . . . to measure their academic performance **Larry:** yeah otherwise how can you see it's an honours student? OK we can put it as . . .
Reading/ re-reading/ assessing writing	Episodes in which the learners simply read or re-read the text they had composed and/or commented on their writing	**Julie:** the average rainfall is calculated by m-m. It can be seen that the average rainfall differs in seasons. There is the most rainfall in summer . . . with the total number of five hundred millimetre . . . winter is . . . while in winter there is the lowest . . . **Emily:** it's too long, do think it's too long **Julie:** no but it's not correct **Emily:** can you, can shorten **Julie:** okay
Other	Episodes dealing with issues such as writing conventions and task management (e.g. Who should be the scribe)	**Mike:** so you do the writing for the first part and I do the writing for the second part **Grace:** yeah okay. We discuss this part

Figure 8.1 Coding of episodes

Table 8.3 Measures of fluency for reports and essays by pairs and individuals

Fluency measures (averaged)	Report task		Essay task	
	Individuals	Pairs	Individuals	Pairs
Words per T-unit	15.86	16.51	16.24	15.55
T-units per task	11.38	10.88	20.29	20.71
Clauses per task	17.42	17.83	42.63	42.17
Words per clause	10.36	10.07	7.73	7.63

Table 8.4 Measures of complexity for reports and essays by pairs and individuals

Complexity measures (averaged)	Report task		Essay task	
	Individuals	Pairs	Individuals	Pairs
Clauses per T-unit	1.53	1.66	2.10	2.02
% subordinate clauses of dependent clauses	66.21	57.14	29.66	34.25
% subordinate clauses per total clauses	22.97	22.76	15.54	17.31
% subordinate clauses per T-unit	35.16	37.82	32.65	35.01

Table 8.4 shows that there was a higher proportion of clauses per T-unit in the essay task, but that a greater proportion of the clauses were subordinated in the report task for both groups. In other words, although the essay task was longer, the report task appeared to elicit more complex language when measured in terms of subordination. These task-based differences required further investigation and are the subject of on going analysis.

Accuracy

Accuracy was measured in global units: error free T-units and error free clauses. The measures for accuracy are reported in Table 8.5.

There were significant differences between the two groups on both measures of accuracy for both tasks, with the pairs producing more

Table 8.5 Measures of accuracy for reports and essays by pairs and individual

Accuracy measures (averaged)	Report task		Essay task	
	Individuals	Pairs	Individuals	Pairs
% error free T-units	32.23	45.09	20.74	33.86
% error free clauses	43.30	57.46	44.67	53.53

accurate error-free T-units ($F = 8.265, p = 0.006$), more error free clauses ($F = 7.119, p = 0.01$). In addition to this, both groups produced more error free T-units on the report task than they did on the essay task, although error-free clauses were similar across both tasks. This is likely to be simply a reflection of the measures where T-units require each individual clause to be error-free in order for the T-unit to be measured as error free.

The process of collaborative composition

In turning to the more qualitative analyses of the learner transcripts, in addition to identifying the types of processes learners were focussing on during the writing activity, we were particularly interested in attempting to illuminate what activities the learners may have been performing in order to enable them to produce texts which were significantly more accurate than those produced by their individual peers. In this section, we outline the process of the collaborative activity, first examining the structure of the interactions overall before moving on to a more finely tuned analysis of the specifically LREs the learners were engaging in.

The first stage of this analysis examined the amount of time spent on planning, composing and revision by the pairs of writers. Time spent on the different phases is shown in Table 8.6.

As Table 8.6 clearly shows, the students spent most of the time on the composition phase. Not all pairs spent time on planning or revising their writing. However, there were differences between pairs and between the tasks. The students spent more time on planning their essays than their reports. Furthermore, there were differences in what the learners focussed on during the planning phase in the two tasks. In the report task, the students deliberated over task clarifications and in particular attempting to understand the graphic prompt. There were also discussions about structure in terms of the order the information should be presented, thus creating a structural framework which guided their subsequent writing. In the essay task, this planning phase consisted largely of brainstorming activities in which the students made notes about the main points they intended to include in their essays They wrote down those ideas in point form, and later

Table 8.6 Proportion of time spent on different phases of the tasks

Average time spent on phases of writing	Report task			Essay task		
	Percentage	*Time*	*Range (mins)*	*Percentage*	*Time*	*Range (mins)*
Planning	10	3 min	0–9	15	9 min	0.5–31
Composing	83	25 min	18–32	78	45 min	25–59
Revision	7	2 min	0–7	7	4 min	0–19

incorporated them into their written text. This probably explains the longer time spent on planning the essays than the reports.

A similar proportion of time was spent on revising the reports and essays (about 7% of total time on task). Where revision was undertaken, it involved re-reading the text, with a major focus on editing for grammatical accuracy. The relative short time spent on revising the written text can be attributable to two factors. Firstly, the participants appeared to be aware of time constraints and these were often mentioned in the dialogue. Secondly, some students took a more recursive approach to their writing and tended to do their revisions throughout the composing process, rather than as a separate, post writing revision phase.

The total number of LREs generated by the tasks and their distribution is summarised in Table 8.7.

Interaction on the report generated a total of 346 LREs, whereas on the essay there were 588 LREs, not surprising given the longer time spent on the essay. The focus of the LREs in both tasks was more on lexis and grammar than on mechanics. L-LREs on both the report and the essay formed over 50% of total LREs (54% on reports and 52% on essays). This is likely to be because the tasks used were selected to be meaning-based tasks rather than grammar-based tasks (compared to dictogloss or text reconstruction tasks used by Swain & Lapkin, 1998; Storch, 2002). Additionally the learners in this study were advanced language learners and hence the need for a focus on grammatical accuracy may not have been as high as for intermediate or lower proficiency learners as used in other studies.

In terms of distribution of LREs, the main concern of L-LREs tended to be with choice of adjectives (e.g. *highest, lowest, least, most*) and some context-specific nouns (e.g. rain vs. rainfall, amount vs. average). Focus on verb choice was limited to the choice of the verb *'to be' versus 'to show'*. Unlike the report, a greater range of verbs (e.g. *perform, improve, enhance, motivate*) and less commonly used nouns (e.g. *benchmarking*) were considered in the essays. The more complex vocabulary used elicited more attention to spelling in the essays than was the case in the report task.

Table 8.7 Language related episodes (LREs)

Types of LRE	Report task		Essay task	
	Number	%	Number	%
Total LREs	346		588	
F-LREs	144	41.6	225	38.3
L-LREs	188	54.3	308	52.4
M-LREs	14	4.0	55	9.3

With F-LREs, on the report the focus tended to be on verb tense, specifically the choice between the simple present or simple past tense. This may have been due to the difficulty students had in combining two verb tenses in the sentence (as in, for example, The table *shows* that rainfall in 2000 *was highest* in ...).

In F-LREs on the essays, the main concern was over word forms (nouns versus adjectives as in *advantage* vs. *advantageous; evaluation* vs. *evaluative*). Deliberations over use of singular or plural nouns also occurred frequently, as students tried to use plural nouns to generalise their statements.

It was difficult to establish whether the amount of time spent on language deliberations correlated with grammatical accuracy, given that only 12 pairs of transcripts were analysed. However, the analysis of the pair work, and in particular the LREs identified, suggests that the availability of peer input and feedback throughout the writing process may explain the greater accuracy found in the pair scripts. The excerpts below, taken from the pair dialogues, illustrate what Donato (1994) refers to as collective scaffolding: instances where learners pool their incomplete knowledge about the L2 in relation to grammar. They also show instances of learners using and reflecting on their language use (Swain, 2000).

As noted in other studies on pair interaction (e.g. Storch, 2002; Swain & Lapkin, 1998) there were great variations noted between the pairs in terms of the amount of attention to language, and in how they approached the tasks. Some pairs paid very little attention to language, and spent the time on task deliberating over and generating ideas. Others spent a considerable amount of time on deliberations over both lexis and grammatical accuracy. For example, in the case of one pair, six LREs were identified in total on the essay task and 14 on the report task. In contrast, in the case of another pair, 93 LREs were identified in their pair talk on the essay task and 44 on their report task.

The F-LREs showed students collaborating over a range of grammatical points. However, unlike the lengthy F-LREs found in the data of the studies by Swain and Lapkin (1998), or Storch (2002), where students engaged in providing each other with explanations, in this study the F-LREs were often quite brief, composed only of two or three turns. In such LREs students deliberate and seek confirmation for choices they make, correct each other, and at times provide explanations for why a particular form should or should not be used. For example, in Excerpt 4, the students confirm for each other the grammatical justification for not using the definite article:

Excerpt 4: Essay
180   **Linda:**   Whether exams
181   **Tracy:**   do we need 'the'?
182   **Linda:**   no, cause I think it's ...
183   **Tracy:**   general
184   **Linda:**   yeah general

Excerpt 5 is a lengthy example which shows deliberating over a range of grammatical and lexical choices, including sentence structure and use of linking words. The students offer suggestions and counter-suggestions, seek and provide feedback to each other and build on each other's suggestions. The process is one of co-construction, of pooling linguistic resources, in the creation of the final sentence.

Excerpt 5: Report

167	**Julie:**	Bucharest
168	**Emily:**	there is
169	**Julie:**	Bucharest has the
170	**Emily:**	No, no, no However
171	**Julie:**	Burcharest
172	**Emily:**	Bucharest
173	**Julie:**	Has, use 'has' again?
174	**Emily:**	Rains
175	**Julie:**	Rains rains most
176	**Emily:**	If you say that I think, however, it rains most in Bucharest
177	**Julie:**	Okay, it rains most ...
178	**Emily:**	In Bucharest in winter

In Excerpt 6, the students deliberate over choice of prepositions: Emily's polar question (line 419) shows lack of certainty over choice of preposition. Although Julie cannot provide her with the required response, Emily works it out by herself. Perhaps the act of verbalising her concern has helped her reach the correct answer. Julie's response 'among yeah' confirms Emily's choice.

Excerpt 6: Essay

416	**Julie:**	Cohesion in the? Of students
417	**Emily:**	cohesion ...
418	**Julie:**	among students
419	**Emily:**	among or of?
420	**Julie:**	cohesion ... cohesion I don't know
421	**Emily:**	teamwork ... I think among
422	**Julie:**	among yeah
423	**Emily:**	among students

Sometimes, students provide each other not only with corrective feedback but also with positive feedback (line 375) about their choices:

Excerpt 7: Essay

| 372 | **Mary:** | because the students expect |
| 373 | **Sue:** | sorry sorry it's supposed to be because they expect right? So we don't ... we don't mention that the words the students again and again |

374 **Mary:**   no it's only once. Exams will motivate them to study ...
375 **Sue:**   oh okay okay very good, excellent
376 **Mary:**   because the students can expect yeah

In the following excerpt, Claire corrects Mary for article use. The explanation is brief – simply highlighting the fact that a specific year is used. Mary accepts the explanation and repeats the phrase with the correct article use:

Excerpt 8: Report
98 **Mary:**   happened in winter ... was the lowest in a year
99 **Claire:** you know in in 'the' year because it's 2000
100 **Mary:**   on in 'the' year

In Excerpt 9, Ivy has identified a gap in her interlanguage:

Excerpt 9: Report
176 **Ivy:**   was a little bit higher than that in ... this in Beijing or that in Beijing?
177 **Penny:** that

She is uncertain which demonstrative pronoun to use. Penny provides the correct answer. Thus, working with another student affords the learners an opportunity to seek and receive feedback about language choices. The same pair, when discussing the essay deliberate over a number of language points simultaneously (noun singular/plural, prepositions), as in Excerpt 10:

Excerpt 10: Essay
219 **Ivy:**   to obtain chance for study ... better chances ...
220 **Penny:** oh better chances for better education
221 **Ivy:**   Ok to obtain a chance ... chances ... for or to?
222 **Penny:** for I think
223 **Ivy:**   I agree with you. For a better education

The next lengthy extract shows how learners deliberate over a number of language issues at the same time, offering suggestions about choices of expression (seasons vs. years), as well as grammatical forms (*city* vs. *cities*) and verb tenses.

Excerpt 11: Report
193 **Eik:**   both city have the same trend throughout the year
194 **Lily:**   yep yep yeah
195 **Eik:**   during the four seasons ... during the four seasons; can I say that? seasons ... both city have
196 **Lily:**   during the year maybe, yeah?
197 **Eik:**   but I don't want to repeat 'throughout the year'
198 **Lily:**   ok ... both cities

199	**Eik:**	both cities you know we should ... we should use past tense always, hea ... Lagos ... had or has? [returns to previously composed sentence]
200	**Lily:**	had.
201	**Eik:**	had ... had throughout the year except in winter which average rainfall was ...
202	**Lily:**	much less than
203	**Eik:**	[continues re-reading previously composed sentences] Bucharest has
204	**Lily:**	has a steady
205	**Eik:**	had
206	**Lily:**	had yeah
207	**Eik:**	had a steady rainfall throughout the year. The average amount of rainfall in 2000 was in the range of 35 to 55

The above excerpts illustrate that when working in pairs, students are able to provide each other not only with corrections but with grammatical explanations to support their claims, as well as reassurance.

As noted earlier, there were also variations in how the pairs approached the tasks. Some pairs adopted a recursive approach. That is, they generated an idea, read and re-read it to evaluate it for accuracy and expression, before proceeding to generate the next idea. Others composed large chunks of the text or the entire text and then evaluated the text composed.

Other variations between the pairs included the nature of input into the decision making process and the use of the L1 in their deliberations. Although this was not frequent in these transcripts, there was occasional use of L1 where pairs self-selected a same language partner. Although the L1 was not translated, previous research has indicated that it can be used for a range of functions (Storch & Wigglesworth, 2003). Most of the pairs collaborated in the creation of the text. That is, they constructed the text by completing each other's ideas (see the example of generating ideas given in Figure 8.1), offering alternative suggestions and feedback. However, in the case of one pair, one student seemed to assume a greater responsibility over task completion, as evident by his longer turns and even use of language (predominant use of the pronoun *I* rather than *we*). This long extract is given in Appendix 8.C. As Donato (2004) reminds us, and as was shown by Storch (2002), interaction does not necessarily mean collaboration.

Conclusion

The use of pair and small group work in the L2 class has received much research attention and the results are supportive of the use of group and pair work in the L2 classroom. In contrast, the use of collaborative writing has received much less attention, partly because of the observed reluctance, perhaps, of students to engage in co-authoring. The results of this study, involving advanced level learners, show that collaboration may not result in longer texts or more complex language but does lead to the production of more accurate texts.

In terms of the process of writing that students engaged in when composing in pairs, an analysis of the dialogues showed that, despite the variations in the approach adopted by the pairs, collaboration afforded the students the opportunity to interact on different aspects of writing. In particular, it encouraged students to collaborate when generating ideas and afforded students the opportunity to give and receive immediate feedback on language, an opportunity missing when students write individually. This may explain why pairs tended to produce texts with greater grammatical accuracy than individual writers. Whether this greater accuracy leads to consolidation of grammatical knowledge for these advanced language learners in the long terms requires further investigation.

In terms of L2 writing pedagogy, the results suggest that there is a place for collaborative writing tasks in the L2 classroom. Collaboration results not only in a greater accuracy of texts produced, but also affords learners the opportunity to engage with and about language. That is, they provide opportunities for language learning and consolidation. They provide a site for language learning.

Acknowledgements

We would like to thank Susy Macqueen for her great assistance with the data collection, Josh Clothier, Tess Dyson and Debbie Loakes for undertaking the seemingly endless task of transcribing the interactions and typing up the writing tasks, and Carsten Roever for statistical assistance. We would also like to thank all the students who participated in this project. This project was supported by an Australian Research Council Grant, DP0450422.

Note
1. Pseudonyms have been used for all participants.

References
Bardovi-Harlig, K. and Bofman, T. (1989) Attainment of syntactic and morphological accuracy by advanced language learners. *Studies in Second Language Acquisition* 11, 17–34.
DiCamilla, F.J. and Anton, M. (1997) Repetition in the collaborative discourse of L2 learners: A Vygotskian perspective. *The Canadian Modern Language Review* 53, 609–633.
Donato, R. (1988) Beyond group: A psycholinguistic rationale for collective activity in second-language learning. Unpublished PhD dissertation, University of Delaware, Newark.
Donato, R. (1994) Collective scaffolding in second language learning. In J.P. Lantolf and G. Appel (eds) *Vygotskian Approaches to Second Language Research* (pp. 33–56). Norwood, NJ: Ablex.

Donato, R. (2004) Aspects of collaboration in pedagogical discourse. *Annual Review of Applied Linguistics* 24, 284–302.

Ellis, R. (1994) *The Study of Second Language Acquisition.* Oxford: Oxford University Press.

Ellis, R. and Barkhuizen, G. (2005) *Analysing Learner Language.* Oxford: Oxford University Press.

Ferris, D. (2003) *Response to Student Writing: Implications for Second Language Students.* Mahwah, NJ: Lawrence Erlbaum Associates.

Foster, P. and Skehan, P. (1996) The influence of planning and task type on second language performance. *Studies in Second Language Acquisition* 18 (3), 299–323.

Foster, P., Tonkyn, A. and Wigglesworth, G. (2000) Measuring spoken language: A unit for all reasons. *Applied Linguistics* 21 (3), 354–375.

Higgins, L., Flower, L. and Petraglia, J. (1992) Planning text together. The role of critical reflection in student collaboration. *Written Communication* 9 (1), 48–84.

Hirvela, A. (1999) Collaborative writing instruction and communities of readers and writes. *TESOL Journal* 8 (2), 7–12.

Hunt, K. (1966) Recent measures in syntactic development. *Elementary English* 43, 732–739.

Keys, C.W. (1994) The development of scientific reasoning skills in conjunction with collaborative assessments. An interpretive study of 6–9th grade students. *Journal of Research in Science Teaching* 3 (9), 1003–1022.

Leki, I. (1993) Reciprocal themes in reading and writing. In J. Carson and I. Leki (eds) *Reading in the Composition Classroom: Second Language Perspectives* (pp. 9–33). Boston: Heinle and Heinle.

Lockhart, C. and Ng, P. (1995) Analyzing talk in ESL peer response groups: Stances, functions and content. *Language Learning* 45 (4), 605–655.

Long, M.H. (1983) Native speaker/non-native speaker conversation and the negotiation of comprehensible input. *Applied Linguistics* 4 (2), 126–141.

Long, M.H. (1996) The role of the linguistic environment in second language acquisition. In B.W. Robinett and J. Schachter (eds) *Handbook of Language Acquisition, Vol 2: Second Language Acquisition* (pp. 446–465). New York: Academic Press.

Nelson, G.L. and Carson, J.G. (1998) ESL students' perceptions of effectiveness in peer response groups. *Journal of Second Language Writing* 7 (2), 113–131.

Polio, C. (1997) Measures of linguistic accuracy in second language writing research. *Language Learning* 47 (1), 101–143.

Richards, J.C., Platt, J. and Platt, H. (1992) *Dictionary of Language Teaching and Applied Linguistics.* Essex: Longman.

Schmidt, R. (1990) The role of consciousness in second language learning. *Applied Linguistics* 11 (2), 192–196.

Schmidt, R. (1994) Consciousness and foreign language learning: A tutorial on the role of attention and awareness in learning. In R. Schmidt (ed.) *Attention and Awareness in Foreign Language Learning* (pp. 1–64). Technical report no. 9. Honolulu: University of Hawai'i Press.

Silva, T. and Brice, C. (2004) Research in teaching writing. *Annual Review of Applied Linguistics* 24, 70–106.

Skehan, P. (1998) *A Cognitive Approach to Language Learning.* Oxford: Oxford University Press.

Skehan, P. and Foster, P. (1999) The influence of task structure and processing conditions on narrative retellings. *Language Learning* 49, 93–120.

Storch, N. (1999) Are two heads better than one? Pair work and grammatical accuracy. *System* 27 (3), 363–374.

Storch, N. (2002) Patterns of interaction in ESL pair work. *Language Learning* 52 (1), 119–158.

Storch, N. (2005) Collaborative writing: Product, process and students' reflections. *Journal of Second Language Writing* 14 (3), 153–173.

Storch, N. and Wigglesworth, G. (2003) Is there a role for the use of the L1 in an L2 setting? *TESOL Quarterly* 37 (4), 760–770.

Swain, M. (2000) The output hypothesis and beyond: Mediating acquisition through collaborative dialogue. In J. Lantolf (ed.) *Sociocultural Theory and Second Language Learning* (pp. 97–114). Oxford: Oxford University Press.

Swain, M. and Lapkin, S. (1998) Interaction and second language learning: Two adolescent French immersion students working together. *Modern Language Journal* 82 (3), 320–337.

Villamil, O.S. and de Guerrero, M.C.M. (1996) Peer revision in the L2 classroom: Social-cognitive activities, mediating strategies, and aspects of social behavior. *Journal of Second Language Writing* 5 (1), 51–75.

Vygotsky, L.S. (1978). *Mind in Society. The Development of Higher Psychological Processes*. Cambridge, Mass: Harvard University Press.

Wolfe-Quintero, K., Inagaki, S. and Kim, H. (1998) *Second Language Development in Writing: Measures of Fluency, Accuracy and Complexity*. Honolulu, Hawai'i: University of Hawai'i at Manoa.

Appendix 8.A

Task 1: Graph report

The graph below shows average rainfall (by season) for four cities. Write a report for a university lecturer describing the information shown below. You should write at least 150 words.

Average Seasonal Rainfall in Four Cities in 2000

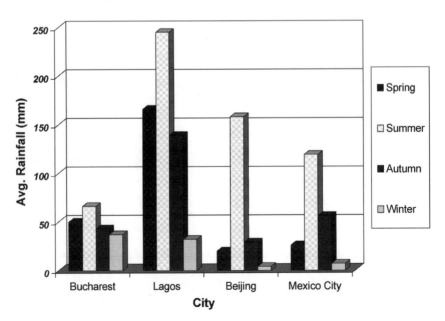

Task 2: Argumentative essay

> Exams are an important part of education in many countries. Discuss the advantages and disadvantages of exams and give your opinion about the role exams should play in education systems.

You should write about 250 words on this topic.

Appendix 8.B

Guidelines for coding and assessing writing

T-units

A T-unit is defined as an independent clause and all its attached or embedded dependent clauses.

e.g. In winter, it is apparent /that Bucharest and Lagos had almost the same amount of rainfall, /which was 43mm or so//

(1 T-unit, the end of which is denoted by // composed of 3 clauses separated by / as shown)

Run-on sentences are counted as 2 T-units (with errors in the first T-unit)

e.g. all of the four cities had the highest rainfall in summer than in the other three seasons//.

on the contrary, they had the lowest rainfall in Winter//.

(2 T-units, each composed of 1 clause)

Clauses

Independent clause: A grammatical structure which contains a subject and a verb and can stand on its own.

Dependent clause: A clause which contains a finite or a non-finite verb and at least one additional clause element of the following: subject, object, complement or adverbial.

Subordinate clause: A dependent clause introduced by an adverbial (e.g. because, while, when), or a relative clause (e.g. Lagos had a high level of rainfal/which was 20 mm//), or a reduced relative clause (e.g. /exams can not properly test the level of knowledge / students have//.

Error identification

Any error excludes a clause from being error free (e.g. omitted plural 's', omitted preposition, omitted articles all count).

Differentiate error free clauses from error free T-units i.e. if the T-unit has two clauses, one may be error free and counts as an error-free clause, the other may have an error, in which case the t-unit is not error free. Error-free T-units are therefore a subset of error-free clauses.

Do not count:

- errors of capitalization;
- errors of lexical choice (e.g. kids vs. children) unless they impede meaning;
- spelling errors of any type;
- punctuation errors.

Appendix 8.C

Sam: That's enough yeah.

Dan: Okay what's next. Beijing, Bucharest and we have Lagos here … how about Mexico City. What is the characteristic of this city. Is there any difference? Things almost the same between Beijing and Mexico City but Beijing has the highest, higher rainfall.

Sam: Rather than Mexico city. Yeah I think we can put it that way. Mexico City has slightly lower average rainfall compared to Beijing.

Dan: How about if we focus to autumn and winter.

Sam: Well I think we should tell the general first and then get on in more details. So I think we better say that Mexico City has slightly lower average rainfall comparing to Beijing. Compares

Sam: Mexico City … has a slightly lower average …

Dan: We need about four more lines I think.

Sam: I think we forget something. I think at first we should say the … the … Lagos is the highest and then Beijing and then Mexico and then finally the smallest one is Bucharest. So that everybody that read the report knows that Lagos has the most and then it followed by Beijing and then it followed by Mexico City and the last one is Bucharest, that has the lowest average seasoned rainfall.

Dan: Umm but how about the conclusion, what should we put it

Sam: Ahh conclusion … I think, I think we should put this slightly lower then put this in here. So I think this is more like the conclusion right …

Dan: Yeah, yeah I think your right

Sam: Oh dear

Dan: So can we put introduction here and this is the one conclusion and this is the content.

Sam: No, no I mean this is a good introduction paragraph and I think …

Dan: We need some more lines here

Sam: Yeah that's right

Dan: Have we finished with the conclusion … or do we need something else.

Sam: Yeah I think … the conclusion is already finished.

Dan: Umm we don't have to mention about the number right ...?

Sam: No I think about the number we can put on the second paragraph, so thins is the third one and this is the first one on the second paragraph we just say that Lagos has the most highest. I mean Lagos has the highest average rainfall is around 200 ... 240 millimeters something like that.

Chapter 9

L2 Vocabulary Acquisition and Reading Comprehension: The Influence of Task Complexity[1]

ELKE PETERS

Introduction

In this chapter, we present a study, in which we tried to manipulate students' attention by altering task instructions. This chapter seeks to address the question whether different task instructions will have differential effects on L2 learners' performance. More specifically, the study focuses on the fact whether an announcement of a vocabulary and/or comprehension test will affect students' look-up behaviour, text comprehension and word retention. It is concluded that it is not evident to manipulate the way students allocate their attentional resources while reading a text. The study is presented and interpreted against the background of theories on tasks and task complexity in particular.

According to Skehan (1998: 99) and Skehan and Foster (2001: 194), task difficulty can be described along the following three axes: code complexity, cognitive complexity and communicative stress. Code complexity refers to language factors, such as linguistic complexity and variety, vocabulary load and variety, or redundancy and density. The second axis, cognitive complexity, relates to cognitive familiarity with a task (e.g. familiarity of topic or familiarity of task) or cognitive processing, i.e. the amount of computation. Finally, communicative stress refers to the performance conditions of a task like time limits, length of the texts used and the number of participants. An important characteristic of tasks might be that they enable 'selective channelling of attention' (Skehan, 1998: 97). How do tasks or task instructions channel learners' attention? Can tasks and task instructions direct learners' attention to particular structures of language such as unknown words or collocations in a text? Another argument given by Skehan (1998: 97) to justify the use of tasks (as defined in a task-based approach) 'is concerned with general information-processing capacities'.

Skehan (1998: 97) states 'that more demanding tasks consume more attentional resources [...], with the result that less attention is available for focus on form'. Consequently, learners who have to carry out a more complex task will have fewer attentional resources left to focus on particular structures or forms such as new vocabulary items.

Robinson (2001: 293–295), on the other hand, advocates that a greater cognitive task complexity can lead to better learning results. In his triadic framework for task complexity, task conditions and task difficulty, a distinction is made between two dimensions in task complexity, *viz.* between the resource-directing and resource-dispersing dimension of task complexity. Increasing task complexity along the former dimension has the potential to direct learners' language resources to specific language structures or forms. For instance, tasks which focus either on the here-and-now or on the there-and-then require L2 learners to distinguish between the present and the past tense on the one hand and to use distinct deictic expressions such as this, that, here, and there on the other hand to talk about a present or a past situation (Robinson, 2005: 5). However, increasing task complexity along the latter, the resource-dispersing dimension, will affect students' language output negatively. In Robinson's Triadic Componential Framework, dual tasks for instance are considered to be cognitively more complex than single tasks because having to carry out two tasks simultaneously will disperse students' attentional and memory resources (Robinson, 2005: 7). As a consequence, students will have fewer attentional resources left to allocate attentional resources to particular forms. This interpretation of the resource-dispersing dimension is reflected in Skehan and Foster (2001) limited attentional capacity system.

So far, most research on task complexity has tended to investigate oral language production as reported in Ellis (2003, 2005), Robinson (2005), and Skehan (1998), whereas few studies have focused on written language production (Ellis & Yuan, 2005; Kuiken *et al.*, 2005). The specific aim of this study is neither on oral nor on written language production but on vocabulary acquisition and reading comprehension. With regard to vocabulary acquisition, it is generally acknowledged that reading texts in a foreign language does lead to vocabulary gains, yet these gains are very low (Horst *et al.*, 1998; Laufer, 2003; Zahar *et al.*, 2001) and probably too low to build a large vocabulary size within a school or educational context. Consequently, L2 learners cannot only rely on reading texts to enlarge their vocabulary size. Therefore, one of the key issues in L2 vocabulary learning is how to create learning opportunities or tasks conducive to lexical development.

The rationale for this study is based on the fact that L2 learners' aim to study a foreign language is often two-fold. Becoming proficient in a foreign language is sometimes not only the aim but it also constitutes a means to acquire knowledge about specific topics related to the target culture. For instance, students who study a foreign language at university do not only need to be proficient in the target language, they should also acquire inter-cultural competence and knowledge about the target culture. Can this dual learning aim of many L2 learners be promoted via specific tasks or task instructions while students have to read a text?

Our focus in this research is on the differential effects of task instruction on students' look-up behaviour, word retention, and reading comprehension. More specifically, we wanted to study the effect of a single and dual task instruction. This study sought to investigate whether it is possible to manip-ulate L2 learners' attention by altering task instructions. We tried to manip-ulate the information processing load the L2 learner engages in when carrying out a dual language learning task. Task complexity is used as theoretical framework to operationalise task instruction. On the one hand, task instruction is manipulated in terms of cognitive complexity and in terms of cognitive processing in particular, according to Skehan's scheme and, on the other hand, in terms of the resource-dispersing dimension of task com-plexity within Robinson's Triadic Componential Framework. Task instruc-tion is operationalised as single versus dual tasks with the dual task being cognitively more complex because of the higher processing load involved.

The outline of this chapter is as follows. Having discussed task com-plexity because it is important for the way we operationalised task instruc-tion, the remaining of the section features our research questions and hypotheses. We will then discuss the design and the procedure of our experiment. Next, we will present the results and discuss them. Finally, we will end this chapter with some first tentative conclusions and suggestions for further research.

Research questions

Our specific research questions are the following:

(1) What is the effect of task complexity on reading comprehension?
(2) What is the effect of task complexity on vocabulary acquisition?
(3) Do students in an intentional learning condition perform better than students in an incidental learning condition?

The difference in terminology between 'incidental' and 'intentional' is used strictly methodologically (Hulstijn, 2001, 2003). In its methodological mean-ing, the label incidental means that students are not forewarned of an upcoming test, whereas the label intentional refers to the fact that students are explicitly forewarned of an upcoming test. In the intentional condition students were forewarned that a vocabulary and/or reading comprehension test would follow, whereas in the incidental condition they were not (see also subsection on Design).

The following research questions were also addressed:

(4)   What is the effect of task complexity on students' look-up behaviour?
(5)   What is the effect of being forewarned of a vocabulary test on students' look-up behaviour?
(6)   What is the effect of looking up a word on word retention and on reading comprehension?

Since the whole experiment was organised electronically, a researcher-developed online-dictionary and a tracking technology were built into a computer programme. On the basis of the log files, provided by the tracking technology, we wanted to find out how task instruction would affect students' look-up behaviour. In addition, we wanted to explore whether L2 learners would look up more words when forewarned of a vocabulary test? Moreover, do learners who click on more words benefit from this more intensive look-up behaviour?

Hypotheses

To begin, we hypothesised that more cognitively demanding tasks such as a dual task would lead to more dispersion of attentional resources as is argued by Robinson (2005). Our expectation was that students who were set a dual task, i.e. text comprehension and vocabulary, would perform worse on both comprehension and vocabulary measures compared to students who received only a single task instruction.

Concerning the third research question, we expected that students who were forewarned of an upcoming vocabulary test would perform better on the vocabulary tests because these students would allocate more attentional resources to vocabulary in general and to unknown words in particular. As a result, they would engage more in word processing than students who were not aware that a vocabulary test would follow. We expected similar results with regard to text comprehension. We assumed that students who were forewarned of an upcoming reading comprehension test would process the text content at a deeper level. Consequently, these students would make more connections between the different parts in the text.

Finally, our last hypotheses concern students' look-up behaviour. The fourth research question focuses on the effect of task complexity on students' use of an online dictionary. We assumed that students who were forewarned of an upcoming vocabulary test would engage in a more intensive look-up behaviour than students who were not aware that a vocabulary test would follow. Our last expectation was that there would be a positive relationship between the number of times a word was looked up and word retention.

Method

Design

An experimental design was adopted with four conditions on the basis of task instruction. Task instruction was operationalised in terms of single and dual tasks. The first group received only a vocabulary task instruction, i.e. the students in this group had to read a text on a computer screen knowing that they would be tested on the vocabulary used in the text (single vocabulary task). The second group was told that they had to read a text on a computer screen in function of a reading comprehension test that would follow afterwards (single reading comprehension task). The third group was aware that having read the text, they would be tested on both vocabulary and reading comprehension (dual task: vocabulary and reading comprehension). Finally, the fourth group constituted the control group. This group received no specific task instructions except reading a text on a computer screen. Being set a dual task, the third group had to perform the cognitively most complex task because this group was forced to divide their attentional resources between text comprehension and vocabulary (see Figure 9.1).

Group 1	+ vocabulary instruction, – reading comprehension instruction
Group 2	– vocabulary instruction, + reading comprehension instruction
Group 3	+ vocabulary instruction, + reading comprehension instruction
Group 4	– vocabulary instruction, – reading comprehension instruction

Figure 9.1 Design of the study

Participants

The participants of this study were 21 students (18 females, three males) studying German as a foreign language at the Katholieke Universiteit Leuven in Belgium. All students had Dutch as their native language, except for one student whose native language was French. This student, however, was not included in the data because a vocabulary pretest showed that s/he knew all the target words. All participants were considered to be at an intermediate proficiency level, as indicated by the proficiency test (see next subsection). Students' mean age was 21 years.

Materials and data collection instruments

The experiment was conducted on computer so a computer programme was developed using the software QuestionMark Perception. A Java-application was written by a computer scientist and added to the software in order to track students' look-up behaviour. We used a slightly adapted text from the German newspaper *Die Zeit*, entitled *Ossis sind Türken* (*Die Zeit*, Staud, 2003: 41). None of the students were familiar with the main idea of the text. The text was shortened to 1026 words and was only available on a computer screen. Forty words in the text could be looked up by clicking on them with the mouse. When clicking on a word, a pop-up window with a German definition and a Dutch translation would appear (see Figure 9.2). Words that could be looked up did not have any visible hyperlinks in order to avoid intensive clicking behaviour (De Ridder, 2000, 2002, 2003). In her study with Belgian university students, De Ridder found that although students are more willing to consult an online dictionary when they read a text with hyperlinks, they do not learn more words nor do they gain a better text comprehension as a consequence of this more intensive clicking behaviour.

The data collection instruments consisted of pretests on the one hand and posttests, administered during the experiment, on the other hand. In order to study possible correlations between learner variables and task complexity, several pretests (proficiency test, vocabulary size test, target words test, and lexical inferencing test) were developed. The placement tests of the Goethe Insititut Inter Nationes in Brussels and of the Centre for Foreign Languages in Leuven were used to assess students' proficiency

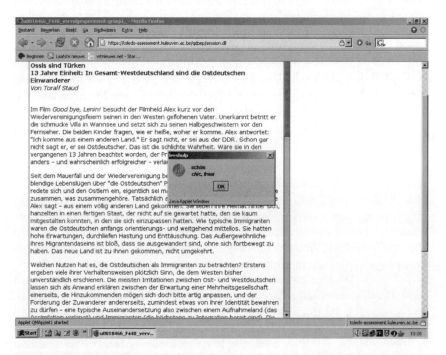

Figure 9.2 Screenshot of text and pop-up window with dictionary information of the adjective *schmuck*

level. Because a student's vocabulary size is correlated positively with vocabulary learning (Horst *et al.*, 1998), a German vocabulary size test (Cronbach alpha = 0.69) was designed on the basis of the frequency list of the IDS-Mannheim and the checklist format or yes/no-format (Meara, 1992; Meara & Buxton, 1987). The vocabulary size test was split up into five parts and was based on the frequency bands from 5000 to 10,000. Each part comprised 40 real words and 20 pseudowords. Furthermore, a self-designed test on the basis of the text *Mode: Die Nation zieht an* (*Frankfurter Allgemeine Zeitung*, November 15, 2003), was used to assess students' inferring ability because it is argued that students who are good at inferring word meanings tend to pick up words in a text more easily (Hulstijn, 1993). Because we had to be sure that our target words were not known, a receptive translation test with 46 items was created. On the basis of this test, 17 target words[2] were chosen. Finally, a questionnaire was developed in order to know more about students' familiarity with computers, text content, and their number of years of German study.

The post-tests comprised vocabulary tests and a reading comprehension test (see Figure 9.3). We were not only interested in how many words students acquired but also in how well they knew the acquired words allowing students to show partial learning of word meanings as Nation (2001) suggests. Therefore students had to take four productive and four receptive vocabulary tests, all of varying difficulty. The four productive tests consisted of two translation tests, of which one test focused on single words and the other one on collocations, and two fill-in-the-gap tests, in which students had to supply a German translation. The four receptive tests consisted of three receptive recall[3] and one receptive recognition test. The first receptive vocabulary test was a translation test in which the target words

Productive vocabulary test 1: Translate the following words into German

Productive vocabulary test 2: Translate the following collocations into German

Productive vocabulary test 3: Fill in the gaps in the text (new context)

Productive vocabulary test 4: Fill in the gaps in the text (original context)

Receptive vocabulary test 1: Translate the following words into Dutch

Receptive vocabulary test 2: Translate the words in bold into Dutch (target words in new context)

Receptive vocabulary test 3: Translate the words in bold into Dutch (original context)

Receptive vocabulary test 4: Match the words with their definition and translation

Figure 9.3 Vocabulary tests

were offered in isolation. The two other receptive recall tests were also translation tests but this time the target words were offered in context, first in a new context and then in sentences as they had occurred in the text. The last vocabulary test, a recognition test, was a matching test in which the word form had to be matched with its German definition and Dutch translation as provided in the online dictionary.

The reading comprehension test was split up in three parts. The first part, which contained five multiple choice and three open, short-answer questions, focused on (literal) facts, whereas the second part consisted of five short-answer questions of an interpretative level. In the final part students had to apply their knowledge of the text to new situations.

Procedure

This study was conducted during two different phases, a pretest session and the experiment. Two weeks prior to the experiment, all students were tested on their German proficiency, receptive German vocabulary size, knowledge of target words, and inferring ability. During the pretest session, students started by filling in a questionnaire, which collected information about gender, age, years of German study and computer familiarity, before taking all the pretests. Except for the inferencing test, all the other tests were administered on computer. All these data were collected in a computer room of the university.

During the experiment, students were randomly assigned to one of the four conditions. They performed the experiment individually in the researcher's office because we wanted to interview the participants immediately after the experiment had taken place. All the students received the instruction that they had to read a German text on a computer screen within a time limit of 20 minutes. Dependent on the group to which the students were assigned, they received the additional instruction that afterwards they would either be (1) tested on vocabulary (group 1), (2) tested on text comprehension (group 2), or (3) tested on both vocabulary and text comprehension (group 3). Students in the control group were only instructed that they had to read a text on a computer screen. Students were shown how they could look up unknown words. However, participants were not aware of the fact that their look-up behaviour was registered in log files.

Students of all four groups had to take all the tests, vocabulary tests as well as the reading comprehension test in order to study possible incidental learning effects and to compare the results between the four groups. Students had to complete eight vocabulary tests, first the four productive vocabulary tests and then the four receptive vocabulary tests. After the vocabulary tests, students took the reading comprehension test, which consisted of three parts. Having completed the tests, students were interviewed about their experiences during the experiment in order to find out how students divided their attention and how they proceeded through the experiment because we were not only interested in the learning product but also in the learning process.

Scoring procedure

The eight vocabulary tests were scored dichotomously, with 1 assigned to a correct answer and 0 to an incorrect one. We disregarded grammar and spelling mistakes both in students' L1 and L2. Because a student's lexical pre-knowledge was taken into consideration when scoring the vocabulary tests, students' scores are reported in fractions instead of students' raw total scores. The reading comprehension questions consisted of multiple choice and open questions. The former questions were corrected automatically by the computer programme, whereas the latter questions were corrected by the researcher. A correct answer received 1 point, a partly correct answer 0.5 point, and a wrong answer 0 point.

Results

What is the effect of task complexity on reading comprehension?

When we compare the results of the reading comprehension tests (see Table 9.1), we can see that the second group with the single task of reading comprehension scored better than the other groups for all three parts of the test. In addition, they manifested the least within-group variation, as reflected in the standard deviation. The next best total score came from the third group who were set a dual task of which one task was a reading comprehension task. The control group, with no specific task instructions, had the lowest total score. The reading comprehension scores of the four groups were subjected to Kruskal–Wallis analyses because the normality assumption was not met. A main effect of task instruction could only be found for the third part of the test (chi-square = 8.63, DF = 3, $p < 0.05$). In order to detect which groups differed significantly from each other, we employed

Table 9.1 Descriptive statistics of reading comprehension test

	Part 1		*Part 2*		*Part 3*		*Total*	
n = 20	*Mean*	*s.d.*	*Mean*	*s.d.*	*Mean*	*s.d.*	*Mean*	*s.d.*
Group 1	6.6	1.34	3.8	0.91	4.2	0.67	14.6	2.56
Group 2	7.2	0.50	4.3	0.84	4.8	0.27	16.6	0.89
Group 3	7.0	1.41	4.0	0.61	3.8	0.84	14.8	1.96
Group 4	7.2	1.30	3.3	1.48	3.5	0.5	14.0	2.32

Note: Group 1 = single vocabulary task, Group 2 = single text comprehension task, Group 3 = dual task, Group 4 = control group.

the parametric ANCOVA (vocabulary size as covariate). A *post-hoc* Tukey–Kramer analysis revealed that the second group (single reading comprehension task) performed significantly better than the control group ($p < 0.05$). The other three groups did not differ significantly from each other. The results are presented in Table 9.1. The first part of the test was scored on eight, the second part on five and the third part also on five, which makes a total of 18.

What is the effect of task complexity on vocabulary acquisition?

In this subsection about vocabulary acquisition, we will first discuss the results of the productive vocabulary tests before moving on to the analyses of the receptive vocabulary tests.

Table 9.2 below illustrates that no consistent pattern developed among the four groups because it was not the same group that obtained the best retention score on each of the four productive vocabulary tests. The first group (single vocabulary task) performed best on the first productive vocabulary test, the control group on the second test, in which collocations needed to be translated. On the third productive vocabulary test, the best retention score was obtained by both the first and the third (dual task) group. Finally, on the fourth productive vocabulary test, students in the third group supplied the most correct translations. None of the scores in the four productive vocabulary tests were normally distributed. Therefore, we conducted the non-parametric Kruskal–Wallis analysis to examine whether task instruction affected students word retention as measured in the productive vocabulary tests. On none of the four productive vocabulary test

Table 9.2 Descriptive statistics of vocabulary tests (in fractions)

	Prodtest1		Prodtest2		Prodtest3		Prodtest4	
$n = 20$	Mean	s.d.	Mean	s.d.	Mean	s.d.	Mean	s.d.
Group 1	0.18	0.10	0.10	0.09	0.15	0.11	0.14	0.10
Group 2	0.10	0.13	0.14	0.10	0.10	0.10	0.18	0.17
Group 3	0.17	0.25	0.14	0.25	0.15	0.13	0.19	0.16
Group 4	0.15	0.10	0.16	0.16	0.09	0.09	0.14	0.11
	Rectest1		Rectest2		Rectest3		Rectest4	
Group 1	0.45	0.13	0.78	0.08	0.91	0.09	0.84	0.08
Group 2	0.44	0.06	0.70	0.12	0.73	0.05	0.86	0.11
Group 3	0.53	0.20	0.73	0.15	0.76	0.14	0.96	0.06
Group 4	0.50	0.12	0.78	0.08	0.78	0.08	0.77	0.18

Note: Group 1 = single vocabulary task, Group 2 = single text comprehension task, Group 3 = dual task, Group 4 = control group. *Prodtest* stands for productive vocabulary test, whereas *rectest* refers to receptive vocabulary test.

did we detect any significant difference between the four groups. Each Kruskal–Wallis analysis yielded a *p*-value higher than the significance level of five percent we presupposed.

The results were better for the receptive than for the productive vocabulary tests. The latter tests were characterised by a bottom effect. The highest scores were found in the fourth receptive vocabulary test in which students had to match the word with the correct definition and translation. This test, a mere recognition test, was considered to be the easiest of all tests by both the designer of the test and the participants. However, no clear pattern across the four receptive vocabulary tests emerged. In the first and fourth receptive vocabulary test, the highest retention scores were found in the third group (dual task), whereas the first group (single vocabulary task) obtained the highest scores on the second and third receptive vocabulary test. However, the control group performed equally well on the second test. In three of the four receptive vocabulary tests, it was the second group (single comprehension task) that retained least words. The results (in fractions) of the vocabulary tests are presented in Table 9.2. It turned out that there was no statistically significant difference in retention score between the four groups on any of the four receptive vocabulary tests. Group means of the first, second, and third receptive test were subjected to an ANCOVA (with vocabulary size as covariate) to determine whether there would be any statistically significant difference between the four groups. For the fourth receptive test, the matching test, a Kruskal–Wallis analysis, the nonparametric version of the ANOVA, was used. Yet no analysis revealed any effect of task instruction.

Incidental versus intentional learning

Concentrating on reading comprehension first, the second and the third group knew that a reading comprehension test would follow. They made up the intentional comprehension condition. Focusing on the overall result, the second group scored best, followed by the third group. When we have a look at each part separately, the best results were each time obtained by the group with a single reading comprehension task. Again the third group with the dual task performed better than the two incidental groups with regard to the first and the second part of the test. To summarize, students who were forewarned of a reading comprehension test performed better than students who were not forewarned.

With regard to word retention, a different picture emerges. The results were not as consistent as was the case for reading comprehension. It was not one group that scored best on all vocabulary tests. In seven of the eight vocabulary tests, however, it was either the first group with a single vocabulary task or the third group with the dual task that performed best. In other words, the intentional vocabulary learning condition obtained higher scores than the incidental vocabulary learning condition but as discussed earlier, these differences were not statistically significant.

What is the effect of task complexity on the look-up behaviour?

It is important to note that students' look-up behaviour regards only the number of clicks on the 17 target words. The computer log files showed that the most intensive clicking behaviour was found in those groups who were set a vocabulary task. Students in the first group clicked on average 10 times on the target words, compared to eight times in the third group, five times in the second group, and three times in the control group. Because the data of students' look-up behaviour were not normally distributed, a non-parametric analysis (Kruskal–Wallis analysis) was used to determine whether any statistically significant difference between the four groups would exist. The Kruskal–Walllis did not yield any statistically significant difference between the four groups ($p = 0.19$). Table 9.3 summarises the look-up behaviour of the four groups. For each group the maximum and minimum number of clicks is given, together with the average number of clicks and the standard deviation.

Students' look-up behaviour can also be analysed in an alternative way. Instead of analysing the look-up behaviour of four conditions, one can regroup the four groups into two groups. The number of lookups of the first (single vocabulary task) and third group (dual task) was combined into the look-up behaviour of the intentional vocabulary learning condition, whereas the number of look-ups of the second (single comprehension task) and fourth group (control group) was combined into the look-up behaviour of the incidental vocabulary learning condition. The incidental vocabulary

Table 9.3 Descriptive statistics of look-up behaviour

n = 20	Number of clicks				
Condition	n	Mean	s.d.	Max	Min
Group 1	5	10.2	9.0	26	4
Group 2	5	5.0	4.9	13	1
Group 3	5	8.2	5.3	14	1
Group 4	5	3.6	1.5	6	2
Alternative condition					
Incidental condition	10	4.3	3.5	13	1
Intentional condition	10	9.2	7.0	26	1

Note: Group 1 = single vocabulary task, Group 2 = single text comprehension task, Group 3 = dual task, Group 4 = control group. n = number of participants, Max = maximum number of lookups, Min = minimum number of lookups.

Table 9.4 Pearson correlation coefficients for look-up behaviour and reading comprehension

n = 20	Part 1	Part 2	Part 3	Total
Words looked-up	0.06	−0.01	0.32	0.14

learning condition looked up an average of nine words, whereas students who were not forewarned of an upcoming vocabulary test, looked up an average of four words. A Wilcoxon two-sample test, which is the non-parametric version of the independent two-sample t-test, was performed to determine whether both groups differed significantly from each other in their number of clicks. The Wilcoxon-two-sample-test showed that the difference in number of lookups between the incidental and intentional vocabulary learning condition was statistically significant ($z = 2.1270, p < 0.05$).

Was students' number of lookups related to students' reading comprehension? Correlation coefficients were calculated for each of the three parts of the comprehension test and for the total score on the comprehension test (= sum of three parts). Only low and non-significant correlations were found as Table 9.4 shows.

Was there a relationship between students' number of lookups and word retention? A Pearson correlation was computed to determine the relationship between students' look-up behaviour and word retention. Moderate to high correlations between students' number of lookups and word retention were found, as reported in Table 9.5. However, not all correlations were significant at the 0.05-level. The Pearson correlation coefficients appear to indicate that students who engaged in more active dictionary use, tended to remain more words.

When a word was looked up, its chances to be retained were different for the several vocabulary tests, being much higher for the receptive than for the productive vocabulary tests. The results range from 18% to 100% with an average of 27% for the productive vocabulary tests and 82% for the receptive vocabulary tests.

Table 9.5 Pearson correlation coefficients for look-up behaviour and word retention

Productive vocabulary test	*r*	*Receptive vocabulary test*	*r*
Productive vocabulary test 1	0.52*	Receptive vocabulary test 1	0.48*
Productive vocabulary test 2	0.26	Receptive vocabulary test 2	0.44*
Productive vocabulary test 3	0.60*	Receptive vocabulary test 3	0.40
Productive vocabulary test 4	0.43	Receptive vocabulary test 4	0.29

*$p < 0.05$.

Discussion

Vocabulary acquisition and reading comprehension

We expected that higher task complexity would lead to more dispersion of attention and hence to worse results on both vocabulary and reading comprehension measures. Students with a dual task did not score better on the vocabulary tests nor on the reading comprehension test, as was expected within Robinson's (2005) Triadic Framework for task complexity. However, because of a lack of significant differences between the four groups with regard to word retention, our first hypothesis was not corroborated. It appears that it is not so straightforward to manipulate students' attention via task instruction since students, irrespective of the condition to which they were assigned, paid primarily attention to the content of the text. In a way, the results point in the direction of Skehan's (1998) limited-capacity processing system, which is also reflected in the resource-dispersing dimension of Robinson's (2005) Triadic Componential Framework. According to Skehan (1998), the limited capacity information-processing system does not have the resources to process in an exhaustive manner all the L2 input which is received. In addition, carrying out two tasks simultaneously will lead to dispersion of attention (Robinson, 2005). Moreover, we doubt whether students in the dual task condition did really carry out the two tasks simultaneously and not consecutively. It seems that they prioritised meaning prior to allocating attention to vocabulary. This is not so surprising because when attentional resources are limited, a selection has to be made (Schmidt, 2001). Consequently, attentional resources are predisposed to prioritise meaning (Schmidt, 2001: 13; VanPatten, 1990: 295). The same results were found by Sercu *et al.* (forthcoming).

Two studies (VanPatten, 1990; Wong, 2001) investigated attention to meaning and to form. Although their concept of focus on form was operationalised in a different way[4] than in our study, both studies point at a priority for meaning and our results seem to confirm this priority for meaning when attending to communicative input. According to VanPatten (1990), there exists a conflict between focus on comprehension and focus on form. In his view, attentional resources are limited and our attention span is too limited to allow both to be emphasised simultaneously. This focus on meaning can be illustrated with two quotations by students who received a dual task instruction:

- 'Although I really had the intention to pay attention to both vocabulary and content, I paid more attention to the content of the text.'
- 'Although you told me that there would follow vocabulary tests, I mainly concentrated on the content of the text.'

Moreover, this priority for meaning did not only apply to students who received a dual task instruction, but also to some students who received a single vocabulary task instruction. One student said: 'I tried to pay attention to vocabulary but I have to admit that while I was reading I started to focus my attention more on the content of the text, I didn't keep on thinking of the vocabulary tests' (quotation by a student in the first group). It seems that other more efficient means are required to have students attend to vocabulary because otherwise learners tend to prioritise meaning regardless of their task instruction. The fact that the target words were not visually enhanced may have contributed even more to dispersion of attention instead of directing learners' attention to relevant linguistic features, *viz.* the target words. Although we assumed that we could manipulate students' attention by altering task instructions, students in the four conditions appear to have approached the experiment similarly. This might explain why the differences in retention scores were so small. In their research about the differential effects of attention concerning different language areas, Gass *et al.* (2003) show that the smallest differences were found in the vocabulary area with the best students. Maybe, this facet could have played a role in our investigation as well. Furthermore, Gass *et al.* (2003: 508) point out that, 'Attention is in the eyes of the beholder.' We may try to manipulate students' attention but students can have their own needs and interests so it remains possible that input does not become intake despite of attention manipulation (Gass *et al.*, 2003; Sharwood-Smith, 1993: 168).

That students had their own needs and goals was further illustrated in the reading comprehension scores. It appeared that all the students in this study approached the task in the way they have been used to approach a task, regardless of the condition to which they were assigned. The participants in this study wanted in the first place to grasp the gist of the text. Vocabulary came in the second place. During the interviews, students indicated that it was impossible not to allocate attentional resources to the content of the text, as is also illustrated in the quotation above by a student in the first group. Students in the control group did not score significantly lower than other students, because of their personal needs and goals as they have been trained during their academic education to prioritise the content of texts and not individual lexical items. The students in the control group also read the text very carefully, even if no reading comprehension test was announced. However, some of these students did expect to be tested on comprehension because of the fact that it was an experiment, as became clear during the interviews.

Incidental versus intentional learning

The hypothesis 'students in an intentional learning condition will perform better than students in an incidental learning condition' appears to be true but this is more the case for reading comprehension than for word retention. Students who explicitly received a reading comprehension task tended to score better than those who were not forewarned of reading comprehension test. Although focused attention is a powerful mechanism for learning (Gass *et al.*, 2003), learning took place incidentally as well. This is best seen in the vocabulary tests. It is possible that students paid attention to vocabulary or content despite the fact that we did not explicitly draw their attention to it. As already mentioned, 'attention is in the eyes of the beholder' (Gass *et al.*, 2003: 508). We expected that a vocabulary task would induce a more intensive look-up behaviour. Students from Group 1 and Group 3 did click significantly more often on target words than students in Group 2 and Group 4, yet this more intensive clicking behaviour in the intentional vocabulary learning condition did not result in deeper word processing. This study provides a first preliminary indication that students who are set a vocabulary task click more intensively on words, yet they do not engage in more word processing.

Look-up behaviour

We expected that a higher task complexity would lead to a greater willingness to consult the online dictionary. Students in the group with a dual task did not look up more words than the group with a single vocabulary task. It seems that it is not task complexity but being forewarned of a vocabulary test which influences students' look-up behaviour, as was already pointed out in the previous subsection. Hence, hypothesis 4 could not be confirmed.

From the log files and the interviews, we also conclude that students did not look up all unknown (target) words, not even the students who were forewarned of an upcoming vocabulary test. The explanations students provided for not looking up an unknown word are in accordance with the claims made by Laufer (2003). According to Laufer, there are two main reasons why students do not look up an unknown word in a dictionary. A first reason is that students do not recognise the unknown word as unknown because they understand the general message of a text. As a consequence, students may not pay sufficient attention to the precise meaning of words. Secondly, students sometimes confuse an unknown word with a similar word, or they see it as a false cognate.

In this study, students made it clear that they sometimes had no urge to look up an unknown word because they understood what was being said in the text. The unknown word did not hamper the general comprehension of the text. Students mentioned that they understood more or less the meaning of the target words while reading the text. For instance, one student said that s/he understood the words when s/he read them in the text, but that s/he could not translate them. However, when having to supply the precise meaning in the vocabulary tests, students realised that they did not always know this precise meaning. This could refer to the fact that not only easy guessing (Mondria & Wit-De Boer, 1991) but also fast reading of dictionary information leads to shallow processing of that information, whereby no form-meaning link is created that is strong enough for long-term memory. In addition, students explained that they found the glosses helpful but not essential for successful text comprehension, which was corroborated by the fact that there was no positive correlation between the look-up behaviour and the comprehension tests. This result is in line with other studies on the influence of electronic glosses on reading comprehension (Chun, 2001; De Ridder, 2002). In this study, another important reason for not looking up a word was that unknown words were not recognised as being unknown e.g. false cognates and synforms (Laufer, 2003: 570). Students thought they knew the meaning of the German word because it resembled a Dutch word or another German word. Let us illustrate this with the target word *Erzeugnisse* (products). One student said: 'when I was sure of the meaning, I didn't look it up. Afterwards however I noticed that these meanings were sometimes not correct, e.g. the German word *Erzeugnis*: I thought it meant "testimony" whereas it actually means "product"'.[5] Words such as *Erzeugnisse* do not draw students' attention because they are recognised at the level of the form. Students know the German morphemes *er-*, *zeugnis-*, and *se*, whereas unfamiliar word forms, which are not recognised at the level of the form, do tend draw students' attention enabling them to notice the lexical gap. One student said that *schikanieren* (to bully, to victimise) caught her attention because this word did not look like a 'normal' word. Lutjeharms (2004: 17) employs the German term *Kontrastmangelphenomen* (phenomenon of a lack of contrast) to describe this phenomenon of not recognising unknown words because of their formal familiarity. Moreover, students' familiarity with other words tends to override contextual factors. They tend to persist in error (Huckin & Bloch, 1993), even when the word's meaning does not fit in the context, as is illustrated in the *Erzeugnisse*-example described earlier.

Students who received a vocabulary task felt that the online dictionary was not only helpful, but also essential to take the vocabulary tests. They were of the opinion that the dictionary helped them learn new words. This is exemplified by the retention chances when a target word was looked up on the one hand and the correlation analyses on the other hand. The findings on the relationship between the total number of lookups and word retention are in line with Knight (1994). Furthermore, the student who looked up the most words in every group had the highest scores on the vocabulary tests. This is true for all groups except the control group.

Conclusion

Though the results in this study do not reflect general tendencies because of the limited sample size, several issues have emerged which deserve further attention and research. First, this study provided preliminary evidence that when set a vocabulary task students tend to look up more words than when not set a vocabulary task. Students' look-up behaviour hardly affects their reading comprehension yet a positive relationship between look-up behaviour and word retention could be found. The effect of forewarning students of a vocabulary tests appeared to be rather quantitative than qualitative in nature since it did not affect students' word retention nor their text comprehension. This study showed that it is an intricate issue to manipulate students' attentional resources via task instruction. Students who were set a single task scored better, yet not significantly better, than students who were set a dual task. The data tend to give evidence for the hypothesis of a limited-processing capacity system in which attentional resources are limited, selective and subject to voluntary control (Schmidt, 2001: 12–13) with a priority for meaning (VanPatten, 1990). Students were not able to process form (words) and content simultaneously at the same level. Even if students are forewarned of a vocabulary test, it remains difficult to have students focus on vocabulary and to create a priority for form, *viz.* vocabulary. Finally, our results suggest that intentional learning might lead to better results, especially with regard to reading comprehension.

Obviously, there were some limitations to this study. One of them is the small size of the sample population as a result of which the results are not statistically significant. Another possible reason for the lack of significant differences could be that there may not have been a difference in task approach between the four groups. As a result of a priority for meaning, students from the first group did not just focus on vocabulary. They read a text and focused on the content of the text as well in order the grasp what the text was about. Their learning behaviour might have resembled the strategies of the third group with a dual task. The control group on the other hand approached the experiment in the same way as the second group with a single reading comprehension task. These students in the control group also took their task, reading a text, seriously, even if no reading comprehension test was announced. So two experimental conditions, *viz.* one group with a reading comprehension task and the other group with a dual task, might have sufficed. Although we want to meet the objection that we confronted the students with an overload of vocabulary tests, we still consider testing partial vocabulary knowledge to be important. Hence, fewer and maybe even only receptive vocabulary tests could still be used. In this experiment only short-term word retention was tested. It would be interesting to study the effects of task instruction on long-term word retention by organising a delayed vocabulary test. Moreover, think-aloud protocols could shed more light on the learning strategies and the cognitive processes underlying the learning activity.

Acknowledgements

I am deeply indebted to Arnoud Wils (Katholieke Universiteit Leuven) for his technical support in creating a tracking technology for the look-up behaviour of the students, to Kornelia Bitzer-Zenner of the Goethe Institut Inter Nationes in Brussels and to the 'Centrum voor Levende Talen, Leuven' for placing the German proficiency test at my disposal, to Ann

Carbonez (Katholieke Universiteit Leuven) for her statistical advice and last but not least to Lies Sercu (Katholieke Universiteit Leuven), Jan Hulstijn (University of Amsterdam) and Madeline Lutjeharms (Vrije Universiteit Brussel) for their invaluable suggestions.

Notes

1. This article is based on a paper presented at the XIV EUROSLA (European Second Language Association) conference held in San Sebastián (Spain) in September (8–11) 2004.
2. The 17 target words were: *anfällig, schlicht, schmuck, überlegen, langfristig, schikanieren, nachlassen, entschwinden, sich erhalten, bekunden, Einzug halten, Verhaltensweise, Währungsunion, Erzeugnis, Prägung, Zusammenprall, über Nacht* (susceptible, simple, neat, superior, long-term/in the long run, to bully, to decrease, to disappear, to maintain, to manifest, to enter, behaviour, monetary union, product, belief/conviction, clash, suddenly).
3. Terminology of recall versus recognition is used as in Laufer *et al.* (2004). 'We will refer to the ability to retrieve the word form as "active" knowledge and to the ability to retrieve the word meaning as "passive" knowledge [...] there is a difference in knowledge between those who can recall the form or the meaning of a word and those who cannot do this, but can recognize the form of meaning in a set of option' (Laufer *et al.*, 2004: 206).
4. VanPatten's (1990) study tested listening comprehension and not reading comprehension. His study was replicated by Wong (2001) who wanted to investigate both reading and listening comprehension. Although her conclusion was that this difference in focus on either content and/or form is not affected in the same way for the written and the aural mode, there exists a priority for meaning.
5. Erzeugnis means 'product'. It was confused with the German word Zeugnis', which means 'testimony', or with the Dutch word 'getuigenis' (testimony).

References

Chun, D. (2001) L2 reading on the web: Strategies for accessing information in hypermedia. *Computer Assisted Language Learning* 14, 367–403.
De Ridder, I. (2000) Are we conditioned to follow links? Highlights in CALL materials and their impact on the reading process. *Computer Assisted Language Learning* 13, 183–195.
De Ridder, I. (2002) Visible or invisible links: Does the highlighting of hyperlinks affect incidental vocabulary learning, text comprehension and the reading process? *Language Learning & Technology* 6, 123–146. On WWW at http://llt.msu.edu/vol6num1/DERIDDER/default.html. Accessed 21.1.03.
De Ridder, I. (2003) *Reading from the Screen in a Second Language. Empirical Studies on the Effect of Marked Hyperlinks on Incidental Vocabulary Learning, Text Comprehension and the Reading Process.* Antwerpen: Garant.
Ellis, R. (2003) *Task-Based Language Learning and Teaching.* Oxford: Oxford University Press.
Ellis, R. (ed.) (2005) *Planning and Task Performance in a Second Language.* Amsterdam/Philadelphia: John Benjamins Publishing Company.
Ellis, R. and Yuan, F. (2005) The effects of careful within-task planning on oral and written task performance. In R. Ellis (ed.) *Planning and Task Performance in a Second Language* (pp. 167–192). Amsterdam/Philadelphia: John Benjamins Publishing Company.

Gass, S., Svetics, I. and Lemelin, S. (2003) Differential effects of attention. *Language Learning* 53, 497–545.

Horst, M., Cobb, T. and Meara, P. (1998) Beyond a clockwork orange: Acquiring second language vocabulary through reading. *Reading in a Foreign Language* 11, 207–223.

Huckin, T. and Bloch, J. (1993) Strategies for inferring word-meanings in context: A cognitive model. In T. Huckin and J. Coady (eds) *Second Language Reading and Vocabulary Learning* (pp. 153–178). Norwood, NJ: Ablex Publishing Company.

Hulstijn, J.H. (1993) When do foreign-language readers look up the meaning of unfamiliar words? The influence of task and learner variables. *The Modern Language Journal* 77, 139–147.

Hulstijn, J. (2001) Intentional and incidental second language vocabulary learning: A reappraisal of elaboration, rehearsal and automaticity. In P. Robinson (ed.) *Cognition and Second Language Instruction* (pp. 258–286). Cambridge: Cambridge University Press.

Hulstijn, J. (2003) Incidental and intentional learning. In C. Doughty and M.h. Long (eds) *Handbook of Second Language Acquisition* (pp. 349–381). Malden, MA: Blackwell.

Institut für deutsche Sprache, IDS-Mannheim. On WWW at http://www.ids-mannheim.de/.

Kaiser, A. (2003, November 14) Mode: Die Nation zieht an. *Frankfurter Allgemeine Zeitung*. On WWW at http://www.faz.net. Accessed 15.11.03.

Knight, S. (1994) Dictionary use while reading: The effects on comprehension and vocabulary acquisition for students of different verbal abilities. *The Modern Language Journal* 78, 285–299.

Kuiken, F., Mos, M. and Vedder, I. (2005) Cognitive task complexity and second language writing performance. In S. Foster-Cohen, M.P. García-Mayo and J. Cenoz (eds) *Eurosla Yearbook*. (Vol. 5) (pp. 195–222). Amsterdam/Philadelphia: John Benjamins.

Laufer, B. (2003) Vocabulary acquisition in a second language: Do learners really acquire most vocabulary by reading? Some empirical evidence. *The Canadian Modern Language Review* 59, 567–587.

Laufer, B., Elder, C., Hill, K. and Congdon, P. (2004) Size and strength: do we need both to measure vocabulary knowledge? *Language Testing* 21, 202–226.

Lutjeharms, M. (2004) Der Zugriff auf das mentale Lexikon und der Wortschatzerwerb in der Fremdsprache. In F.G. Königs and E. Zöfgen (eds) *Fremdsprachen lehren und lernen. Themenschwerpunkt: Wortschatz–Wortschatzerwerb–Wortschatzlernen*, 33, 10–26.

Meara, P. (1992) *EFL Vocabulary Tests*. Swansea: Centre for Applied Language Studies.

Meara, P. and Buxton, B. (1987) An alternative to multiple choice vocabulary tests. *Language Testing* 4, 142–154.

Mondria, J.A. and Wit-De Boer, M. (1991) The effects of contextual richness on the guessability and the retention of words in a foreign language. *Applied Linguistics* 12, 249–266.

Nation, I.S.P. (2001) *Learning Vocabulary in Another Language*. Cambridge: Cambridge University Press.

QuestionMark Perception. On WWW at http://www.questionmark.com.

Robinson, P. (2001) Task complexity, cognitive resources, and syllabus design: A triadic framework for examining task influences on SLA. In P. Robinson (ed.) *Cognition and Second Language Instruction* (pp. 287–318). Cambridge: Cambridge University Press.

Robinson, P. (2005) Cognitive complexity and task sequencing: Studies in a componential framework for second language task design. *IRAL* 43, 1–32.

Schmidt, R. (2001) Attention. In P. Robinson (ed.) *Cognition and Second Language Instruction* (pp. 3–32). Cambridge: Cambridge University Press.

Sercu, L., De Wachter, L., Peters, E., Kuiken, F. and Vedder, I. (forthcoming) The effect of task complexity and task conditions on foreign language development and performance. Three experimental studies. *ITL, Review of Applied Linguistics*.

Sharwood Smith, M. (1993) Input enhancement in instructed SLA. *Studies in Second Language Acquisition* 15, 165–179.

Skehan, P. (1998) *A Cognitive Approach to Language Learning*. Oxford: Oxford University Press.

Skehan, P. and Foster, P. (2001) Cognition and tasks. In P. Robinson (ed.) *Cognition and Second Language Instruction* (pp. 183–205). Cambridge: Cambridge University Press.

Staud, T. (2003) Ossis sind Türken. 13 Jahre Einheit: In Gesamt-Westdeutschland sind die Ostdeutschen Einwanderer. *Die Zeit*, 41/2003, On WWW at http://www.Zeit.De. Accessed 2.10.03.

VanPatten, B. (1990) Attending to content and form in the input: An experiment in consciousness. *Studies in Second Language Acquisition* 12, 287–301.

Wong, W. (2001) Modality and attention to meaning and form in the input. *Studies in Second Language Acquisition* 23, 345–368.

Zahar, R., Cobb, T. and Spada, N. (2001) Acquiring vocabulary through reading: Effects of frequency and contextual richness. *The Canadian Modern Language Review* 57, 541–572.

Chapter 10

Task-Effect on the Use
of Lexical Innovation Strategies
in Interlanguage Communication

ELSA GONZÁLEZ ÁLVAREZ

Introduction

When speakers of a language fail to find in the established lexicon a term which gives 'immediate satisfaction' to their communicative needs, a new word may be coined, which may be permanently incorporated in the language providing that certain requirements are met (Bauer, 1983). A similar behaviour can be found in first (L1) or second (L2) language learners when gaps are noticed when searchig for an expression with which to fulfil a particular communicative goal. Thus, the phenomenon of word formation in language learning has been dealt with both by those interested in the process of acquisition of knowledge and skills to produce new words (Broeder *et al.*, 1996; Clark, 1993; Pavesi, 1998), and also by those focused on how learners apply this knowledge to overcome lexical deficits during L2 communication, that is, on the research area of communication strategies (henceforth, CS) (Dewaele, 1998; González-Álvarez, 2004; Ridley & Singleton, 1995; Singleton & Little, 1991; to name a few).

An important issue in CS studies has been the identification of the factors that influence the selection of particular strategy types, among which proficiency- and task-related factors have received special attention. From a different perspective, a fair amount of task-based research has also tried to determine the effect of manipulating specific task features on the different dimensions of performance.

After reviewing notions and findings from both approaches, the present study will investigate the impact of task-related factors on the selection and use of mechanisms of lexical innovation in interlaguage (IL) communication.

Lexical Innovation in Second Language Acquisition (SLA) Research

In the context of lexical CS research, different labels have been given to the strategy of lexical innovation,[1] broadly defined as the creation of new words (i.e. not previously present in the learners' interlanguage lexicon) by combining known elements to compensate for gaps in the L2 lexicon. Few studies have dealt specifically with this strategy, probably because of its reported low frequency of application compared to other types (Bialystok, 1983; González-Álvarez, 1999; Poulisse, 1987; Poulisse & Bongaerts, 1994). However, it has been shown that this is a key aspect in lexical development since it contributes to improving learners' fluency and strategic competence (Robinson, 1994). Moreover, the fact that learners are able to exploit their knowledge of word structure in the creation of acceptable (although often non-attested) L2 forms suggests that the reported underuse of this ability may be due to their unawareness of the potential of their IL resources (González-Álvarez, 2004).

Definition and categorisation

A basic underlying distinction between so-called 'conceptual' and 'code' strategies can be identified in most taxonomies proposed to date, defined as follows: conceptual strategies 'manipulate the individual's knowledge of the properties of the concept itself', whereas code strategies 'manipulate the user's knowledge of word form by the construction of *ad hoc* labels for referents via languages other than the L2, or via derivational rules within the L2' (Kellerman & Bialystok, 1997: 34).

Following Yule and Tarone's (1997) comprehensive taxonomy, code strategies can be further subdivided into two main groups: (a) word coinage, by which new words are formed by recombining known L2 elements (often yielding non-attested forms in the L2); and (b) transfer, which includes borrowing (or language switch), literal translation and foreignizing, defined as the morphological or phonological modification of L1 forms to adapt them to the L2 norm (or what the learner perceives as such), resulting in forms that are frequently non-existing and even not possible in the L2.[2]

The different strategy types have been characterized along three dimensions: communicative effectiveness, cognitive load and linguistic demands imposed on the learner. Trying to determine how effective and informative the different types were, Poulisse (1993) asked a group of native speakers to guess the meanings of different CS samples within their original context. Reconceptualisation strategies – listing conceptual features of the referent, combining two lexical items into a new word, and adding background information – tended to be the most successful, followed by substitution plus – including (grammatical) word coinage and foreignising – and substitution (approximation and, especially, code-switching). However, and more importantly, Poulisse concluded that task-related factors can vary the intrinsic comprehensibility of a particular strategy, which 'depends so heavily on the amount of specific information contained in the CS itself and on the informativeness of the context in which it is embedded' (Poulisse, 1993: 166).

Communication strategies can also be characterised according to the demands they impose on the learners' resources. In general, we can say that L2-based strategies place considerably greater demands than L1-based ones (Bialystok, 1990). Following Poulisse (1993), CS types can also be ranked according to the amount of processing effort required: substitution strategies appear as less cognitively demanding than substitution plus strategies, since the latter involve non-automatic encoding procedures; even more demanding are reconceptualisation strategies, which involve 'more drastic changes in the preverbal message' (Poulisse, 1993: 182). Often, the more clear and comprehensible a CS is, the less economical it is, i.e. the more linguistic and/or processing effort it will require.

Factors in the selection of communication strategies

Research in this field has also tried to determine the factors that influence the selection of a particular problem-solving mechanism in interlanguage oral communication, among which proficiency level, personality or cognitive style, cultural background, nature of the task and communicative situation have been identified (*cf.* Bialystok, 1983, 1990).

Learner factors: Proficiency level

Proficiency level in the L2 was one of the first factors to be identified, the claim being that less proficient learners use more CS, and also more L1-based strategies (Poulisse, 1993), which is only natural since they are likely to be confronted with more lexical problems, and since 'some [strategies] may be too sophisticated for less advanced language learners' (Bialystok, 1990: 48). As for lexical innovation, Ridley and Singleton (1995: 141) compared the use of this strategy by four learners and, albeit a 'relatively minor feature of the *ab initio* learners' performance', found the highest percentages of innovations in the solution of lexical problems in all tasks in the subjects with the poorest lexical proficiency. L1-based lexical inventions turned out to be more frequent in less proficient learners in Dewaele's (1998) and Poulisse and Bongaerts' (1994) studies.

Task factors

It has also been suggested that task demands affect CS choice more than proficiency level (Bialystok, 1990; Poulisse, 1993, 1997). Ridley and Singleton (1995) observed that interviews yielded the lowest number of examples of lexical innovation for every subject, and that inter-subject variation was more evident in tasks which allowed subjects more freedom in lexical choice. Similarly, Pavesi (1998) observed that L2 learners' spontaneous word coining does not normally start until they have reached advanced levels, favouring other strategies, such as paraphrases or L1 transfer to refer to the desired concepts. Learners at intermediate levels, however, are already capable of forming new words when specifically asked to do so in elicitation tasks. Singleton and Little (1991) also investigated the strategy of creativity as a response to L2 lexical problems, and concluded that innovations, especially L1-based ones, tended to be associated with the more problematic test items and difficult tests.

The interaction between task-type and proficiency level has been illustrated by Poulisse's (1993) reports of the findings from the Nijmegen project. She observes that, although proficiency-related differences appeared as expected, cross-group differences in the relative frequency of application of the different CS types varied across tasks. Thus, whereas only a few transfer strategies were used in referring to photographed objects by all the groups, all of them used this strategy type in approximately 20% of the cases in the interview. Clear proficiency-related differences in the use of L1-based strategies were found only in the story-retell task.

The integration of CS use in a model of verbal communication, adapted from Levelt's (1989), allows Poulisse (1993, 1997) to account for this task-related variation in CS. According to the principles of clarity and economy, speakers strive for a maximally comprehensible message while investing minimal processing effort (from both speaker and listener). Similarly, when the most effective means of communication – i.e. the concept's conventional name – is not available, learners will still try to adhere to these principles and produce references as clear and effective as, 'but no more informative than' necessary (Poulisse, 1997: 52).

Several task-related factors have been identified as potential influence for the selection of more or less demanding strategy types. Among these, Poulisse (1993) lists task demands, the opportunity to get feedback from an interlocutor, cognitive complexity of the task, or time constraints. Thus, when a balance between clarity and economy is not possible and learners need to choose, the importance of the communicative goal pushes them to an extra effort in getting the message across, athough obviously determined by the availability of resources. Learners will also take advantage of all situation- or task-related factors that allow them to reach their communicative goals (relatively) effortlessly.

Thus, when task demands are high and subjects perceive the importance of being accurate and specific, they will be ready to use more comprehensible, even if more demanding, CS. This claim is supported by the proportionally higher use of more demanding strategies in object reference tasks, which required greater referential explicitness (Poulisse, 1993).

The presence of an interlocutor, and the possibility to obtain feedback as to the comprehensibility of the message, allows the speaker to use more demanding strategies only if necessary. The effect of this factor is so strong,

Poulisse (1993) argues, that all level groups in her study made a similar (relatively high) use of transfer strategies in the interview task.

A related interlocutor-effect on the choice of linguistic means used is the interlocutor's L1. Grosjean (1998) takes it into account to explain the different states of activation of the bilingual's languages, seen as 'modes' or stages along a monolingual–bilingual continuum (from one language spoken primarily to a high level of activation of both languages). The language mode would be controlled by such factors as 'who the bilingual is speaking or listening to, the situation, the topic, the purpose of the interaction and so on' (Grosjean, 1998: 136).

As for situation or context, Dewaele (1998) compared the frequency of lexical inventions in formal and informal interviews with L2 and L3 French subjects, and found that code-switching was in general avoided in the formal interviews (not so much in the informal ones), 'probably because they feared they would be penalized' (Dewaele, 1998: 487).

Finally, cognitive complexity and time constraints would also favour the selection of less demanding strategies, so that the learner's attention is freed to be directed to other aspects of the task, as the higher frequency of L1-based strategies in the interview task in Poulisse's (1993) study suggests.

Task-Based Research

We have seen above how the type of task used to elicit SLA data influences the output, particularly the type of strategies used. Several authors working outside the context of CS research have also tried to determine the effect of varying the complexity of a task on L2 performance, and its potential consequences for task-based pedagogy and L2 learning.

Effects of task complexity: Information-processing approaches

It should be noted that tasks can be studied from a wide range of perspectives, depending on the different theoretical views of language learning and performance.[3] From an information processing perspective, the focus of researchers has been on how task difficulty affects the way attention is allocated during task performance, on which task factors influence allocation of resources, and on the impact on actual performance. Although there is general agreement on the fact that tasks differ in the demands they make on our attention, and that 'varying these attentional demands may systematically affect the accuracy, fluency, and complexity of learner speech' (Robinson, 2003: 643), two opposing views have been held as to its effect on performance, based on two different understandings of the attentional capacities of the learner.

Thus, Skehan (1998) and Skehan and Foster (2001) contend that speakers' information processing capacities are limited, and consequently we cannot direct the same amount of attention to competing areas of performance such as fluency (content-focused) and accuracy and complexity (form-focused); therefore, priorities have to be set. Given the choice, learners tend to prioritise content over form. It follows that tasks which are cognitively complex in their content divert attentional resources from form, fostering the use of automatically-processed simpler language, and lowering the degree of accuracy of still non-automatic language forms.

Skehan's work is based on a model of language learning according to which L2 knowledge is stored and accessed by means of a dual system which is both rule- and exemplar-based. The first system draws upon lexical elements on which rules are applied creatively, so that meanings can be expressed precisely; these operations involve higher processing demands, thus drawing attentional resources from those aspects of performance that enhance fluency. The exemplar-, memory-based system, on the contrary, stores lexical items together with relatively fixed phrases which can be quickly accessed with little processing demands; attentional resources are thus freed to be directed to other areas, more often those which favor fluency, disregarding accuracy and complexity.

Building on claims and findings in areas such as cognitive linguistics, differential and cognitive psychology, and L1 development and cognition, Robinson (2001, 2003, 2005) puts forward the Cognition Hypothesis of task-based L2 learning, which questions the utility of single-resource, limited-capacity models, and adopts a multiple resource theory which admits that there are different separate resource pools, while accommodating interference models that explain trade-off effects between different aspects of performance in terms of processes which control information flow.

As regards the effects of task complexity on performance, Robinson (2003, 2005) suggests that some task features disperse attention between resource pools (resource-dispersing dimensions) while others direct attention 'to specific needed areas of the L2 within a pool' (Robinson, 2003: 646) (resource-directing dimensions). Increasing complexity along any of these dimensions increases the demands on learners' cognitive resources. In the first case, however, particular features of language code can be utilised in meeting these demands, and so resources are potentially directed to such features, leading to qualitative increases in accuracy, fluency and complexity. In the second case, since the demands cannot be met through the use of any particular language feature, this extra effort is wasted, which may result in the kind of trade-offs described by Skehan and others. 'Increases in task complexity along multiple dimensions will not degrade output, perception of input, and intake, and may lead to qualitative increases in all three relative to performing simpler tasks' (Robinson, 2003: 651).

Dimensions of task complexity

Several task features have been claimed to influence the different dimensions of task complexity. A brief summary is given here of those proposed by Skehan, on the one hand, and Robinson, on the other, since they are generally taken to be representative of the abovementioned contrasting views on attentional capacity.

Robinson (2001, 2005) considers that it is important to distinguish between task complexity (cognitive factors), task conditions (interactional factors) and task difficulty (learner factors). Interactive demands of the task involve two types of variables: participant (same/different gender; familiar/unfamiliar; power/solidarity) and participation (open/closed; one-way/two-way; convergent/divergent), while both affective and ability variables are included within learner factors. Task complexity is affected by processing demands, which are dependent on task characteristics, such as [+/− few elements]; [+/− here-and-now]; [+/− reasoning demands], included among resource directing dimensions; and [+/− planning], [+/− single task], and [+/− prior knowledge], among resource-dispersing dimensions.

Skehan (1998) also analyses task complexity in three areas: code complexity, cognitive complexity and communicative stress. The first one, code complexity, is determined by the complexity and variety of linguistic structures and vocabulary needed to successfully complete the task. The second area, cognitive complexity or manipulation of the task's content, is broken down into: (a) cognitive familiarity (including familiarity and predictability of topic, of discourse genre and of task), which is assumed to reduce the cognitive load of the task; and (b) cognitive processing, affected again by several factors, such as organisation, clarity and sufficiency, as well as type of task-relevant information provided to learner, and amount of computation or manipulation of information needed.

Several researchers (Bygate, 1998; Ellis, 1987; Foster & Skehan, 1996) investigated the effect of pre-task planning conditions on performance, the assumption being that pre-task planning would reduce the cognitive load of a task and result in improved performance. Interesting results were obtained by Ellis (1987), who observed that decreasing pre-task planning time results in less availability of on-line processing capacity, which results, in turn, in declined accuracy of (non-automatic) syntactic performance, but not so much of lexical performance.

A structured organisation of relevant information has been shown to ease the processing demands of a task. Skehan and Foster (1999) found that tasks with clear inherent structure yielded more fluent and accurate performance. No effect on complexity was observed.

Finally, several sources of communicative stress related to task conditions that could affect performance are identified. Time limits and time pressure on getting a task finished are assumed to make attention to form more difficult, increasing the likelihood of resorting to memory-based communication (Skehan, 1998). Modality or stakes, i.e. the perception of the importance of successful completion of a task, may direct learners' attention to accuracy. Iwashita *et al.* (2001), who used test-tasks to elicit data, ascribed the lack of consonance between their results and previous research to the fact that in testing contexts subjects focus primarily on accuracy regardless of other task-conditions.

In spite of the undeniable value of this approaches, some weaknesses have also been pointed out, such as the lack of a single measure of task performance or the general disregard of learner factors, setting or teacher's role (Ellis, 2000).

The Present Study

The present study investigates the influence of task-type on the frequency of application of lexical innovation strategies used by Spanish L2-learners of English in oral communication. The tasks used in the study as well as the different strategy types considered are assumed to vary in the degree of linguistic and cognitive demands imposed on the learner. The effect of proficiency level on the relationship between task and strategy type will also be assessed.

The study is motivated, in the first place, by the realisation that lexical innovation, in spite of being an important part of lexical development, has been shown to be an underused strategy type. However, the fact that learners are able to use it and create acceptable L2 items when 'forced' to do it (as in elicitation or particular kinds of tasks) suggests that this reported underuse may be partly due to their not being aware of its potential. Secondly, although several task features have been suggested to affect performance and CS use, contradictory results as to the effect of manipulating different task dimensions have been reported.

Accordingly, the main objective of the study is to find out if and which specific task-types and task-features have a significant impact on the use of lexical innovation strategies, especially of L2-based word coining. Pedagogically, the interest lies in the possibility of selecting and designing tasks which promote the appplication of lexical creativity, which can be implemented (1) to make learners aware of the potential positive effect of exploiting their knowledge of word structure on performance and acquisition, and (2) to give them the opportunity of putting this knowledge into practice and improving their command of L2 word-formation processes.

Hypotheses

Drawing on the preceding discussion and the findings of previous research, the following hypotheses were formulated:

- *Hypothesis 1*: The degree of lexical freedom and code complexity of a task will have an impact on the frequency of application of the different code strategies under consideration (i.e. word coining, foreignising and code-switching).
- *Hypothesis 2*: The relative frequency of application of the different strategy types will vary across tasks.

- *Hypothesis 3*: Task-related differences in the relative frequency of application of the different strategy types will vary as a function of proficiency level.

Method

Participants

A language placement test (Allan, 1992) was administered to 100 undergraduate students of L2 English at the University of Santiago de Compostela (Spain), with different proficiency levels in English. They were aged between 18 and 30. Their L1 was Spanish. Three level groups were established according to test results as follows: elementary (EL) (scores from 111 to 130), intermediate (INT) (from 131 to 150), and advanced (ADV) (from 151 to 170). Ten subjects with similar test results were selected from each level, rendering a total of 30 students taking part in the rest of the tasks.

Materials and procedures

The participants were asked to perform three different tasks which imposed different linguistic, communicative and cognitive demands, ranging from less naturalistic to more spontaneous and natural communication: picture description (T1), story-telling (T2) and interview (T3).

In the picture description task the participants had to locate some referents highlighted by the researcher in five different pictures depicting everyday scenes, so that another student who would later listen to their description could place them correctly in a similar picture. The interviewer gave the students the initial instructions and only asked questions when they failed to refer to any of the targets. It was predicted that subjects would be forced to refer to some entities which were suspected to be difficult even for the more advanced learners. It was hypothesised that this feature would direct their attention to the formal or linguistic aspects of the task and would increase the code complexity and communicative demands.

For the second task, story-telling, the participants were asked to tell a very well-known fairy tale, 'Cinderella'. A simple picture book was used to help them remember the story and make sure they would not leave out any detail. It also allowed the interviewer to ask some questions based on the pictures only when the subjects omitted or avoided referring to particular targets. Prior knowledge was assumed to reduce the cognitive, though not the linguistic, demands of the task.

Finally, a semi-structured interview of about 30 minutes was held between the researcher and each student individually. The cognitive complexity of this task as compared to the other two was assumed to lie in the time pressure of a dialogue condition and in the unpredictability of the questions, as well as in the fact that different skills (listening and speaking) are involved in this task to a higher extent than in the other two. On the other hand, there was more lexical freedom, since there were no elements to which the subjects had to refer obligatorily, which was assumed to reduce the linguistic complexity and referential demands of this task.[4]

Data selection, classification and analysis

The recorded material was transcribed and carefully analyzed in order to identify all the examples of lexical innovation. The main criterion used in the selection of examples was basically the non-existence of the form provided by the learner, since this was considered to be the best way to ensure that the student was making a creative use of a given word formation device, and not only repeating an unanalysed lexical unit. Examples of existing forms were included when there was evidence that the learner had spontaneously coined the word at the moment he was performing the task (*cf.* González-Álvarez, 2004).

An explanation of the kind of evidence to be included in this study seems in order, given the different kinds of data that have been gathered by researchers working on lexical innovation from different perspectives. I decided to concentrate on strategies classified under the main category of code strategies by Yule and Tarone (1997). Under the label 'lexical innovation' I included examples of what has been previously called foreignizing or L1-based word coining (L1WDC), since the bases 'manipulated' by learners are L1 lexical items, and 'morphological creativity' or L2-based word coining (L2WDC) because, formally, the lexical items used or 'manipulated' belong to the L2 lexicon. Code-switching (CDSW) was also considered within the category of L1-based code strategies for two reasons. Firstly, because, although not the product of creative construction of lexical items, it is somehow similar to non-adapted borrowings in natural languages. Another reason is the fact that some authors (Poulisse & Bongaerts, 1994) include within the category of code-switching both morpho-phonologically adapted and non-adapted L1 forms as examples of bilinguals' simultaneous activation of two languages.

Building on previous research, the three types were characterised in terms of the linguistic and cognitive demands imposed on the learner, as well as of comprehensibility, or communicative effectiveness. Therefore, as regards linguistic complexity and cognitive load, L2-based word coining was characterised as more demanding than foreignising, in turn more demanding than code-switching. In terms of communicative effectiveness, the same hierarchy was established, although, as it has been pointed out, the intrinsic effectiveness of a CS is also determined by contextual factors.

Results and Discussion

Effect of task type on relative frequency of lexical innovation

Lexical creativity has been associated with problematicity and low degree of lexical freedom (Ridley & Singleton, 1995), and with elicited more than with spontaneous communication (Pavesi, 1998). In the present study,

T1 (picture description) was characterised as more controlled than the other two tasks, since it required subjects to refer obligatorily to many 'difficult' referents, followed by T2 (story-telling), where the number and difficulty of elements of obligatory reference was reduced. Finally, T3 (interview) gave the subjects more freedom to choose both the contents and the linguistic expression.

In order to test H1, the mean frequency of application of lexical innovation CS (both L2-based word coining and L1-based foreignising) was calculated relative to the number of lexical problems experienced by the subject in each task. Code-switching and other solutions (including different instances of holistic – approximation and semantic contiguity – analytic, and reduction and interactive strategies) were also taken into account for the analysis. Table 10.1 shows the mean frequencies for each task and reveals that T1 yielded the highest mean frequency of L2-, L1-, and L2- plus L1-based lexical innovation. T2 displays a higher frequency than T3 as regards L2- and L2- plus L1-based lexical innovation. The lowest frequency of these two types is found in T3. ANOVA and post-hoc analyses revealed that differences in the mean frequency of L2- and L2- plus L1-based coining were significant only between T1 and T3 ($p = 0.026$ and $p = 0.049$, respectively).

In view of these results H1 is confirmed: more controlled and lexically difficult tasks favour the application of innovations as solutions to lexical

Table 10.1 Descriptive statistics for the percentage of communicative strategy types and other solutions relative to the total number of lexical problems per task

Task		L2WDC	L1WDC	L2WDC + L1WDC	CDSW	Code strategies (L2WDC + L1WDC + CDSW)	Other solutions
T1	Mean	18,20	5,73	23,93	2,93	26,87	73,27
	n	30	30	30	30	30	30
	s.d.	12,91	4,94	12,05	4,39	11,86	11,82
T2	Mean	13,93	3,63	17,57	2,33	19,90	80,20
	n	30	30	30	30	30	30
	s.d.	16,29	8,31	16,70	5,71	17,84	17,83
T3	Mean	6,70	5,43	12,13	10,03	22,17	71,10
	n	30	30	30	30	30	30
	s.d.	19,86	13,94	24,87	22,71	32,48	37,36
Sig.		0.029	0.669	0.054	0.060	0.475	0.338

L2WDC: L2-based word coining.
L1WDC: L1-based word coining (foreignising).
CDSW: code-switching.

problems to a higher extent than less controlled and more spontaneous tasks, which allow for reduction strategies, since learners could avoid referring to certain concepts. The reported results also suggest that the differences in degree of lexical freedom and control between T1 and T2, on the one hand, and T2 and T3, on the other, may be too small to yield significant results. The fact that T2 is placed in between, and almost equidistant from T1 and T3 reflects its intermediate position in terms of degree of difficulty and lexical freedom.

These results support previous findings on the acquisition of L2-word formation, where lexical innovation in spontaneous tasks was harder to find than in elicited tasks (Pavesi, 1998), and also those reflected in Ridley and Singleton (1995) and Singleton and Little (1991), who respectively reported that the number of lexical innovations was higher in story-telling than in interview tasks and that innovations were associated with problematicity and linguistic difficulty.

Task effect on the selection of L1- vs. L2-based processes

Table 10.2 shows the effect of task-type on the distribution of L1- and L2-related creations, and of foreignizing and code-switching within the first group. Percentages are here calculated relative to the total number of L2- and L1-based innovations and code-switching found in each task. Figure 10.1 features the distribution of L2- and L1-based word coining and code-switching across tasks:

Table 10.2 Descriptive statistics for percentage of L2-, L1-based word coining and code-switching relative to the total number of word coining and code-switching per task

Task		L2WDC	L1WDC	CDSW	L1 (WDC + CDSW)
T1	Mean	**63,86**	**24,89**	**11,04**	**36,14**
	n	30	30	30	30
	s.d.	28,29	19,88	17,22	28,29
T2	Mean	**68,28**	**19,88**	**11,83**	**31,72**
	n	21	21	21	21
	s.d.	42,09	34,41	25,49	42,09
T 3	Mean	**19,78**	**31,78**	**48,44**	**80,22**
	n	15	15	15	15
	s.d.	30,30	41,22	48,43	30,30
Sig.		0.00	0.520	0.00	0.00

L2WDC: L2-based word coining.
L1WDC: L1-based word coining (foreignising).
CDSW: code-switching.

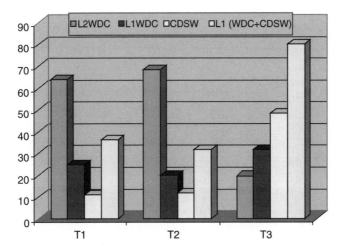

Figure 10.1 Distribution of L2-, L1-based word coining and code-switching across tasks

We can see that T2 presents the highest mean percentage of L2-based innovations, closely followed by T1. The figures for L2-based processes in T3 are the lowest, and, conversely, T3 stands out as regards L1-based strategies, especially code-switching. ANOVA tests confirmed that differences in L1 vs. L2 use were significant between T1 and T3 ($p = 0.000$), and between T2 and T3 ($p = 0.000$), but not between T1 and T2 ($p = 1.000$). No significant differences were found in the use of foreignising strategies across tasks, which was highest in T3, followed by T1, and T2 in this order. As for code-switching, T1 elicited the lowest percentage, followed by T2, followed in turn by T3; differences were significant between T1 and T3 ($p = 0.001$) and between T2 and T3 ($p = 0.001$).

H2 is thus confirmed, since these results demonstrate that task-type has an impact on the relative frequency of use of L2- vs. L1-based strategies, especially as regards code-switching within the latter category.

Comprehension of single items and identification of 'difficult' referents was more important in the picture description task (T1), and to some extent in the storytelling (T2), than in the conversation task (T3), described as the least demanding from a linguistic and referential point of view. This task feature allowed learners to rely on 'easier' or less demanding (L1-based) strategies in T3. Conversely, the need to be more specific in T1 and T2 contributed to the increase in learners' attention and care when choosing an expression, as it is reflected in the higher use of more demanding and communicatively effective L2-based word coining.

These data reveal a tendency opposite to that in Singleton and Little (1991), who observed that use of L1-based innovations increased with task difficulty, but confirm the results obtained by Poulisse (1993), who reported the highest frequency of transfer strategies in the interview task. They also agree with Robinson's (1995, 2005) claims regarding the effect of decontextualised task conditions on performance, since he found that the absence of supporting visual context, which required greater referential explicitness, resulted in greater lexical complexity and density and a strong trend towards accuracy. Poulisse's (1993) findings regarding learners' use of strategies which required a greater processing effort when it is important to get the message across are also supported. This kind of demands can likewise be related to Robinson's (2005) resource-directing dimensions of task complexity, since the subject's attention in T1 and T2 is directed to elements of the L2 system that can contribute to the successful completion of the task.

The significant differences in the mean frequency of L2-based strategies found between T1 and T3, and T2 and T3 can therefore be interpreted as confirming that increased linguistic complexity leads to a higher frequency of L2-based CS. However, this claim seems to be countered when we compare the results for the two monologic tasks and observe that, even though the differences were very small and not statistically significant, T2 – characterised as less referentially and linguistically demanding – elicited more L2-based word coining than T1. This apparent contradiction can be interpreted in two ways: either the linguistic difficulty of the two tasks is very similar, so they cannot be compared to test the effect of this dimension, or increasing complexity along this dimension does not have the suggested effect on CS use. However, since clear and significant differences were found between two unequivocally distinct tasks regarding code and referential complexity (T1 and T3), it could still be claimed that these results provide some support to Poulisse's (1993) findings and Robinson's (1995, 2005) claims as regards greater attention to linguistic features when the task demands high referential accuracy, but also to the increased use of more demanding CS when cognitive load is reduced by increased prior knowledge, as shown below.

The higher amount of interaction generated in T3 between the researcher and the learners was another factor which enabled the latter to use less demanding and intrinsically less comprehensible L1-based strategies, since they could get feedback from the interlocutor and check whether their utterances were sufficiently informative, using a more demanding strategy only if necessary (*cf.* Poulisse, 1997). Further support for this line of argumentation can be found in Robinson (2005), who found that syntactic complexity and accuracy were not significantly affected by task complexity, which was put down to the fact that 'this was an interactive task, in which partners made frequent use of comprehension checks [which] mitigated against the speaker, direction-givers' attempts at complex syntax' (Robinson, 2005: 14).

Grosjean (1998) has proposed that the states of activation of a bilingual's languages vary along a continuum from monolingual to bilingual mode, which is controlled by factors such as the interlocutor, among others. The fact that in the present study there was more interaction with the interviewer – who they knew was a native speaker of their L1 – in T3 than in the other two may have contributed to increasing their awareness of her presence and, thus, to a higher activation of the learners' L1 in this task.

The more 'relaxed' and informal character of T3 probably played a role in raising the learners' L1 level of activation. Likewise, the fact that the subjects had more freedom in their answers probably added to the perception that content was more important than linguistic accuracy (*cf.* Dewaele, 1998). On the contrary, the pressure of having to name many difficult referents in T1 and T2 probably added to the perception of these tasks as a kind of test by informants, who therefore devoted more attention to linguistic accuracy and avoided L1 use, which they might feel would be interpreted as a sign of lower L2 proficiency level. In this regard, Iwashita *et al.* (2001: 431) observed that 'a focus on accuracy may be paramount in the testing situation regardless of the conditions under which the task is performed, and this in turn may affect the fluency and complexity of candidates' speech'.

Time pressure, the fact that more than one skill was involved, and the unpredictability of the researcher's questions characterised T3 as more cognitively demanding than the other two. The unplanned nature and particular rhythm of the interview gave subjects less time to think about the linguistic expression, favouring a reduction in attention and effort devoted to the encoding process, and leading to an increased used of 'easier', L1-based strategies. In the other two tasks, where the subjects had more time for lexical retrieval, proportionally more L2-based strategies were applied. The significant differences in the use of L1 and L2-based strategies between T3 and T1, and between T3 and T2 support Skehan's (1998) claims about the appropriateness of exemplar-, memory-based communication when time pressure is high, and are also in accordance with Ellis' (1987) findings regarding the effect of reducing planning time on rule-based, non-automatic performance, but not so much on lexical performance. The tendency to favor code-switching over word coining in T3 also supports these claims, since very little processing demands are involved in accessing an L1 term, compared to those needed for non-automatic processes such as application of L2 derivational rules, which makes of code-switching a suitable strategy for time-pressing communicative situations where precision is not the main goal.

It could also be claimed that, to a certain extent, T1 was more cognitively demanding than T2, since it was a more unfamiliar kind of task, and required from subjects some cognitive computation to analyse and organise the pictures and select relevant referents for identification of targets. Telling a well-known story with a clear structure (the picture book even eliminated the effort of remembering the sequence of events) was thought to be the simplest task. And although differences were not significant between these two tasks, the higher use learners made of L1-based word coining in T1 would suggest that increasing the cognitive demands leads to an increased use of L1-based strategies.

Effect of proficiency level on task-related CS selection

In order to investigate the interaction between proficiency level and task-type on the selection of L1- vs. L2-based strategies, the relative frequency of innovations of each type was calculated across level groups and tasks, as shown in Table 10.3 and Figure 10.2.

We can see that the Elementary group uses proportionally more L1-based strategies in all the tasks, when foreignising and code-switching are considered together. However, when the three strategy types are considered separately, a higher mean frequency of L2-based word coining is revealed in T1, but not in the other two. The Intermediate and Advanced groups used more L2-based strategies in T1 and T2, but not in T3, where foreignising and code-switching were more frequent that L2-based innovations.

Although we can conclude that task type affects CS selection in the three level groups, task-related differences in the mean use of the three strategy types reveal that this variation is small in the Elementary group, but increases in the other two groups, where it is more clearly marked. It may be the case that below a certain level of proficiency, task-type does not have as much influence on CS selection as it has at higher levels.

Cross-group differences seem to be particularly marked in T2: whereas the Elementary group produced considerably more L1- than L2-based innovations (78% vs. 21.99%), the reverse tendency is observed in the Intermediate

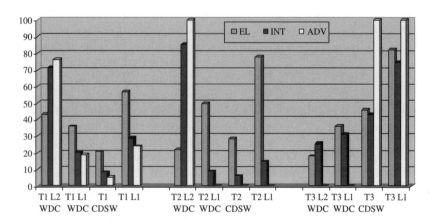

Figure 10.2 Relative frequency of the different strategy types across tasks and level groups

Table 10.3 Descriptive statistics for relative frequency of the different strategy types across tasks and level groups

	T1												T2												T3											
	L2 WDC			L1 WDC			CDSW			L1			L2 WDC			L1 WDC			CDSW			L1			L2 WDC			L1 WDC			CDSW			L1		
	Mean	s.d.	n	Mean	s.d.	n	Mean	s.d.	n	Mean	s.d.	n	Mean	s.d.	n	Mean	s.d.	n	Mean	s.d.	n	Mean	s.d.	n	Mean	s.d.	n	Mean	s.d.	n	Mean	s.d.	n	Mean	s.d.	n
EL	43,23	28,16	10	35,85	20,95	10	20,9	20,2	10	56,76	28,16	10	21,99	37,8	7	49,65	44,4	7	28,34	36,09	7	78	37,8	7	17,91	25,75	8	36,25	44,05	8	45,83	50,19	8	82,08	25,75	8
INT	71,24	22,52	10	20,32	16,07	10	8,42	16,3	10	28,75	22,52	10	85	22,67	8	8,75	18,07	8	6,25	17,67	8	15	22,67	8	25,55	38,96	6	31,11	42,51	6	43,33	49,66	6	74,44	38,96	6
ADV	75,89	24,19	10	19,1	19,57	10	5	11,24	10	24,10	24,19	10	100	0,00	6	0,00	0,00	6	0,00	0,00	6	0,00	0,00	6	0,00		1	0,00		1	100		1	100		1
Sig.	0.015			0.108			0.091			0.015			0.000			0.009			0.095			0.000			0.744			0.738			0.578			0.744		

and the Advanced groups, which produced L1-based innovations with a mean frequency of 15% and 0% respectively (differences were significant between Elementary and Intermediate ($p = 0.002$), and between Elementary and Advanced ($p = 0.002$) groups). As for T1, the three groups show the same tendency to increase the use of L2-based strategies, if results are compared with those for T3, although, again, the more limited resources of the Elementary group made them use a lower proportion of this type than the other groups (significant differences were found between Elementary and Intermediate and Elementary and Advanced groups). Finally, all the groups used more L1-based word coining and code-switching than L2-based innovations in T3, and no significant differences were found in this task as regards the use of the three strategy types.

The particular characteristics of each task, especially those related to the amount of detail needed, have been shown to influence the selection of particular strategy types. When performing tasks with inherent features that aid to the comprehension of the message, learners will not need to use very successful strategies in terms of comprehensibility. According to Poulisse (1997), the possibility of feedback from the interlocutor in interview tasks favours the use of L1-based strategies so much that proficiency related differences as regards their use almost disappear, because even advanced students take advantage of the possibility of using easier strategies. In T2, some of the factors (more relaxed character or less amount of detail needed than for T1) should lead students to use L1-based strategies. However, since it is nearer the monologue condition (with very little interlocutor's intervention) than T3, probably intermediate and advanced students still felt that they needed to expend extra effort in being clear, and as they had the resources, they used more L2-based strategies. Elementary students, however, because of their more limited resources, would take advantage of those task features that favor the use of L1-based strategies, opting for economy to the expense of clarity. It seems that CS choice is not only affected by task demands or features but also by the resources available to the learners; the ideal balance between clarity and economy is more easily reached by students with more resources. In fact, Poulisse (1997) remarks that learners are more likely to experience the 'imbalance' between the two principles than native speakers, who have more resources to find the most effective and economical means. We can conclude that the interaction between task features and learners' factors influences the selection of a particular strategy type, and, therefore, confirm H3.

Summary and Conclusions

The observed tendencies in our data suggest that more controlled and linguistically demanding tasks favour the creation of new terms, whereas less controlled tasks would allow subjects to use alternative mechanisms, such as reduction or avoidance strategies.

Task-related factors have also been shown to influence the selection of the different types of lexical innovation strategies, that is, L1- vs. L2-based, as defined in this study. The former were characterized as linguistically and cognitively less demanding, and the latter were assumed to be the most communicatively effective. Thus, tasks with high code complexity and referential demands, T1 and T2, elicited significantly more L2-based strategies than T3 in all level groups, since learners probably perceived the importance of accuracy and clarity. Low time pressure in these tasks also allowed subjects to select significantly more strategies with higher processing demands, such as those involving application of L2 word formation rules.

On the contrary, higher time pressure and lower referential demands in the interview task promoted the use of automatic processes, such as the selection of morphologically non-adapted L1 items. The more frequent intervention of the interlocutor in the conversation task similarly favored the introduction of L1-based strategies, since subjects could obtain feedback as to the comprehensibility of the message, and also raised the degree of activation of the learners' L1. Significant differences were found between T3 and the other two tasks. The strong influence of this particular factor in this task was confirmed by the fact that no proficiency-related differences were found here.

The tendency to increase the use of L2-based word coining in T2 compared with T1 was interpreted as suggesting that prior knowledge reduced the cognitive load of T2, allowing subjects to concentrate on formal aspects. Clear proficiency-related variation was observed in this task, since the Elementary group showed a strong preference for L1-based word coining followed by code-switching, whereas the Intermediate and Advanced groups overwhelmingly chose L2-based innovations. This variation was put down to the fact that T2 is placed in a middle position along the continua of [+/− referential and linguistic demands] and [+/− dialogue condition] which in turn influences its position along the bilingual-monolingual mode continuum.

Finding out if (and which) kinds of tasks and task features promote the application of lexical creativity could have interesting implications for pedagogy. If this ability is to be fostered and developed, it would be desirable to select tasks which 'force' learners to put this knowledge into practice, and push their capacities further.

The present study has shown that task-type has an influence on the selection and frequency of use of different strategy types. However, further research is required to determine unequivocally which task-features favour the use of L2-based lexical innovation, since the fact that the tasks in this study represented more than one dimension made it difficult on occassions to determine the origin of the observed task-related variation. Similarly, it would be desirable to investigate the extent to which increasing opportunity for using L2-based lexical innovation leads to correct acquisition of L2 word-formation processes, that is, to determine the relationship between CS use and acquisition of target features.

Acknowledgements

This research was supported by the Spanish Ministry of Science and Technology and the FEDER funds (BFF 2002-02441) and by the Galician government (Xunta de Galicia) (PGIDT03PXIC20403PN).

I would like to thank Juan C. Estevez for his valuable advice on the statistical analyses. Needless to say, the author is entirely responsible for any inaccurate interpretation of the data.

Notes

1. See Yule and Tarone (1997) for a general overview of the different approaches regarding CS taxonomisation, and Poulisse (1993) and Kellerman and Bialystok (1997) for a comparison between the Nijmejen two-strategy and Poulisse's three-strategy taxonomies. See also González-Álvarez (2005) for a review of the treatment of lexical innovation in SLA research.
2. A further distinction is established by some authors (Dörnyei & Kormos, 1998; Poulisse, 1993) between semantic word coinage, a conceptual strategy, and grammatical word coinage or derivation, a code or linguistic strategy. Kellerman and Bialystok (1997: 34) observe in this regard that 'some utterance tokens may well be the product of both conceptual and code strategies (...) And some utterances will be ambiguous'.
3. See Ellis (2000) for an overview of the different approaches in task-based research.
4. See González-Álvarez (2004) for a thorough description of the tasks and procedures.

References

Allan, D. (1992) *Oxford Placement Test*. Oxford: Oxford University Press.
Bauer, L. (1983) *English Word-Formation*. Cambridge: Cambridge University Press.
Bialystok, E. (1983) Some factors in the selection and implementation of communication strategies. In C. Faerch and G. Kasper (eds) *Strategies in Interlanguage Communication* (pp. 100–118). London: Longman.
Bialystok, E. (1990) *Communication Strategies. A Psychological Analysis of Second Language Use*. Oxford: Blackwell.
Broeder, P., Extra, G. and Van Hout, R. (1996) Word-formation processes in adult language acquisition: A multiple case study on Turkish and Moroccan learners of Dutch. In K. Sajavaara and C. Fairweather (eds) *Approaches to Second Language Acquisition* (pp. 15–24). Jyväskylä: University of Jyväskylä.
Bygate, M. (1998) Units of oral expression and language learning in small group interaction. *Applied Linguistics* 9, 59–52.
Clark, E.V. (1993) *The Lexicon in Acquisition*. Cambridge: Cambridge University Press.
Dewaele, J.-M. (1998) Lexical inventions: French interlanguage as L2 versus L3. *Applied Linguistics* 19 (4), 471–490.
Dörnyei, Z. and Kormos, J. (1998) Problem-solving mechanisms in L2 communication. A psycholinguistic perspective. *Studies in Second Language Acquisition* 20, 349–385.
Ellis, R. (1987) Interlanguage variability in narrative discourse: Style-shifting in the use of past tense. *Studies in Second Language Acquisition* 9, 12–20.
Ellis, R. (2000) Task-based research and language pedagogy. *Language Teaching Research* 4 (3), 193–220.

Foster, P. and Skehan, P. (1996) The influence of planning and task type on second language performance. *Studies in Second Language Acquisition* 18, 299–323.

González Álvarez, E. (1999). Análisis de los errores léxico-semánticos. In L. Iglesias Rábade (ed.) *Análisis de los Errores del Examen de Inglés en las Pruebas de Acceso a la Universidad en el Distrito Universitario de Galicia* (pp. 207–270). Santiago de Compostela: ICE-Universidade de Santiago de Compostela.

González Álvarez, E. (2004) *Interlanguage Lexical Innovation*. Munich: Lincom.

González-Álvarez, E. (2005) Lexical creativity in SLA research. In I. Moskowich-Spiegel and B. Crespo (eds) *Re-Interpretations of English. Essays on Language, Linguistics and Philology (II)* (pp. 203–225). A Coruña: Servicio de Publicacións da Universidade da Coruña.

Grosjean, F. (1998) Studying bilinguals: Methodological and conceptual issues. *Bilingualism: Language and Cognition* 1, 131–149.

Iwashita, N., McNamara, T. and Elder, C. (2001) Can we predict task difficulty in an oral proficiency test? Exploring the potential of an information-processing approach to task design. *Language Learning* 51 (3), 401–436.

Kellerman, E. and Bialystok, E. (1997) On psychological plausibility in the study of communication stratregies. In G. Kasper and E. Kellerman (eds) *Communication Strategies: Psycholinguistic and Sociolinguistic Perspectives* (pp. 31–48). London: Longman.

Levelt, W.J.M. (1989) *Speaking: From Intention To Articulation*. Cambridge, MA: MIT Press.

Pavesi, M. (1998) 'Same word, same idea.' Conversion as a word formation process. *International Review of Applied Linguistics* 36, 213–231.

Poulisse, N. (1987) Problems and solutions in the classification of compensatory strategies. *Second Language Research* 3, 141–153.

Poulisse, N. (1993) Theoretical account of lexical communication strategies. In R. Schreuder and B. Weltens (eds) *The Bilingual Lexicon* (pp. 157–191). Amsterdam: John Benjamins.

Poulisse, N. (1997) Compensatory strategies and the principles of clarity and economy. In G. Kasper and E. Kellerman (eds) *Communication Strategies. Psycholinguistic and Sociolinguistic Perspectives* (pp. 49–64). London: Longman.

Poulisse, N. and Bongaerts, T. (1994) First language use in second language production. *Applied Linguistics* 15 (1), 36–57.

Ridley, J. and Singleton, D. (1995) Strategic L2 lexical innovation: Case study of a university-level *ab-initio* learner of German. *Second Language Research* 11 (2), 137–148.

Robinson, P. (1994) Universals of word formation processes: Noun incorporation in the acquisition of Samoan as a second language. *Language Learning* 44, 569–615.

Robinson, P. (1995) Task complexity and second language narrative discourse. *Language Learning* 45, 99–140.

Robinson, P. (2001) *Cognition and Second Language Instruction*. Cambridge: Cambridge University Press.

Robinson, P. (2003) Attention and memory during SLA. In C. Doughty and M.H. Long (eds) *The Handbook of Second Language Acquisition* (pp. 631–678). Oxford: Blackwell.

Robinson, P. (2005) Cognitive complexity and task sequencing: Studies in a componential framework for second language task design. *International Review of Applied Linguistics* 43, 1–32.

Singleton, D. and Little, D. (1991) The second language lexicon: Some evidence from university-level learners of French and German. *Second Language Research* 7 (1), 61–81.

Skehan, P. (1998) *A Cognitive Approach to Language Learning*. Oxford: Oxford University Press.

Skehan, P. and Foster, P. (1999) The influence of task structure and processing conditions on narrative retellings. *Language Learning* 49 (1), 93–120.

Skehan, P. and Foster, P. (2001) Cognition and tasks. In P. Robinson (ed.) *Cognition and Second Language Instruction* (pp. 183–205). Cambridge: Cambridge University Press.

Yule, G. and Tarone, E. (1997) Investigating communication strategies in L2 reference: Pros and cons. In G. Kasper and E. Kellerman (eds) *Communication Strategies: Psycholinguistic and Sociolinguistic Perspectives* (pp. 17–30). London: Longman.

Chapter 11

Fostering EFL Learners' Awareness of Requesting Through Explicit and Implicit Consciousness-Raising Tasks

EVA ALCÓN SOLER

Introduction

Interlanguage pragmatic research has shown some differences regarding opportunities offered for learners' acquisition of pragmatic competence in second and foreign language contexts. According to Kasper (2001), the second language context offers rich exposure to the target language and opportunities to use it for real-life purposes. In contrast, learners in a foreign language learning environment lack opportunities to be engaged in everyday life interaction. Thus, as reported by Lörscher and Schulze (1988), the typical interaction patterns observed in foreign language contexts restrict opportunities to practise discourse organisation strategies. In addition, Rose (1999) claims that large classes, limited contact hours, and little opportunity for intercultural communication are some of the features of the English as a foreign language (EFL) context that hinder pragmatic learning. Bardovi-Harlig and Hartford (1993) and Nikula (2002) also illustrate how the input offered to learners in academic contexts may not result in pragmatic learning. On the one hand, Bardovi-Harlig and Hartford (1993) point out that the requests teachers made to students were status-bound, and as a consequence they could not serve as direct models for the learner. On the other hand, Nikula's (2002) study focuses on how pragmatic awareness is reflected in the use of modifying elements of speech by two non-native speakers (NNSs) in EFL and content-based classrooms. Findings of this study reveal a tendency towards directness in teachers' performance which is explained in terms of the constraints of the classroom and the teacher's status compared to that of students. Apart from the analysis of the input, other studies have examined whether textbooks present pragmatically accurate models for learners (Alcón & Safont, 2001; Bardovi-Harlig, 1996; Crandall & Basturkmen, 2004; Salazar & Usó, 2001; Vellenga, 2004). Results of these studies have shown that the way speech acts or conversational functions are considered in textbooks is not the most appropriate, since presenting a list of linguistic forms is highly unlikely to result in pragmatic learning.

As a consequence of the above-mentioned difficulties involved in dealing with pragmatic competence in foreign language learning contexts, the use of authentic audiovisual input and the role of instruction have received special attention in research on pragmatic development. As regards authentic audiovisual input, the use of video, films and TV has been reported as being useful to address knowledge of a pragmatic system and knowledge of its appropriate use. The studies conducted by Rose (1997), Rose and Ng Kwai-Fun (2001), Grant and Starks (2001) and Washburn (2001) were motivated by the assumption that both pragmalinguistic and sociopragmatic awareness are particularly difficult for those studying in an EFL context. From this perspective, the authors claim that authentic audiovisual input provides ample opportunities to address all aspects of language use in a variety of contexts. Besides, as reported by Rose (1997), audiovisual material first offers language teachers the possibility of choosing the richest and most suitable segments, analysing them in full and then designing software to allow learners to access pragmatic aspects as needed. Secondly, it may be useful to expose learners to the pragmatic aspects of the target language. Thirdly, pragmatic judgment tasks can be based on audiovisual discourse analysis and prepare learners for communication in new cultural settings. This last aspect takes into account the issue of task design and task implementation, which in turn is related to the role of instruction on pragmatic learning.

Research has shown that instruction positively affects acquisition when compared to exposure to the target language (Long, 1991; Doughty, 2001, 2003). Moreover, an analysis of what type of instruction is the most effective for language learning has also been addressed. From this perspective, and taking into account the differences between learning with or without awareness (Schmidt, 2001; Dekeyser, 2003) and drawing on Dekeyser's (2003) definition of explicit versus implicit learning, Norris and Ortega (2000) review the empirical research dealing with the effectiveness of instruction. Findings from this review point out that grammatical rules are better learned under explicit conditions. Similarly, focusing on pragmatics, the advantage of explicit teaching over the implicit approach is reported, among others, in House (1996), House and Kasper (1981) and Takahashi (2001). House and Kasper's (1981) study involved German EFL university students and focused on a variety of discourse markers and gambits. The authors designed two versions of the same communicative course, one explicit and one implicit, which provided learners with adequate input and opportunities to practise. However, learners in the explicit version of the course received metapragmatic information and participated in discussions related to their performance in the role plays. Results of the study indicate that an improvement took place in both groups but the explicit group had an advantage over the implicit one. Similar findings are reported in House (1996), since both the explicit and implicit group benefit from instruction focused on developing pragmatic fluency, but the explicit group used a greater variety of discourse markers and strategies. Focusing on requests, Takahashi (2001) also reported explicit instruction as being more effective. After examining the effect of four input enhancement conditions (explicit teaching, NS-learners request comparison, NS-NNS request comparison, and reading comprehension) on Japanese EFL learners' development of request strategies, the author reports that the explicit group outperformed the other three groups in the use of the four request strategies addressed in the study.

From the above mentioned studies, as well as taking into account Kasper's (2001) review of pragmatic instructional interventions, there seems to be an agreement on accepting that explicit instruction includes all types in which rules are explained to learners, whereas implicit instruction makes no overt reference to the rules. However, while bearing in mind Long's (1991) paradigms in instruction (i.e. focus on meaning, focus on forms and focus on form), Doughty (2003) suggests the need to further explore the relationship between the concept of explicit and implicit and the type of instruction adopted. In the pragmatic realm, Bardovi-Harlig (2001) provides evidence that a non-interventionist, or focus on meaning, approach is insufficient to develop learners' pragmatic competence. Regarding the other two interventionist approaches, most of the studies dealing with the effect of pragmatic instruction have adopted a focus on forms paradigm. Among many others, Takashahi (2001), Tateyama (2001) and Safont (2005) are examples of studies where the pragmatic features are presented, explained, discussed and, in some cases, finally practised. Paying attention to the focus on form paradigm, some recent studies have tried to illustrate how this instructional approach can be operationalised in the interventional research on pragmatic learning by adopting a pro-active focus on form (Alcón, 2005; Fukuya & Clark, 2001; Fukuya *et al.*, 1998; Martínez-Flor, 2004). On the one hand, Fukuya *et al.* (1998) implemented recasts as implicit feedback on learners' production of requests. The authors employed an interaction enhancement technique consisting of showing a sad face to indicate a sociopragmatic error followed by repetition of the student's inappropriate utterance with rising intonation. Results of the study did not support the hypothesis that implicit feedback would be efficient in comparison to the explicit group that received explicit instruction on the sociopragmatic factors affecting appropriateness of requests in different situations. On the other hand, Fukuya and Clark (2001) and Martínez Flor (2004) used input enhancement techniques to draw learners' attention to the target features. In Fukuya and Clark's study, learners of English as a second language (ESL) were randomly assigned to one of the three groups: focus on forms, focus on form, and a control group. While learners in the focus on forms group were provided with explicit instruction on the socio-pragmatic features affecting mitigation in requests, typographical enhancement of the mitigators appeared in the version presented to the focus on form group. Findings from the three groups' performance did not reveal any significant differences in learners' pragmatic ability. From a similar perspective, Martínez-Flor (2004) used a combination of implicit techniques to analyse the effect of explicit and implicit treatments on the speech act of suggesting. Results of her study showed that both implicit (operationalised by the combination of input enhancement and recasts) and explicit (teachers' explanation of suggestions) instructional groups outperformed the control group in awareness and production of the speech act of suggesting. Moreover, there were no significant differences in learners' pragmatic ability in the implicit and explicit treatment conditions. Similar to the results reported by Martínez-Flor (2004), Alcón's (2005) study showed an advantage of explicitly and implicitly instructed learners over uninstructed ones in their awareness and production of requests. However, the author points out the need to consider the delayed effect of explicit and implicit teaching approaches on pragmatic learning in future research.

Based on the positive effects of pragmatic instructional interventions and the debate over the operationalisation of explicit and implicit teaching, our study analyses the effect of explicit and implicit consciousness-raising tasks in focus on forms versus focus on form instruction. From this perspective, the present investigation provides empirical evidence on the effectiveness of consciousness-raising tasks for pragmatic learning. Additionally, it attempts to shed light on the way explicit and implicit teaching techniques benefit the development of learners' pragmatic awareness. Thus, the study aims to answer the following two research questions:

(1) Are consciousness-raising tasks effective in increasing learners' noticing of requesting?
(2) Do learners benefit from explicit and implicit instruction on requests? And, if so, are learners' gains in awareness at the level of noticing and understanding sustained after the instructional period?

Considering the above research questions, the empirical evidence on the pragmatic teachability hypothesis (Kasper, 2001), and the results of the effect of implicit versus explicit techniques on pragmatic learning (Alcón, 2005; Fukuya & Clark, 2001; Fukuya *et al.*, 1998; Martínez-Flor, 2004), we formulated the following hypotheses:

Hypothesis 1: Both explicit and implicit consciousness-raising tasks will draw learners' attention towards requests. As a consequence, learners' noticing in both the explicit and implicit group will be higher in the post-test than in the pre-test, but this will not be the case for the control group.

Hypothesis 2: There will be significant differences between the two treatment groups (explicit and implicit) in their pragmatic awareness of requests.

Research Design

Subjects

The study involved 132 students, all between 17 and 18 years of age, who were in the last year of their secondary education in a state high school in Spain. The 95 females and 37 males taking part in the study had studied English between seven and 10 years, and did not differ with regard to student ethnicity or academic background. Three groups of 44 students whose level of proficiency, as measured by the school level placement test, was not statistically significant were randomly formed.[1] One group (explicit group) was provided with focus on forms instruction based on the use of explicit consciousness-raising tasks on requests, and provision of metapragmatic feedback. Another group (implicit group) received focus on form instruction by means of input enhancement on pragmalinguistic and sociopragmatic factors involved in requesting, and made use of implicit consciousness-raising tasks. The third group, the control group, did not receive any instruction on the use of requests. Two English language teachers also participated in the study. While teacher A met the three groups two hours a week for 15 weeks, teacher B developed research tasks and observed the lessons in order to indicate, should it happen, any bias shown by teacher A for or against any of the groups. Both teachers scored the pre-test and post-test individually and reached an agreement on the grades of the tests.

Procedure and material

The three groups were exposed to excerpts taken from different episodes of the series *Stargate* throughout 15 self-study lessons. The aim of the self-study lessons in the two treatment groups was to make students aware of the sociopragmatic and pragmalinguistic aspects involved in making requests, while in the control group the focus was on comprehension and production of the English language. The structure of the self-study lessons that constitute the data of our study was as follows:

Lesson 1: After watching the whole episode, students were exposed to a film excerpt with a focus on requests. The excerpts included direct requests, conventionally indirect and nonconventionally indirect requests (Blum-Kulka, 1987). The students were then provided with a scripted version of the episode and were asked to identify the phrases used to ask people to do something, as well as being asked why they thought particular linguistic

formulas were used. The aim of this task was to measure learners' awareness and metapragmatic awareness of requests in a pre-test.

Lessons 2 to 14: During these weeks the control group did not receive
any instruction on the use of requests. Presentation of the video was followed by comprehension questions and self-correction of them. In contrast,
the two treatment groups (explicit and implicit) received two different
types of instruction, accompanied by specific tasks focussed on awareness
and production of requests in different situations. Instruction was in
English, but tasks were translated into Spanish when students had some
trouble with task performance. The instructional treatment focused on the
following expressions: Use of *imperative*, *I want + infinitive*, and *will
you + infinitive* for direct requests; *can/could + subject + infinitive?*, *I'd
like + infinitive*, *would you mind if I ... ?*, and mitigated want statements *If you
could + infinitive* for conventionally indirect requests; and finally statements
which could be understood as requests only by considering the situational
context were used to focus on non-conventionally indirect requests (see
Example D in Appendix 11.A for the use of non-conventionally indirect
requests). The instructional treatment was conducted as follows:

Instructional treatment for the explicit group

This instructional treatment adopted a sequential method consisting of
the following material: (a) the presentation of the selected excerpts from the
series *Stargate*; (b) the scripted versions of the excerpts; (c) a set of explicit
consciousness-raising tasks; and (d) request production tasks elaborated on
the basis of the type of requests presented in the video (see Appendix 11.A).
Finally, the answers to the tasks, together with written metapragmatic
explanations on the use of requests, were given for learners' self-correction.

Instructional treatment for the implicit group

The treatment for the implicit group consisted in a parallel method to that
of the explicit group. The same extracts from the series *Stargate* that were presented to the explicit group were also employed for the implicit treatment.
However, the request strategies appeared in bold on the scripts. In addition,
the sociopragmatic factors involved in each except appeared in capital letters
and in bold. Regarding the tasks, students were provided with a set of
implicit consciousness-raising tasks and request production tasks elaborated
on the basis of the type of request presented in the video (see Appendix 11.B).
Finally, the possible range of answers was handed out for learners' self-
correction, but written metapragmatic explanations were not provided.

Lesson 15: At the end of the instructional period, and similar to the pre-
test, participants were asked to identify the requests formulae from the film
excerpts as well as to explain why a particular type of language was used.
This task was employed to measure individual achievement on request
awareness in a post-test and in a delayed post-test administered three
weeks after finishing the instructional treatments (see Appendix 11.C).

Operationalisation of awareness

Although in cognitive psychology awareness is usually linked to the ability to verbally report a subjective experience (Leow, 1997; Schmidt, 2001; Tomlin & Vila, 1994), most second language acquisition (SLA) studies dealing with the role of instructional techniques to draw learners' attention to formal aspects of the input, assess what is attended to by means of post-exposure tasks (Fotos, 1993; Leow, 1997, 2000). In line with these studies, students' post-tests were coded taking into account the following levels of awareness defined by Schmidt (1993):

(a) Awareness at the level of *noticing*, which was operationalised as an adequate identification of the request strategy without any mention of the rules.
(b) Awareness at the level of *understanding*, which was operationalised as an explicit formulation explaining the contextual factors that triggered specific request realisation strategies.

Results and Discussion

The effect of consciousness-raising tasks on developing learners' pragmatic awareness of requests was measured first by analysing learners' identification of requests in the post-test. We were interested in comparing the three groups (explicit, implicit and control) simultaneously to see if there were any meaningful differences among them. Thus, we applied the one-way ANOVA statistical test. As illustrated in Table 11.1, the amount of variability between groups (SS between = 859.879) is greater than the amount of variability within the groups (SS within = 93.364), which indicates that there is some difference in the groups. Moreover, the F ratio (with two degrees of freedom) is larger than the observed value of F (202.009), which indicates that significant group differences were found with regard to identification of requests at a probability level of 0.000 ($p < 0.001$).

However, can the difference in the post-test be linked to instruction? In order to answer this question we need to examine hypothesis 1 which concerned the effect of instruction by means of consciousness-raising tasks on learners' noticing of requests. Hypothesis 1 claimed that both explicit and implicit consciousness-raising tasks would improve learners' identification

Table 11.1 ANOVA for learners' identification of requests in the post-test

	SS	*df*	*MS*	*F*	*p*
Between	859.879	2	429.939	594.045	0.000
Within	93.364	129	0.724		
Total	953.242	131			

of requests in the post-test as compared to of the pre-test, but this would not be the case in the control group. Thus, we compared the pre-test and the post-test to ascertain whether instruction had been effective. In order to account for statistical differences in test performance, we chose a matched *t*-test, as we were interested in the performance of one group on two different measures, that is, before and after the instructional period. This parametric statistical procedure allows us to see how significant the difference in noticing request strategies was in the two moments selected.

As shown in Table 11.2, *t*-test analysis of results did not report any statistical difference in the control group before and after the instructional period. However, there were differences in the treatment groups. The *t* value ($t = -23.934$) denotes statistically significant differences that point to $p = 0.000$ probability level for the explicit group. Likewise, the *t* value ($t = -38.529$) and the probability level ($p = 0.000$) also denote statistically significant differences for the implicit group in noticing request realisation strategies at the beginning and end of the instructional period. Although both explicit and implicit instruction improved learners' identification of requests in the post-test as compared to the pre-test, we were also interested in investigating whether the use of explicit and implicit consciousness-raising tasks in focus on forms versus a focus on form instruction had had an effect on subjects' noticing the speech act of requesting at various levels of directness. Thus, we considered the total number of direct (*Infinitive, I want + infinitive, will you + infinitive*), conventionally indirect (*Can/Could + subject + infinitive?, I'd like + infinitive, would you mind if I . . . ?, If you could + infinitive*) and non-conventionally indirect request strategies (hints and contextually blended requests) identified by learners in the *Stargate* episode used in the post-test. The difference in frequency in the three groups was analysed using a chi-square test. Statistical analysis revealed that the difference in the total number of adequate identifications of direct request strategies made by learners in the explicit, implicit and control groups was statistically significant ($\chi^2 = 50.65$; $df = 6$; $p = 0.000$). In relation

Table 11.2 Learners' differences in noticing request realisation strategies at the beginning and end of the instructional period

Group	*Test*	*M*	*s.d.*	*t*	*Sig*
Explicit	Pre-test awareness	2.4	0.8748	−23.934	0.000
	Post-test awareness	7.8	1.0475		
Implicit	Pre-test awareness	2.7	0.7649	−38.529	0.000
	Post-test awareness	7.5	0.6583		
Control	Pre-test awareness	2.5	0.6973	1.654	0.105
	Post-test awareness	2.3	0.8004		

to the identification of conventionally indirect requests, statistical analysis revealed that there was an overall significant difference between the total number of adequate identifications between the groups ($\chi^2 = 54.76$; $df = 4$; $p = 0.000$). Finally, the difference in the number of expected interpretations of non-conventionally indirect requests was not significant between the three groups ($\chi^2 = 13,66$; $df = 3$; $p = 0.135$).

Chi-square analysis of results seems to indicate that instruction needs to consider the level of directness as a variable. It seems that while instruction, through explicit and implicit consciousness-raising tasks, has a positive effect on learners' noticing direct and conventionally indirect request strategies, the identification of non-conventionally indirect requests is a bigger problem for both explicitly and implicitly instructed learners. Following Cook and Liddicoat (2002), this finding can be explained from a language processing perspective. In the case of direct and conventionally indirect requests, learners can rely on their linguistic knowledge to identify the request strategies. Nevertheless, as the level of indirectness increases, it seems to demand sufficient processing capacity to activate both linguistic and contextual knowledge. In this sense, it is possible that through instruction, utterances such as *I want + infinitive, will you + infinitive, can/could + subject + infinitive? I'd like + infinitive, would you mind if I ... ?* have become automatic to allow processing capacity to focus on additional contextual information. In contrast, in the case of non-conventionally indirect strategies, where the speaker's request is not made explicit in the utterance, either by using a direct or conventionally indirect request, learners can not rely on pragmalinguistic conventions, and they seem to have problems in decoding the expected meaning of the utterance.

Moreover, Figure 11.1 also shows that learners' sociopragmatic awareness on request realisation strategies increased after having received focus on forms (explicit group) and focus on form (implicit group) instruction. However, and in contrast to the two instructional groups, learners in the control group do not show an increase in sociopragmatic awareness in requesting. In fact, the number of reasons provided by the control group is lower than in the pre-test.

The following examples, which accompany this extract from the *Stargate* series, illustrate the reasons given by students in the explicit, implicit, and control group to explain why the requests in italics, previously identified by learners, were used:

TEALC: For whom do you pledge this remembrance?
ALAR: My father. Through his vision, our nation has survived.
TEALC: I see
ALAR: It is custom among our people to formalize new alliances such as ours. In exchange for all of our knowledge, technologies,

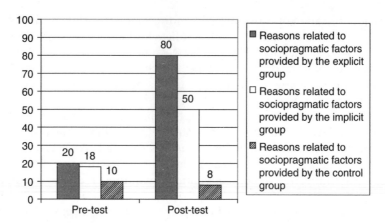

Figure 11.1 Learners' awareness of sociopragmatic factors affecting requests

medicines ... Earth will provide us with however much 'Heavy Water' as we require to end this war once and for all. *Do not be alarmed*; Colonel, merely three or four times what you have just provided, on a daily basis.

CARTER:	That adds up to several metric tons a year, sir.
ALAR:	A small price to pay for what we offer in return.
FARRELL:	Alar. *Listen*
ONEILL:	What?
ALAR:	*Silence*. I hardly recognize it.
ALAR:	When at full strength ... our defence field makes us as invulnerable as when I was a boy. I propose that we write into words what we already share in our hearts.
DANIEL:	Um, before we do that, *would you mind if I ask a question*.
ALAR:	It's all right ...

Students' explanation in the explicit group:
'Imperatives are used to ask people to do things (listen, silence), and the expression would you mind indicates that Alar is superior to Daniel. He wants to be polite. Other expressions could be used, for example: "I'd like to stay, if you don't mind."'

Students' explanation in the implicit group:
'Different expressions are used in the situation where the Colonel and his friends talk: "Listen", "do not be alarmed", 'would you mind if I ask a question...."'

Students' explanation in the control group:
'They wanted to know how the war started and are discussing and negotiating the end of the war.'

The above examples illustrate the way the explicit group outperformed
the implicit one in the number of reasons related to sociopragmatic factors.
While both the explicit and implicit groups show an increase in pragmalinguistic awareness, only explicit instructional learners seem to be aware
of the influence of variables such as interlocutor social distance or degree
of imposition on the use of specific request strategies. This result is in line
with the findings reported in Rose and Ng Kwai-fun (2001), who compared
the use of inductive and deductive approaches to the teaching of compliments and compliment responses to university learners of English in Hong
Kong. Similar to our study, a deductive and inductive approach proved
effective as far as pragmalinguistics is concerned. However, the deductive
approach involving metapragmatic discussion proved to be more effective
in developing learners' sociopragmatic competence.

To sum up the findings related to Hypothesis 1, we can claim that our
results indicate that consciousness-raising tasks may be effective for
increasing learners' noticing of requesting. In line with previous research
on the positive effect of instruction on learners' development of pragmatics
(Morrow, 1995; Olshtain & Cohen, 1990; Safont, 2005), our work seems to
confirm previous studies that show that pragmalinguistic features can be
taught through consciousness-raising activities (Billmyer, 1990; Clennell,
1999; House, 1996). Additionally, the use of both explicit and implicit
consciousness-raising tasks proved to be effective in improving learners'
noticing of pragmatically appropriate requests after the instructional
period. In this sense, our data support Schmidt's (1993, 2001) noticing
hypothesis, since learners in the instructional treatment groups, in contrast
to the control group, need to pay attention to relevant forms, to their pragmalinguistic functions and, albeit to a lesser extent, to the sociopragmatic
constraints these particular forms involve in requesting. It seems, therefore,
that Doughty's (2001) micro-processes, which potentially contribute to
learning, selective attention and cognitive comparison can be activated in
focus on forms and focus on form instruction, through explicit and implicit
pragmatic consciousness-raising tasks. However, as far as sociopragmatics
is concerned, a focus on forms approach seems to be more effective than the
focus on form type of instruction, which was conceptualised in this study
by using input enhancement techniques (request strategies in bold and
written self-correction answers with no metapragmatic information).

Hypothesis 2 concerned the effectiveness of the two types of instructional treatments employed in the study. In order to analyse which type of
instruction on requests proved more effective (explicit versus implicit), we
compared the post-test identification of request strategies in the explicit and

Table 11.3 Learners' gains in noticing in the explicit and implicit groups

Test	Group	n	M	T	Sig
Post-test awareness	Explicit	44	7.84	1.462	0.147
	Implicit	44	7.59		

implicit group (see Table 11.3). As we were dealing with the effect of two types of instruction on one independent variable (learners' noticing of requesting in the post-test), we applied the *t*-test for independent sample data as our statistical procedure. As shown in Table 11.3, there was almost no difference in the students' mean scores in the post-test. Participants in the explicit treatment condition had a mean of 7.9 (s.d. = 1.04) in noticing requests, while participants in the implicit treatment group had a mean of 7.5 (s.d. = 0.65). A *t*-test analysis of the differences between means yielded a *t* of 1.462. When we compared the *t* value with the critical value for the *t*-test (with 86 *df*), no significant difference between learners' gain in noticing in the explicit and implicit groups was found.

Our findings do not seem to confirm previous research on the advantage of explicit over implicit teaching of pragmatics (House, 1996; House & Kasper, 1981; Safont, 2005; Takahashi, 2001; among others). On the contrary, and in line with Fukuya *et al.* (1998) and Martínez-Flor (2004), our study indicates that the use of explicit and implicit consciousness-raising tasks in focus on form and focus on forms instruction helps learners notice specific request realisation strategies, and as a result may have promoted learning. However, further analysis was carried out in order to ascertain if learners' gains in noticing of request strategies were sustained in time. Thus, following the instructional period adopted in the study, three weeks after finishing the instructional treatment a delayed post-test was administered. Students were asked to identify the request formulae from a *Stargate* episode and to provide an explanation of why this type of language was used (see Appendix 11.C). Taking into account Schmidt's (1993) position on two levels of awareness, that is awareness at the level of noticing (referring to the target forms without mentioning any rules) and awareness at the level of understanding (referring to the explicit formulation of rules), learners' adequate identification of request strategies was used to measure two types of gains. On the one hand, we examined learners' gains in awareness at the level of noticing (see Table 11.4) and, on the other hand, learners' adequate explanations of the type of language use were understood as a sign of gains in awareness at the level of understanding (see Table 11.5). As shown in Tables 11.4 and 11.5, *t*-test analyses were performed to determine whether there were any statistically significant differences between explicit and implicit learners' noticing and understanding in the delayed post-test. Results of the *t*-test indicate that there is a significant difference between

Table 11.4 Learners' delayed gains in noticing in the explicit and implicit groups

Test	Group	n	M	T	Sig
Delayed post-test in noticing	Explicit	44	7.72	7.018	0.000
	Implicit	44	6.31		

Table 11.5 Learners' delayed gains in understanding in the explicit and implicit groups

Test	Group	n	M	T	Sig
Delayed post-test in understanding	Explicit	44	3.77	13.035	0.000
	Implicit	44	1.25		

learners' gains both in noticing and understanding requests in the delayed post-test.

To sum up, results related to Hypothesis 2 were partially confirmed. On the one hand, following Schmidt's (1993) concepts of noticing and focus on form in relation to processing pragmatic input, the study supports the idea that instruction can explicitly and implicitly help learners to focus on pragmatic aspects and to notice them. More specifically, it appears that instruction (through the use of explicit and implicit consciousness-raising tasks) and feedback (metapragmatic explanations and positive feedback) are effective for noticing requests in contexts. However, whether that knowledge of requests is retained over time is more questionable for implicitly instructed learners. Results of our study seem to indicate that the effects of explicit instruction are sustained in time more than the effects of implicit instruction at both levels of awareness: noticing and understanding. However, care should be taken not to misinterpret the results of this study, since it is possible that even awareness at the level of understanding may be insufficient to gain absolute proficiency at the pragmatic level. Additionally, in our research we have aimed to provide evidence on the way explicit and implicit teaching techniques benefit learners' pragmatic awareness of requests, but the way explicit and implicit instruction influence learners' production is an area which requires further examination. As suggested by Koike and Pearson (2005), it is possible that explicit and implicit instruction and feedback contribute in different ways to pragmatic awareness and production of selected target forms.

General Discussion and Conclusion

Our investigation contributes to previous research on the positive effect of instruction on second and foreign language learning (Doughty, 2003;

Norris & Ortega, 2000). More specifically, it aimed to examine the benefits of instruction through explicit and implicit consciousness-raising tasks on EFL learners' gains in pragmatic awareness of requests. Results of the study support the positive effects of instruction in interlanguage pragmatics (Bouton, 1994; House, 1996; Rose & Ng Kwai-fun, 2001). Likewise, the present investigation confirms the advantage of explicit instruction by reporting the positive delayed effect of explicit consciousness-raising tasks on learners' awareness of requests at both the noticing and understanding levels. These findings can be explained from a cognitive perspective and may provide pedagogical implications for teaching pragmatics in foreign language contexts.

From a cognitive perspective, our study is based on one of the tenets of SLA theory that claims that attention to input determines intake. Drawing on Schmidt's (1993) theoretical framework, which points out the need to implement pedagogical intervention on pragmatic issues, the results of our study address Schmidt's (1993) noticing hypothesis, where it is claimed that learners' noticing of the target features is a requirement for further second language development. Thus, in the present study, learners' gains in the instructional treatment groups, in contrast to the control group, can be explained by the effect of instruction on drawing learners' attention to request strategies, which resulted in learners' noticing the direct and conventionally indirect request strategies. As previously mentioned, while learners in the control group are exposed to input on requesting, learners in the explicit and implicit treatment groups need to pay attention to relevant forms, to their pragmalinguistic functions, and to the sociopragmatic constraints these particular forms involve in requesting. It seems, therefore, that Doughty's (2001) micro-processes, which potentially contribute to learning, selective attention and cognitive comparison, are activated in our study through both direct and indirect pragmatic consciousness-raising tasks.

Findings of the study also shed light on the debate regarding the possibility of learning without awareness, often conceptualised in terms of explicit and implicit learning. In our study, we have followed DeCoo (1996), who points out that the differences between explicit and implicit instruction or deductive and inductive learning are to be understood as part of a continuum rather than as opposite terms. From this perspective, in this paper, learners in the explicit learning conditions are instructed to look for rules of language use, while in the implicit learning group conditions for learning are created through manipulation of the linguistic input. Moreover, following Izumi's (2002) suggestion of using a combination of implicit techniques to help learners notice the target features, input enhancement of pragmalinguistic and sociopragmatic factors are used together with positive feedback to help implicitly instructed learners to pay attention to pragmatic features of the language. Bearing in mind the way explicit and implicit learning has been operationalised in the present study, the lack of significant differences in noticing request strategies between explicitly and implicitly instructed learners seem to confirm previous research reporting that implicit learning by means of manipulation of input enhancement techniques and feedback contributes to paying more attention to the grammatical (Robinson, 1997) and pragmatic (Alcón, 2005; Martínez-Flor, 2004) features of the target language. Furthermore, results of the study also confirm previous research which shows that higher levels of awareness are assured by manipulating input, even in implicit input conditions (Rosa & O'Neill, 1999). However, the superior delayed effect of explicitly instructed learners on pragmatic awareness of requests (both at the level of noticing and understanding) may suggest that awareness of target pragmatic features without an explicit formulation of their rules is not sufficient to learn them (see also Rose & Ng Kwai-fun, 2001). Thus, it could be claimed that it was explicit rule presentation and metapragmatic feedback rather than manipulation of input and positive feedback that created a difference in the delayed effect of the instructional treatments. In this line, it could be hypothesised that implicit and explicit teaching techniques may create opportunities for noticing pragmatic issues and this may influence intake, that is to say the initial stage of acquisition. However, as shown by the results of the delayed post-test, explicit instruction may trigger higher levels of awareness necessary for learning to take place.

In relation to the pedagogical insights which are likely to be drawn from this research, it should be pointed out that, in line with SLA research, the focus of this study is not to transform results into pedagogical ideas. Nevertheless, some implications can be drawn. Firstly, planned pedagogical action seems likely to be implemented in the foreign language context by providing learners with authentic audiovisual input, opportunities to become aware of language use and feedback about language norms in particular settings. Due to the pitfalls involved in the presentation of pragmatic issues in the textbooks (Alcón & Safont, 2001; Boxer & Pickering, 1995; Vellenga, 2004), more reliable data can be obtained from authentic audiovisual input, and awareness and comprehension of different pragmatic meanings can be achieved by drawing attention to the linguistic forms and the sociopragmatic variables of selected speech events. However, although this approach will provide opportunities to develop an understanding of target pragmatic issues, care should be taken to urge learners to adopt the sociocultural norms as one's own. We believe it is necessary to inform learners about the social function of requests and the significance of different degrees of indirectness, but the language learner is entitled to consciously choose a divergent pragmatic system. As reported by Bardovi-Harlig (2001), adopting a sociocultural norm as one's own is an individual decision, which could be a possibility only when the pedagogical decision of providing information about the culture and the way is expressed through language has already been taken. Secondly, the use of consciousness-raising tasks or input enhancement techniques, which in the past have proved effective for developing learners' linguistic competence, present new challenges for those who need to acquire pragmatic competence in a target language. This seems particularly relevant in foreign language contexts, where the lack of naturally occurring input and direct or indirect feedback on pragmatic issues make the task of pragmatic language learning especially difficult. Thirdly, although the present study does not focus on EFL teachers' pragmatic awareness, it is worth pointing out that understanding the nature of interlanguage pragmatics may have implications for language teaching. Karatepe's (2001) study on Turkish EFL teachers' awareness and production of indirect requests is an example which illustrates non-native speakers' difficulty in assessing the contextual factors affecting the speech act of requesting. Thus, we believe that the literature focused on raising teachers' language awareness (see Trappes-Lomax & Ferguson, 2002) should include pragmalinguistic and sociopragmatic issues as a way to increase language awareness in teacher education. Similarly, the theoretical conditions for pragmatic learning and the research on ILP development should be incorporated into teacher training programmes (see also Bardovi-Harlig, 1992; Martínez-Flor, 2003).

Finally, further research needs to be conducted to investigate some limitations of the present study. Among these, in this investigation we have focused on the operationalisation of the implicit and explicit teaching of requests using direct and indirect consciousness-raising tasks; however different teaching approaches need to be operationalised and implemented taking into account particular educational contexts. Likewise, the study reports indirect evidence of the role played by attention and awareness on pragmatic language learning, but more direct assessment of attention and awareness (by using think-aloud protocols, for instance) should be included in further research so as to be able to make claims regarding learners' internal processes. Moreover, since the effect of different instructional treatments may vary depending on learners' individual variables, in line with Takahashi (2005), it would be wise to conduct further studies that examine the extent to which pragmatic awareness is related to such individual variables.

Acknowledgements

This paper is a part of a research project funded by (a) the Spanish *Ministerio de Educación y Ciencia* (HUM2004-04435/FILO), co-funded by FEDER, and (b) *Fundació Universitat Jaume I* and *Caixa Castelló-Bancaixa* (P1.1B2004-34). I would like to thank Alicia Martínez-Flor for her suggestions on an earlier version of this paper and Teresa Mora for her advice on the statistical analyses.

Notes

1. By using a one-way ANOVA statistical test, we examined the differences between the means obtained in the placement level test in the three groups. Results of the analysis allowed us to consider that the three groups did not differ with regard to their level of English language.

References

Alcón, E. (2005) Does instruction work for learning pragmatics in the EFL context? *System* 33 (3), 417–436.

Alcón, E. and Safont, P. (2001) Occurrence of exhortative speech acts in ELT materials and natural speech data: A focus on request, suggestion and advice realization strategies. *Studies in English Language and Linguistics* 3, 5–22.

Bardovi-Harlig, K. (1992) Pragmatics as a part of teacher education. *TESOL Journal* 1 (3), 28–32.

Bardovi-Harlig, K. (1996) Pragmatics and language teaching: Bringing pragmatics and pedagogy together. In L.F. Bouton (ed.) *Pragmatics and Language Learning* (vol. 7) (pp. 21–39). Urbana, IL: University of Illinois at Urbana-Champaign.

Bardovi-Harlig, K. (2001) Empirical evidence on the need of instruction in pragmatics. In K.R. Rose and G. Kasper (eds) *Pragmatics in Language Teaching* (pp. 13–32). Cambridge: Cambridge University Press.

Bardovi-Harlig, K. and Hartford, B.S. (1993) Learning the rules of academic talk: A longitudinal study of pragmatic development. *Studies in Second Language Acquisition* 15, 279–304.

Billmyer, K. (1990). I really like your lifestyle: ESL learners learning how to compliment. *Penn Working Papers in Educational Linguistics* 6 (2), 31–48.

Blum-Kulka, S. (1987) Indirectness and politeness in requests: Same or different? *Journal of Pragmatics* 11, 131–146.

Bouton, L.F. (1994) Can NNS skill in interpreting implicature in American English be improved through explicit instruction? – A pilot study. In L.F. Bouton (ed.) *Pragmatics and Language Learning, vol. 5* (pp. 88–109). Urbana, IL: Division of English as an International Language Intensive English Institute, University of Illinois at Urbana-Champaign.

Boxer, D. and Pickering, L. (1995) Problems in the presentation of speech acts in ELT materials: The case of complaints. *ELT Journal* 49, 44–58.

Clennell, C. (1999) Promoting pragmatic awareness and spoken discourse skills with EAP classes. *ELT Journal* 53 (2), 83–91.

Cook, M. and Liddicoat, A.J. (2002) The development of comprehension in interlanguage pragmatics: The case of request strategies in English. *Australian Review of Applied Linguistics* 25 (1), 19–39.

Crandall, E. and Basturkmen, H. (2004) Evaluating pragmatics-focused materials. *ELT Journal* 58 (1), 38–49.

DeCoo, W. (1996). The induction-deduction opposition: Ambiguities and complexities of the didactic reality. *International Journal of Applied Linguistics* 34, 95–118.

Dekeyser, R. (2003) Implicit and explicit learning. In C. Doughty and M.H. Long (eds) *The Handbook of Second Language Acquisition* (pp. 313–348). Oxford: Blackwell.

Doughty, C. (2001) Cognitive underpinnings of focus on form. In P. Robinson (ed.) *Cognition and Second Language Instruction* (pp. 206–257). Cambridge: Cambridge University Press.

Doughty, C. (2003) Instructed SLA: Constraints, compensation, and enhancement. In C. Doughty and M.H. Long (eds) *The Handbook of Second Language Acquisition* (pp. 256–310). Oxford: Blackwell.

Fotos, S. (1993) Consciousness-raising and noticing through focus on form: Grammar task performance versus formal instruction. *Applied Linguistics* 14, 385–407.

Fukuya, Y.J. and Clark, M.K. (2001) A comparison of input enhancement and explicit instruction of mitigators. In L.F. Bouton (ed.) *Pragmatics and Language Learning* (Vol. 10) (pp. 111–130). Urbana, IL: Division of English as an International Language Intensive English Institute, University of Illinois at Urbana-Champaign.

Fukuya, Y.J., Reeve, M., Gisi, J. and Christianson, M. (1998) Does Focus on Form work for teaching sociopragmatics? Paper presented at the 12th International Conference on Pragmatics and Language Learning, University of Illinois at Urbana-Champaign (ERIC Document Reproduction Service No. ED 452736).

Grant, L. and Starks, D. (2001) Screening appropriate teaching materials. Closings from textbooks and television soap operas. *International Review of Applied Linguistics* 39, 39–50.

House, J. (1996) Developing pragmatic fluency in English as a foreign language. *Studies in Second Language Acquisition* 18, 225–253.

House, J. and Kasper, G. (1981) Zur Rolle der Kognition in Kommunikationskursen. *Die Neueren Sprachen* 80, 42–55.

Izumi, S. (2002) Output, input enhancement, and the noticing hypothesis: An experimental study on ESL relativization. *Studies in Second Language Acquisition* 24 (4), 541–577.

Kasper, G. (2001) Classroom research on interlanguage pragmatics. In K.R. Rose and G. Kasper (eds) *Pragmatics in Language Teaching* (pp. 33–60). Cambridge: Cambridge University Press.

Karatepe, C. (2001) Pragmalinguistic awareness in EFL teacher training. *Language Awarenenes* 10, 178–188.

Koike, D.A. and Pearson, L. (2005) The effect of instruction and feedback in the development of pragmatic competence. *System* 33 (3), 481–501.

Leow, R.P. (1997) Attention, awareness, and foreign language behaviour. *Language Learning* 47, 467–505.

Leow, R.P. (2000) A study of the role of awareness in foreign language behaviour. *Studies in Second language Acquisition* 22, 557–584.

Long, M.H. (1991) Focus on form: A design feature in language teaching methodology. In K. de Bot, R. Ginsberg and C. Kramsch (eds) *Foreign Language Research in Cross-Cultural Perspective* (pp. 39–52). Amsterdam: John Benjamins.

Lörscher, W. and Schulze, R. (1988) On polite speaking and foreign language classroom discourse. *International Review of Applied Linguistics* 26, 183–199.

Martínez-Flor, A. (2003) Input in the EFL setting: A focus on teachers' awareness and use of requests, suggestions and advice acts. *VIAL: Vigo International Journal of Applied Linguistics* 0, 73–101.

Martínez-Flor, A. (2004) The effect of instruction on the development of pragmatic competence in the English as a foreign language context: A study based on suggestions. PhD thesis, Universitat Jaume I, Castellón.

Morrow, C.K. (1995) The pragmatic effects of instruction on ESL learners' production of complaint and refusal speech acts. PhD thesis, Buffalo, State University of New York.

Nikula, T. (2002) Teacher talk reflecting pragmatic awareness: A look at EFL and content-based classroom settings. *Pragmatics* 12 (4), 447–467.

Norris, J. and Ortega, L. (2000) Effectiveness of L2 instruction: A research synthesis and quantitative meta-analysis. *Language Learning* 50 (3), 417–528.

Olshtain, E. and Cohen, A.D. (1990) The learning of complex speech act behavior. *TESL Canada Journal* 7 (2), 45–65.

Robinson, P. (1997) Generalizability and automaticity of second language learning under implicit, incidental, enhanced, and instructed conditions. *Studies in Second Language Acquisition* 18, 27–68.

Rosa, E. and O'Neill, M.D. (1999) Explicitness, intake, and the issue of awareness. *Studies in Second Language Acquisition* 21, 511–556.

Rose, K.R. (1997) Pragmatics in the classroom: Theoretical concerns and practical possibilities. In L.F. Bouton (ed.) *Pragmatics and Language Learning* (Vol. 8) (pp. 267–295). Urbana, IL: University of Illinois at Urbana-Champaign.

Rose, K.R. (1999) Teachers and students learning about requests in Hong Kong. In E. Hinkel (ed.) *Culture in Second Language Teaching and Learning* (pp. 167–180). Cambridge: Cambridge University Press.

Rose, K.R. and Ng Kwai-fun, C. (2001) Inductive and deductive approaches to teaching compliments and compliment responses. In K.R. Rose and G. Kasper (eds) *Pragmatics in Language Teaching* (pp. 145–170). Cambridge: Cambridge University Press.

Safont, M.P. (2005) *Third Language Learners. Pragmatic Production and Awareness.* Clevedon: Multilingual Matters.

Salazar, P. and Usó, E. (2001) The speech act of requesting in ESP materials: An example based on Tourism course books. In S. Posteguillo, I. Fortanet and J.C. Palmer (eds) *Methodology and New Technologies in Language for Specific Purposes* (pp. 95–105). Castelló: Servei de Publicacions de la Universitat Jaume I.

Schmidt, R. (1993) Consciousness, learning and Interlanguage pragmatics. In G. Kasper and S. Blum-Kulka (eds) *Interlanguage Pragmatics* (pp. 21–42). New York: Oxford University Press.

Schmidt, R. (2001) Attention. In P. Robinson (ed.) *Cognition and Second Language Instruction* (pp. 3–33). New York: Cambridge University Press.

Takahashi, S. (2001) The role of input enhancement in developing pragmatic competence. In K.R. Rose and G. Kasper (eds) *Pragmatics in Language Teaching* (pp. 171–199). Cambridge: Cambridge University Press.

Takahashi, S. (2005) Noticing in task performance and learning outcomes: A qualitative analysis of instructional effects in interlanguage pragmatics. *System* 33 (3), 437–462.

Tateyama, Y. (2001) Explicit and implicit teaching of pragmatic routines. In K.R. Rose and G. Kasper (eds) *Pragmatics in Language Teaching* (pp. 200–222). Cambridge: Cambridge University Press.

Tomlin, R. and Vila, V. (1994) Attention in cognitive science and second language acquisition. *Studies in Second language Acquisition* 16, 183–203.

Trappes-Lomax, H. and Ferguson, G. (2002) *Language in Language Teacher Education.* Amsterdam: John Benjamins.

Vellenga, H. (2004) Learning pragmatics from ESL and EFL textbooks: How likely? *Teaching English as a Second or Foreign Language* 8 (2), 1–13.

Washburn, G.N. (2001) Using situation comedies for pragmatic language teaching and learning. *TESOL Journal* 10 (4), 21–26.

Appendix 11.A: Example of Some of the Activities Used with the Explicit Group

(1) *Read the following information about making requests. Then, find an example of this request type in the* Stargate *excerpt and justify your choice.*

    (A) Imperatives are used to ask people to do something when one of the interlocutors has a higher position or they know each other very well.

Example: In making his request O'Neill uses an order (*Daniel, shut up*), which shows that he knows Daniel well.

Other examples:

(B)　In making requests the less you know someone or the higher the position someone has, the more polite and formal you need to be.

Example: O'Neill has a higher position than Carter, so he uses a conditional tense to indicate more polite language (*if you're gonna go back and tell General Hammond, I would like to stay here and take a look at their fusion technology*)

Other examples:

(C)　The language you use when requesting also depends on the type of tasks you want the other person to do.

Example: Daniel says *I'd like to know more about your enemy*, since this is a bigger favour he is asking for. As indicated by Alar's reply, this type of request was not expected.

Other examples:

(D)　Sometimes people make requests in an indirect way. In this way the context and the whole conversation can help us to notice that people are asking us to do something.

Example: In Act five, O'Neill, the colonel, says: *Enemy bombers approach the perimeter*. However, what he is giving is an order to engage the bombers.

Other examples:

(2)　*Write a request for the following situations*:

(A)　Colonel O'Neill asks Daniel to find information about the time the war started.

(B)　Daniel asks Alar to provide them with evidence to formalise a new alliance.

(C)　Colonel O'Neill asks Alar to let Jaffa return.

Appendix 11.B: Example of Some of the Activities Used with the Implicit Group

(1)　*We use a variety of ways to ask people to do something. Here you have different examples of requests taken from the* Stargate *excerpt you have seen. Find them in the printed version, and complete them*:

Listen...

Perhaps you'll...

Would you mind if...

I'd like to...

I want to...

(2)　*Make a request for the following situations*:

(A)　Colonel O'Neill asks Daniel to find information about the time the war started.

(B) Daniel asks Alar to provide them with evidence to formalise a new alliance.

(C) Colonel O'Neill asks Alar to let Jaffa return.

Appendix 11.C: Delayed Post-Test

(1) *Choose the phrases or set of phrases used to ask people to do something in the* Stargate *episode. Explain the type of language used in each of your choices.*
Request 1
Why do they use this type of language?
Request 2
Why do they use this type of language?
Request 3
Why do they use this type of language?
Request 4
Why do they use this type of language?

Chapter 12

Interactive Task Design: Metachat and the Whole Learner

MARIE-NOËLLE LAMY

Introduction

In this chapter I focus on conversations about language between adult learners online, in synchronous and asynchronous[1] postings. I use socio-affective and social-semiotic perspectives, thus distancing myself some-what from cognitive ways of looking at tasks. I developed an interest in the pedagogical potential of metalinguistic conversations for two reasons. Because adults come to the task with diverse knowledge of both L2 and L1, I expected that metalinguistic interaction would enable them to swap expert and novice roles with each other within the constantly changing dynamics of the classroom (Dias, 1998: 25; Morita, 2004: 598), which would advance an educational agenda favouring learner-directedness. Secondly, as metalinguistic conversations developed in directions that the learners felt like following, greater contingency could arise. This I regarded as moti-vational for adults, and also as progressive, following Van Lier (1996: 180) for whom in a contingent conversation 'the agenda is shared by all partici-pants and educational reality may be transformed'. However, in seeking to satisfy his condition of contingency, the problem of designing tasks for greater spontaneity proved difficult (Lamy & Goodfellow, 1999b: 60).

Here I provide an ethnographic account of metalinguistic conversations by learners engaged in an online task, *Simuligne*, designed to address this difficulty. After studying data from the project forums, chat rooms and emails, I introduce a new perspective on the function of these conver-sations, which holds pointers for task design.

Metachat

Van Leeuwen (2004) outlines two ways of understanding metalanguage. In the first the emphasis is on form and on metalanguage as a register of specialist terminologies, whose use for language teaching, prestigious in 19th and early 20th century academic settings, was contested by the communicative movement and deleted from the repertoire of most language teachers. In the second approach the 'metalinguistic function is seen as one of several simultaneous functions of linguistic communication. [...] As a result, metalanguage is here not a scientific register. No special training is needed to communicate about communication' (Van Leeuwen, 2004: 108). I adopt this functional interpretation of metalanguage and I concentrate on its use in conversation, calling it 'metachat' to reflect its interactive and informal qualities.

Here are examples to illustrate different types of metachat.

Directed metachat

This example is from an asynchronous forum thread in Lamy and Goodfellow's (1999b) study. The task involved:

- selecting any L2 text (the only condition being that students found it interesting);
- studying it individually; then
- discussing its language with peers on a tutor-facilitated asynchronous forum.

Student 1 chose a page from *Vol de Nuit*, by Saint-Exupéry, and reported to the forum his puzzlement about the word *apprivoiser* (to tame). A conversation followed, (Appendix 12.A), in which participants collaborated in refining their understanding of the verb's functioning in this context.

In such a reflective task, the pitfalls of traditional instructed metalinguistic activity are avoided, i.e. the teacher's expertise is backgrounded, and metalinguistic talk is not decontextualised. Instead it is contextualised within a process of personal inquiry and inter-personal engagement, which is considered to be one of the requirements for initial learning, see Batstone (2002: 3).

Although the conversation flowed from Student 1's personal interests, the *apprivoiser* metachat was not spontaneously triggered, but was 'directed', i.e. a metalinguistic task was prescribed: conversing about vocabulary. Judging from this example, the design of the task had been successful. However, many other learners in the study had actually failed to engage in the task. Those who commented metalinguistically did so in simple responses to their teachers, and the informal student-directed talk that we hoped to 'seed' via the task did not generally materialise, hence our remark: 'the difficulty lies in creating the conditions for learners to be [...] gradually led towards "fully contingent" conversational interaction which is nonetheless reflective on language and learning issues' (Lamy & Goodfellow, 1999b: 60).

Spontaneous metachat

This example is also taken from the 1999 study and shows metachat happening serendipitously rather than instructed within the task. A teacher had declared herself 'sidérée' (stunned) by the quality of learners' work. Learners C. and E. metachatted to discover the meaning of '*sidérée*' (Table 12.1).

Semi-spontaneous metachat

Between a 'directed' exchange like the *apprivoiser* discussion, and the 'spontaneous' conversation about *sidérée* is a category which I call 'semi-spontaneous metachat'. Here the task provides the conversational orientation, but the learners are allowed freedom and time in order to develop both task-convergent and task-divergent (contingent) threads. Thus in the current data, metachat about *foot and mouth disease* developed from a remark about *pig swill*, brought on by shared reminiscences of school food. The 'directed' task was to talk about differences between *schools* in the UK and *écoles* in France.

Table 12.1 Spontaneous metachat in a forum discussion

C.	Je pense que 'sideral' a quelque chose à voir avec les étoiles, c'est-à-dire, l'astronomie. Peut-être il est associé avec le temps et le mouvement. Je suis certaine qu'il y a des scientifiques ou des ingénieurs qui le sauront plus mieux que moi! Amitiés.
E.	Comme scientifique, j'essayerai d'expliquer le mot sidéral. En anglais, sideréal veut dire "des étoiles". Un jour sidéral est un peu plus court qu'un jour solaire, d'ou viens la nécessité pour avoir une année bonde dans une dans quatre pour réassigner le temps solaire avec le temps sidéral. Allez voir http://www.astro.virginia.edu/~eww6n/astro/SiderealDay.html (malheureusement en angliais) pour une explication meillure.
C.	Que je sois dans le ruisseau, je regarde les etoiles (mes excuses a Oscar Wilde!) Sidéré est frappé comme on regarde une étoile. Selon moi, une explication parfaite.
C.	*I think that 'sideral' has something to do with stars, that is with astronomy. It may be related to time and movement. I'm sure there are scientists or engineers here who will know a lot more about this than I do. All the best.*
E.	*As a scientist, I'll try to explain the word sidéral. In English 'sidereal' means 'of the stars'. A sidéral day is shorter than a solar day hence the need for a leap year out of four to realign solar time with sidereal time. Have a look at http://www.astro.virginia.edu/~eww6n/astro/SiderealDay.html (sadly in English) for a better explanation.*
C.	*I may be in the gutter but I'm looking at the stars (with apologies to Oscar Wilde). Sidéré is struck as if looking at a star. To me, a perfect explanation.*

The Study

Research aims and questions

Earlier I proposed a gradation from 'directed' to 'free' along a dimension of control, which is a task parameter. Differences between controlled and free conversations can also be theorised so as to highlight their social functions. Eggins and Slade (1997) distinguish between 'pragmatic' and 'casual' conversations, the former tied to a transaction (commercial or educational), the latter 'simply for the sake of talking'. They claim that although casual talk presents a 'sometimes aimless appearance and apparently trivial content', nevertheless casual conversations, like pragmatic ones, are 'highly structured, functionally motivated semantic activit[ies]' (Eggins & Slade, 1997: 6). In this chapter, I explore metachat in various controlled, freer, pragmatic and casual contexts, to understand how it constructs the participants' online social world and what learning opportunities it affords them. I investigate how different tasks from the online project *Simuligne* help generate and sustain metachat. Various responses, from formal written production to spontaneous conversations, were elicited to see whether metachat would occur, including spontaneous sustained metachat. I ask the following questions:

(1) Whereabouts in the online environment did the metachat occur? (e.g. did directed metachat occur within the more tightly instructed tasks, and did spontaneous metachat happen in what Bannink (2002: 281) calls the 'cracks and seams' of the task?)
(2) What was the metachat about and how did this relate to the learner's experience overall? (e.g. did learners metachat differently when exchanging messages 'in character' within role plays, and when socialising?)

From these reflections I derive epistemological insights into the role of metalanguage and draw pedagogical implications about its facilitation through task design.

The participants

During April to July 2001, 40 part-time intermediate-to-advanced learners of French volunteered to take part in a project run by the UK Open University in collaboration with the University of Franche-Comté, France. Participants were UK-based and mainly (though not exclusively) native speakers of English. They were split into three groups, each with an online tutor. Each group included two French Native Speaker Helpers (NSHs), who were to act as cultural informants, taking care to avoid overlapping with the 'official' tutorial function.

The task

The project consisted of two tasks: a structured simulation (*Simuligne*, which gave its name to the overall project) and a semi-structured cultural task (*Interculture*). *Simuligne* was a 'simulation globale' (Caré & Debyser, 1995), in which communication is supported by a scenario requiring that learners consensually create a small community through role plays and other activities including collaborative assignment production. *Simuligne*'s scenario was based on the competitive creation of imaginary French cities possessing the attributes required for hosting a residential course. Table 12.2 summarises the simulation's phases.

Five of the 16 subtasks in Table 12.2 were designed to elicit metachat. These were expected to generate:

- onomastic and toponymical discussions [sub-tasks 5 and 6];
- talk about jobs vocabulary and associated pragmatics [sub-task 7];
- grammar and style negotiations (consistent with collaborative writing) [sub-tasks 8 and 9].

At three points during the 10 weeks, learners, tutors and NSHs also took part in *Interculture*, a web-based exercise coupled with an open-ended forum discussion, inspired by *Cultura* (Furstenberg *et al.*, 2001). This task could be completed in L1 if participants preferred. It was made up of these steps:

- UK learners and French NSHs individually answered questionnaires designed to bring emotions into play: free-associating with vocabulary likely to resonate with adults (e.g. *patriotism/patriotisme*, or

Table 12.2 Timing and content of the phases of the simulation (metachat-oriented tasks in bold)

Phase 1	*Phase 2*	*Phase 3*	*Phase 4*	*Phase 5*
2–22 Apr	*30 Apr–13 May*	*14 May–3 June*	*4–23 June*	*25 June–6 July*
Get connected	(1) How to chat in a forum (2) Introduce yourself	(3) Research four French cities (4) Imagine a city (5) **Collaboratively name your fictitious city.** (6) **Create and name your character.** (7) **Create your character's role in the community**	(8) **Describe the city** (9) **History/ anthem of the city** (10) Making contact (11) Interactions (12) Unplanned incidents	(13) View and vote (14) Publish vote results (15) Feedback (16) Award presentation

freedom/liberté), a sentence-completion task (e.g. *a hero is someone who ...*), and 10 provocative situations to react to by saying what you would do next (e.g. *You see a woman slapping a child in the street*).
• Participants consulted a Web form which juxtaposed the responses of the two groups. Juxtaposition allowed them to immediately 'see' similarities and differences in attitudes. They then debated the results asynchronously.

Neither in *Simuligne* nor in *Interculture* were students explicit told to talk about words. The aim in *Interculture* was to have metachat emerge 'naturally' from talk about other topics. As Gardner and Wagner (2004: 2) observe: 'experimental settings focus on second language speakers' lack of competence and often make them look less competent and resourceful than naturally occurring data show them in fact to be'. Although the context of the study was educational and not 'naturally-occurring' language, by backgrounding the nature of my research focus I aimed to avoid the anxiety that language learners associate with the technical terminologies which many assume are needed in order to talk about language.

The design and planned function of the various 'spaces' of the online environment are represented in Figure 12.1. Vertical black lines show where the less and more structured spaces of the project were. Grey oval shapes symbolise unplanned inter-communication between spaces, as participants carried conversation topics across from their group forum into the plenary forum, or from a chat session into an email, etc.

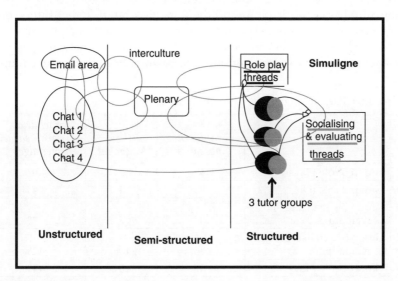

Figure 12.1 The spaces for discussion and their relationship to the activities

Data Collection and Analysis

All interaction data, including private emails,[2] were collected. Firstly I produced a broad content analysis of the learners' messages (i.e. excluding those from tutors and from NSHs), to assess how much metachat appeared in the different spaces and tasks of the project. Secondly I analysed the metachat qualitatively, using a coding system distinguishing between directed, semi-spontaneous and spontaneous metachat.

Quantitative analysis

Messages containing metachat represented 43% of the total learners' postings ($n = 1894$), contributed by 13 individuals out of the total population of 40. Table 12.3 shows the quantity of metachat in the tutor group forums (the other spaces will be examined later).

The tutor groups yielded low and high percentages of metachat, which prevents a clear picture from emerging, though in general Group 2 and Group 3 produced no or little metachat while role playing, and slightly more while socialising (before the role plays) and evaluating (afterwards). In contrast, Group 1 produced metachat during all these phases. Scrutiny of the content revealed that Groups 2 and 3's metachat exclusively reflected their preoccupation with naming the technological features (e.g. the French for *smiley*, *download*, or *hyperlink*). When the table was rewritten omitting the technology-related metachat from all groups, the pattern was clearer.

Table 12.4 shows that Group 2 rarely metachatted and Group 3 never did. Group 1 is very productive of metachat. Given that the groups had the same number of participants and the same task but different tutors, one explanation of the differences could relate to tutors (although the analysis of tutoring issues is beyond the scope of this paper). Instead I suggest another explanation, related to group membership. Two members of Group 1

Table 12.3 Participation in the tutor group forums

		Total learner messages	Metachat	Metachat as % of total learner messages
1	Group 3 role plays	45	0	0%
2	Group 2 role plays	90	4	4%
3	Group 2 socialising and evaluating	100	7	7%
4	Group 3 socialising and evaluating	86	10	12%
5	Group 1 role plays	57	8	14%
6	Group 1 socialising and evaluating	249	41	16%

Table 12.4 Tutor group participation, excluding technology-related postings

		Total learner messages	*Metachat*	*Metachat as % of total learner messages, excluding ICT-related*
1	Group 3 role plays	45	0	0%
2	Group 2 socialising and evaluating	100	0	0%
3	Group 3 socialising and evaluating	86	0	0%
4	Group 2 role plays	90	4	4%
5	Group 1 role plays	57	8	14%
6	Group 1 socialising and evaluating	249	37	15%

(M. and G.) had also participated in an earlier project run for 12 months in 2000–2001, reported in Lamy and Hassan (2003), where they had been keen communicators. Two other assiduous participants in the 2000–2001 study, N. and H., are also among the present cohort. Membership of the 2000–2001 project is relevant to the present cohort's participation patterns, as confirmed by Figure 12.2, which shows total language-focused messages for each of the 13 individuals who metachatted. Veterans from the 2000–2001 study are identified by letters, everyone else by number. G., M., N. and H. are clearly more productive than newcomers, except number 3.

Table 12.5, which includes the synchronous chat room sessions data, shows the extraordinary productiveness of the chat session in row 10. This

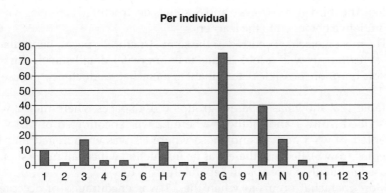

Figure 12.2 Language-focused messages per metachatting individual

Table 12.5 Participation in all 'spaces' of the project

		Total learner messages	Metachat	Metachat as % of total learner messages, excluding ICT-related
1	Group 3 role plays	45	0	0%
2	Group 2 socialising and evaluating	100	0	0%
3	Group 3 socialising and evaluating	86	0	0%
4	Chat room session 2 [N. and Gp 2]	151	1	1.5%
5	Chat Room session 1 [N. and Gp 2]	108	2	2%
6	Gp2 role plays	90	4	4%
7	Chat Room session 4 [N. and Gp 2]	45	5	11%
8	Group 1 role plays	57	8	14%
9	Group1 socialising and evaluating	249	37	15%
10	Chat Room session 3 [M., G. and tutor]	237	60	25%

featured a chat between two of the veterans discussed above, G. and M., and their tutor.

Factors other than group dynamics also impacted. To show this, I now revisit the data, using task-design related criteria involving the parameters 'structuring' and 'control'.

Table 12.6 shows the extent to which the task involved a directed process and required structured outcomes. Row 1 shows interactions that were highly structured, because they were integral to the role plays. The next group (rows 2, 3 and 4) shows more loosely structured interactions. In these, instructions were issued but the expected outcomes were open-ended. The third group (rows 5 and 6) shows unstructured activities where the initiative belonged to the learners.

The most metachat occurred in the semi-structured spaces, particularly in *Interculture* (row 2). I look at this task in greater detail shortly. First, I explore one more possible determinant of metachat productivity: the use of the L1.

Table 12.7 shows as separate groups those spaces where the L2 was prescribed (rows 1 and 2), those where L2 was encouraged but L1 was accepted (rows 3 and 4), and those where L1 was encouraged and L2 accepted (row 5). Because there was no instruction which language should be used in emails, these appear separately (row 6).

More metachat occurred when the L1 was encouraged or accepted. Row 5 shows that encouragement to use L1 (both as a means of expression

Table 12.6 Participation in each 'space', according to degree of task structuring

	RP = role plays	*Total learner messages*	*Metachat*	*Metachat as % of total learner messages*
	Highly structured, RP			
1	Tutor group forums (role plays)	192	12	**6%**
	Semi structured, not part of RP			
2	Plenary forum (*Interculture*)	360	52	**14%**
3	Tutor group forums (socialising and evaluating)	435	37* (58)	**8.5%** (13%)
4	Plenary forum (final evaluation)	99	8	**8%**
	Unstructured, not part of RP			
5	Chat rooms	735	70	**10%**
6	Emails	73	2	**3%**

*Asterisked figures exclude messages about naming features of the technology. The effect of adding these is shown in brackets.

and as a resource) produces the highest result (14%). The next highest impact is in the chat sessions, in row 3 (10%), where the choice of language of communication was free and code-switching was frequent.

In sum, task design parameters influencing levels of metachat are:

- task content (role plays, socialising, technological chat);
- complexity of task structuring;
- language used in the task.

Implications for task design are drawn later.

Qualitative analysis

I started the qualitative analysis by studying metachat content produced under varying conditions of task prescription: in *Simuligne* (highly-structured, with a prescribed outcome), in *Interculture* (semi-prescribed, with an open-ended outcome), and in task-free spaces (chat rooms, emails). I searched for differences between messages exchanged 'in character' when role-playing, and others. It soon emerged that no such differences existed, as participants posted messages 'indiscriminately', i.e. metachat could occur in any space in the environment. So I moved my focus from degree

Table 12.7 Language-focused messages in decreasing order of prescription of L2 use

		Total learner messages	Metachat	Metachat as % of total learner messages
	L2 prescribed			
1	Tutor group forums (RP)	192	12	6%
2	Tutor group forums (socialising and evaluating)	435	37* (58)	8%*(13%)
	L2 encouraged, L1 accepted			
3	Chat rooms	735	70	10%
4	Plenary forum (final evaluation)	99	8	8%
	L1 encouraged, L2 accepted			
5	Plenary forum (Interculture)	360	52	**14%**
	No prescription of L1 or L2			
6	Emails	73	2	**3%**

*Asterisked figures exclude messages about naming features of the technology. The effect of adding these is shown in brackets.

of task structuring to degree of spontaneity, using the categories 'directed metachat', 'semi-spontaneous metachat' and 'spontaneous metachat', summarised in Table 12.8.

Content of directed metachat

The *Simuligne* role play forums yielded some metachat as expected in sub-tasks 5, 6, 7 and 9 (see Table 12.2 *supra*): creating the roles and producing the assignments. The collaborative construction of an anthem triggered discussion of the false friend *vers* (which means 'line', not 'verse'). When creating fictitious characters, learners explored vocabulary. For example, a participant decided to become 'Mme Moreau', commenting:

> Moreau. Tête de Maure, c'est la couleur brun foncé. Ce n'est pas un nom imaginaire – c'est la couleur des cheveux. [*Moreau. Moor's head, referring to the colour dark brown. It's not a fantasy name, it refers to hair colour.*]

Content of semi-spontaneous metachat

Interculture provided the opportunity for learners to start with a prescribed topic and move on contingently. The prescribed topics that generated the most sustained contingent metachat were *famille/family* and

Table 12.8 Types of learner input

Directed metachat: learner applies task instructions:
(1) to create identities as part of *Simuligne* role play
(2) to explore language provided as part of *Interculture* task
Learner evaluates own linguistic progress (in response to explicit instruction)
Semi-spontaneous metachat
Learner queries/explores new linguistic material
(1) encountered in the task instructions
(2) encountered indirectly, while doing the task
(3) produced contingently in L1 while doing the task
Spontaneous metachat
Learner initiates or responds to non-task-related metalinguistic comment
Learner makes general comment about language or languages
Learner self-queries or self-corrects

école/school, providing rich conversational environments in which learners reminisced about their childhood and plugged cultural gaps for NSHs. Discussion of a pair like *communauté/community* led on to personal narratives about one's role in one's community, going on to metachat, e.g.:

> Mon travail s'agit plus d'eviter les accidents que les crimes. Vous savez sans doute que le mot «securite» se traduit en deux mots anglais. [*My work is more about avoiding accidents than preventing crime. As you probably know, the word 'sécurité' has two translations in English.*]

Content of spontaneous metachat

Four productive mechanisms were identified in the spontaneous metachat: emotion, self-deprecation, taboos and linguistic advice.

(a) Emotion: i.e. postings about how to convey emotions experienced within the online community, such as frustration or, as in the forum below, laughter.

> **D:** I also chuckled (comment on dit en français?) [*I also chuckled (how do you say this in French?)*]
>
> **NSH:** Ça pourrait être 'j'ai pouffé de rire' [*It could be 'I burst out laughing'*]
>
> **D:** J'ai pouffé de rire I believe would translate in English as 'to burst out laughing' or 'to be in stitches (fam)'. The Oxford dictionary definition of chuckle is 'chuckle v. laugh quietly or inwardly; n. a quiet or suppressed laugh'. Entre autres mots, deux genres de rire, un est bruyant, l'autre est discret

(chuckle). [*In other words, here are 2 kinds of laughter, one noisy, the other quiet (chuckle)*]

G: I looked up my dictionary and found there is a difference between 'un rire étouffé' (a chuckle, smothered laughter) and 'étouffer de rire' (to choke with laughter). I learn something new every day with this Simuligne . . .:-)

D: Simuligne is now a daily tonic for me. I am learning so much and I laugh so much each morning. Thus I have found the following in Oxford/Hachette: [he then quotes 16 lines of examples, idiomatic phrases and proverbs from the semantic field of *rire* to be found in this source] Bonne dimanche!

G: All different kinds of 'rire' here: http://clicnet.swarthmore.edu/rire/lexique/r/rires.html

(b) Self deprecation: by calling themselves *oddball, bonkers, plonker, cinglé* (mad) or *tarte* (idiot), both national groups triggered explanations and translations.

(c) Taboos: words like *Gollywog* (Debussy's piano piece) or *dick* (spotted dick) triggered queries, hypotheses, suggested translations and multilingual comparisons.

(d) Learners provided linguistic expertise to NSHs. Typically, a learner would use an English phrase which a NSH then queried. These exchanges led to interlingual comparisons and sociolinguistic comments.

In sum, task design parameters influencing levels of metachat are:

- degree of control embedded within task instructions (directed process versus spontaneous process);
- task content (cultural comparison, personal revelations, emotion and taboos);
- language used in the task (learner linguistic expertise).

Implications for task design will be drawn later.

Summary of findings

I now map these findings onto my research questions. The answer to the first question (where in the online environment did the metachat occur?) is: everywhere, but mainly in the spaces reserved for more loosely structured tasks, where L1 was tolerated, particularly when the participants had had a prior opportunity to become acquainted with each other, albeit online only.

Relating to my second question (what was the content of the metachat and how did this relate to the learner's experience overall?), I found that through metachatting, participants explored their identity and familial biographies. I also found that the conditions that led to longer exchanges were those in which NSHs were involved, not – as had been planned – because they 'helped' learners access the L2 culture, but because they put themselves in the position of novices, allowing learners to display L1 linguistic and sociolinguistic expertise.

Redefining the term 'context' in communicative pedagogies, authors such as Batstone (2002), Belz (2001), Breen (2001) and Yonge and Stables (1998) have argued in favour of broadening it considerably, to include pre-task and post-task activities, as well as what goes on during the task but isn't directly related to it, thus accepting 'as educationally valid the more complex, mitigative, interweaving of social and cognitive material' produced in the context of the educational experience (Yonge & Stables, 1998: 67). My scrutiny of the wider context of interaction among the learners in this project has shown that metachat and L1 use belong to that socio-cognitive material. However, to support the notion that this material is educationally valid, we should also, as Verschueren (2004: 54) says, 'demonstrate that the reflexivity involved is neither fortuitous nor trivial'. To do this, I now offer a social semiotic perspective on some of my findings, highlighting the socio-cohesive function served by metachat, and the importance of L1 tolerance in sustaining threads.

Discussion

Like Gardner and Wagner (2004) and Belz (2002) I view the adult L2 speaker in educational settings not as a conversational beginner but as a fully fledged conversationalist whose panoply of linguistic, pragmatic and strategic resources is different but not inferior to that of a native speaker, and 'whose focus is on the successful prosecution of their activities, using whatever means available' (Gardner & Wagner, 2004: 3). This is particularly true of adults who, as the literature on the post-compulsory sector stresses, bring to the learning their experience as professionals, family members and citizens, shifting in and out of these roles recursively and dynamically.

Epistemological and pedagogical consequences flow from this. To start with the pedagogical: the teacher no longer focuses on helping learners acquire the resources that are assumed to be possessed by native speakers, but on organising a setting in which they can successfully prosecute their activities and constructively confront their resources with those of others. Metachat is one of the means available to them in this endeavour, as it allows them to exercise agency through enacting real roles such as linguistic novices seeking support or linguistic experts conferring it, co-constructing knowledge from resources that are textual (the messages in the project), intertextual (books or web sites alluded to) and autobiographical, thus promoting their self-expression and self-construction as 'whole' learners.

Epistemologically, I propose that we can understand the function of metachat by looking upon conversations as semiotic processes (for the participants involved in them) and semiotic objects (from the point of view of the analyst). In the semiotic process we use 'the formal elements of language, the linguistic signifiers, as a resource for "doing something with words", where "doing" includes, of course, representation', (Van Leeuwen, 2004: 123). *Simuligne* participants represented language and, through this representational function, they 'did something with words', i.e. they 'enacted' group relationships.

Applying a social semiotic perspective to four examples from my data, I suggest that metachat incorporates the learner's representational activity as well as his/her enacting of relationships with other resource-holders. The first example shows an Anglo-Colombian participant using her multilinguality to aid the semiotic process:

> C'est a dire concubinage? Est-ce que vous utilisez ce mot en francais? En espagnol est un mot tombé en désuétude. [*Does this mean concubinage? Do you use this word in French? In Spanish it's an obsolete word.*]

Acquisitionists, might theorize code switches in terms of interlanguage, socio-cultural theorists in terms of intercultural awareness, and critical discourse analysts in terms of resistance (Norton, 2001). A social semiotic interpretation additionally accommodates the construct of identity, seen as created through the meaning-making processes that underpin discourse. For example this learner represents the signifier *concubinage* in order to query both its denotation and its sociolinguistic status, marshalling her Hispanic resources to contrast *concubinage* with its Spanish cognate. Also, through her use of the plural 'vous', instead of 'tu' (used universally to single addressees elsewhere in the forum), she is enacting her relationship to some community.[3] By choosing 'vous', she is constructing her identity as an outsider, while through other pragmatic input (asking a direct question, offering relevant information), she simultaneously signals her readiness to work collaboratively with the resource-holders in that community. Further, to quote Belz's (2002: 32) study of learners playfully hybridising L1 and L2, our learner is also 'conceptualising herself as a multicompetent language user with respect to all languages she knows, as opposed to a deficient communicator with respect to only her L2(s)'.[4]

The learner in the second example, a musician, is sending her tutor an audio file of one of her recordings, during the pre-task socialisation phase.

> Voici un tout petit morceau de 'Golliwog Cake Walk' by Debussy. La traduction du titre n'est pas très polie, donc, je le laisse en anglais. [*Here's a very short extract from Debussy's 'Golliwog Cake Walk'. The translation of the title is not very polite, so I'll leave it in English.*]

Her academic resource is her knowledge of the sociocultural value of the word *Golliwog* in English. By displaying this form, while hinting at its taboo status, she is enacting some form of social relation[5] to the tutor and to the group, who responded by requesting (tutor) and offering (group) clarification about its connotations.

Here are two more examples, showing longer interactions. The first comes from a thread devoted to discussing the words *France/United Kingdom*. One of the discussions concerned the phrase *Union Jack*. Note the code switch at line 3.

Learner 1: il a des connotations négatives [*it has negative connotations*]
Learner 2: ça me fait penser au Front National [*it reminds me of the National Front*].
Learner 3: I differ. I am proud to be English
[Learner 3 goes on to explain his role in WW2 as well as the radical changes in society since those days]
Learner 2: I hope that nobody takes what I say TOO seriously
Learner 4: Just to lighten the tone a bit! I remember a French girl getting very upset at the term Great Britain. She thought the British were being arrogant, saying that their country was 'great'... An interesting linguistic misunderstanding!

[In subsequent threads, all return to using the L2]

Here the metachat supported the enactment of relations of power (over whose vision of 'Britishness' is more legitimate), but also of loyalty to the group and concern for its continuing welfare (see Learner 4's reference to the emotion in the thread and her stated desire for a return to a calmer tone).

The following example also involves identity-building, as G. concludes a discussion by making a statement on behalf of the community.[6]

N: At first glance, the french concept of 'Communauté' seems to have rather broader boundaries than the english one of 'Community'. Does this reflect the stereotypical concept of the english as essentially parochial

NSH: Je ne comprends pas le terme 'parochial'? [*I don't understand the word 'parochial'*]

G: Parochial: ça veut dire qu'on est pas très ouvert sur le monde [...]
[*Parochial: it means you're not very open to the world [...]*]

H: G. a dit la vérité ---- Ça vient de parish (en France paroisse) ça veut dire un petit secteur desservi par une église, un curé. Mais, c'est vrai que la connotation est d'un esprit étroit et conservateur. [*G. is right, it comes from 'parish' which means a small area served by a church, a priest. But it's true that the connotation is of narrow-mindedness and conservatism*]

G: Il faut dire aussi que le sens du mot 'parochial' que nous avons utilisé ici n'a rien à voir avec l'église - on n'est pas tellement religieux ici! [*It has to be said that the meaning of 'parochial' that we've been using has nothing to do with the church - we're not very religious here*]

Code-switching may effect various processes:

- cognitive, e.g. 'scaffolding assistance' (Storch & Wigglesworth, 2003: 760);
- sociodynamic, e.g. integrating oneself into a group or helping outsiders to come in (Mondada, 2004: 38);
- socio-political, e.g. gaining 'the other party's trust' (Morgan, 1997: 433).

I have shown that metachatting in different languages creates these affordances and additionally allows participants to exercise agency while transforming their understanding of their relationship to each of the languages that make up the wider context within which they operate.

Task Design Implications

I now turn the findings of this study into proposals for integrating metachat into learning programmes. How much of a learning programme should be dedicated to metalinguistic work is a question that only teachers can answer, so my suggestions are qualitative only.

I have shown that learners can turn any topic into an opportunity for metchatting. I will now identify the conditions under which this happens and I will draw some implications from three perspectives:

- task parameters (task structuring and control, task sequencing, face validity and task modelling);
- time and space for interaction;
- reinforcement of learner control and reduction of learner anxiety.

Task parameters

Structuring and control

Tasks characterised by simple structures and lighter control from teachers should be favoured. Avoid building in many stages requiring what Crooks and Gass (1993: 19) call 'convergence'. Role-plays pressurise participants into resolving issues 'in character' hence may inhibit free exploration. Simulations demand completion of sub-tasks by certain milestones to ensure the timely progress of the collaborative outcome, risking curtailing student-led exploration. But as several writers have observed teachers may feel uncomfortable in reducing controls, through fear of loss of focus during class. For Furstenberg *et al.* (2001: 82), teacher control produces 'a reassuring expectation [...] that at some point the chapters will have been covered, the relevant questions asked and answered. With *Cultura*, of course, the questions are many and the book is being written as the course unfolds. The data produced by students varies and is enriched from day to day, making the process of interpretation itself the focus of the class'. Norton (2000: 145) addresses the issue from her point of view as teacher of English to speakers of other languages but identifies a similar dilemma: 'the lived experiences and identities of language learners need to be incorporated into the formal curriculum. I have noted, however, that essentializing student experience will compromise the conditions necessary for reflection', unless a mechanism is created to foster this reflection. Like Furstenberg and Norton, I consider that tasks in which pressure to cover the teacher's programme is removed or lessened, such as inquiry-based tasks or open-ended discussions, including tasks legitimating the adduction of personal memories, are supportive of this reflective aim. Metachat fulfils these requirements whilst additionally offering L2 knowledge enhancement.

Task sequencing

To further contain possible loss of focus, sequences should be constructed as a mix of cognitive, discursive and social concerns, which as *Cultura* and *Interculture* have shown are better than mono-parameter tasks at leading learners to assume control. A good pattern would be to start with a reflective cognitive phase, requiring analysis and comparison, followed by a phase dedicated to both cognitive and socio-affective exchanges. A consequence of taking seriously the teacher's new role, i.e. facilitating the creation of a setting in which learners can authentically work with their own resources and those of their peers, is that emotions and contentious topics should be viewed not as conversational parasites, but as part of the context that supports the learning. Teachers should be encouraged to work with rather than against these sensitive topics.

Face validity and task modelling

Tasks should have face validity. They should 'be contingent upon learners sharing an interpersonal orientation to context which supports and *validates* [interpersonal] behaviour' (Batstone, 2002: 6, my emphasis). Face validity is important in shaping a shared orientation to metachat, as this participant comment illustrates: 'We're learning from each other. Though in a sense you could say we are not focused, we're dilettante-ing around, wandering from one thing to the next.' A strategy for legitimating metachat to the learners might be to introduce the project via sessions aimed at raising awareness about metalanguage, using electronic sources as stimuli. For credibility and entertainment value, short topical pieces from a popular expert could be used (with the proviso that this will not give students the opportunity to 'see' a thread in action and model their interactivity on it). Examples for French are Alain Rey's column at: http://www.radiofrance.fr/chaines/ franceinter01/information/chroniques/chronique/archives_rey.php? chronique_id=50, and the CIEP's (International Centre for Pedagogical

Studies) page at http://www.ciep.fr/chroniq/index.htm. To provide an interactive task model, conversational extracts from electronic discussion lists could also be proposed, following Fant (2001: 91) (with the proviso that learners will need to be warned that content is not always authoritative). A non-moderated example for French is *Franc-Parler*, a portal for 'the world community of teachers of French', at http://www.francparler.org/forum/. A moderated example for multilingual debate through the medium of English is LANTRA-L, a free password-protected email list for translaters and interpreters (joining information at http://www.geocities.com/Athens/7110/lantra.htm).

Time and space for interaction

This study has confirmed Lamy and Goodfellow (1999a: 468) in showing that the more time is allowed for social induction and the establishing of group membership, the higher the number reflective interactions. Conference access should be arranged so that learners 'meet' socially before course start. The induction phase will hold different interest for distance learners, for whom this is an opportunity to counter their isolation, and for campus-based students who may know each other well already. For these too, however, community-building is valuable, though it may rely rather more on sharing immediate concerns such as local activities and events.

Data analysis and Figure 12.1 have shown that metachat occurred in different spaces of the project, and were not confined to sub-tasks that were meant to produce a metalinguistic outcome. Students metachatted wherever and whenever the opportunity arose, which supports the requirement for flexibility of task structure. However, we also know that good practice in online conferencing involves strong structuring of forums, with thread topics clearly identified by appropriate headers. To resolve this dilemma, provide the architecture and navigational aids (for reassurance), but expect them to be subverted and be prepared to support the metachat wherever it occurs.

Reinforcement of learner control and reduction of learner anxiety

Insights can be drawn from the way that, in this project, three sources of anxiety were addressed.

First, there was no pressure to use technical linguistic terminology. Task instructions should be written with no explicit requirement to use meta-language. A priority on cultural comparison or personal experience will, without contriving a metalinguistic exercise, produce sufficient lexical gaps to foster metachat.

Second, there was time to discuss technology-related anxieties. A mixed strategy involving task design and teacher training can be used:

- Ensure that sufficient time was available, both before and during the task, for learners to discuss technological procedures. Some will spontaneously adopt expert roles and provide procedural guidance to their peers. A space could also be created for FAQs, to be populated by participants' contributions.

• Teachers should refrain from providing the technological answers, but instead encourage L2 peer advice and if appropriate be prepared to make the technological processes themselves a metalinguistic focus of the class.

Finally, participants' mastery over more than one language was valued and legitimated.

• Build the use of L1 into some of the tasks. In *Interculture*, use of L1 is triggered by a sequence involving a specially-designed lexico-semantic task and sentence-completion exercise, leading to an information-gap-based metachat. Alternatively, use a different lead into the metachat: for example close analysis of a text or film extract.
• Where possible, take advantage of group multilingualism by seeking pre-sessional information about participants' linguistic profiles and arranging groups so as to maximise cross-linguistic contact. Web-based environments make this easy to organise, as L3 populations and materials can be harnessed more easily.

Reducing anxiety in these different ways helps learners to seize control of all the meta-linguistic resources available within the group, express their identity and exercise their agency.

Conclusion

Working from a socio-cultural framework towards one informed by social semiotics, I have presented metalinguistic conversations as vehicles for the simultaneous pursuit of cognitive and socio-affective negotiations, and the realisation of learners' sense of self and orientation to the community (whether the local learning community or the wider target language community). In this outlook, the metachatting learner's role shifts from recipient (to whom the information is transmitted) to autonomous agent. Through analysis of interactive learner data, I have demonstrated that metachat is 'neither fortuitous nor trivial', and offers rich possibilities for identity-building and enactment of agency within social settings, while discharging its traditional function as a source of information on the L2. Accordingly I have made suggestions for task designers and teachers who are interested in adding metachat to their L2 teaching repertoire.

Notes

1. Online synchronous exchanges happen in real time. They may be written (e.g. 'textchat') or spoken (e.g. Internet telephony). Asynchronous exchanges happen

as and when the user wishes to communicate. They may be written (e.g. discussion groups on the Internet) or spoken (e.g. audio file attachments).
2. With participants' permission.
3. 'Some' community, because it is not clear whether 'vous' represents the NSHs in the project, or the French in general. Picking up on Norton (2001)'s terminology, we could say that 'vous' is the 'imagined community' of which this learner is not a member.
4. In the plural in the original.
5. A finer-grained interpretation, specifying the effects of the learner's pragmatic choices in this situation (e.g. to hold back an explanation of 'Gollywog', thus excluding the tutor from the expert group, and to affirm membership of the L1 community by displaying her adherence to its sociocultural codes) is beyond the scope of this paper.
6. This community may be the turn-takers in the discussion, the tutor group or the UK population.

References

Bannink, A. (2002) Negotiating the paradoxes of spontaneous talk in advanced L2 classes. In C. Kramsch (ed.) *Language Acquisition and Language Socialization* (pp. 266–88). London–New York: Continuum.

Batstone, R. (2002) Contexts of engagement: A discourse perspective on 'intake' and 'pushed output'. *System* 30, 1–14.

Belz, J.A. (2001) Institutional and individual dimensions of transatlantic group work in network-based language teaching. *ReCALL* 13 (2), 213–231.

Belz, J.A. (2002) Second language play as a representation of the multicompetent self in foreign language study. *Journal for Language, Identity, and Education* 1, 13–39.

Breen, M.P. (2001) Overt participation and covert acquisition in the language classroom. In M.P. Breen (ed.) *Learner Contributions to Language Learning: New Directions in Research* (pp. 112–140). Harlow: Longman Pearson Education.

Caré, J.M. and Debyser, F. (1995) *Simulations Globales.* Paris: Centre International d'Etudes Pédagogiques.

Crookes, G. and Gass, S. (eds) (1993) *Tasks and Language Learning.* Clevedon: Multilingual Matters.

Dias, J. (1998) The teacher as chameleon: Computer-mediated communication and role transformation. In P. Lewis (ed.) *Teachers, Learners, and Computers: Exploring Relationships in Call* (pp. 17–26). Nagoya: The Japan Association for Language Teaching, Computer-Assisted Language Learning National Special Interest Group.

Eggins, S. and Slade, D. (1997) *Analysing Casual Conversations.* London: Equinox.

Fant, L. (2001) Creating awareness of identity work in conversations: A resource for language training. In M. Kelly, I. Elliott and L. Fant (eds) *Third Level, Third Space* (pp. 79–93). Bern: Peter Lang.

Furstenberg, G., Levet, S., English, K. and Maillet, K. (2001) Giving a virtual voice to the silent language of culture: The Cultura project. *Language Learning and Technology* 5 (1), 55–102.

Gardner, R. and Wagner, J. (eds) (2004) *Second Language Conversations.* London, New York: Continuum.

Lamy, M.-N. and Goodfellow, R. (1999a) Supporting language students' interactions in Web-based conferencing. *Computer-assisted Language Learning* 12 (5), 457–477.

Lamy, M.-N. and Goodfellow, R. (1999b) Reflective conversations in the virtual language classroom. *Language Learning and Technology* 2 (2), 43–61.

Lamy, M.-N. and Hassan, X. (2003) What influences reflective interaction in distance peer learning? Evidence from four long-term online learners of French. *Open Learning Journal* 18 (1), 39–59.

Mondada, L. (2004) Ways of "Doing being plurilingual" in international work meetings. In R. Gardner and J. Wagner (eds) *Second Language Conversations* (pp. 18–39). London–New York: Continuum.

Morgan, B. (1997) Identity and intonation: linking dynamic processes in an ESL classroom. *TESOL Quarterly* 31 (3), 431–450.

Morita, N. (2004) Negotiating participation and identity in second language academic communities. *TESOL Quarterly* 38 (4), 573–603.

Norton, B. (2000) *Identity and Language Learning. Gender, Ethnicity and Educational Change.* Harlow: Longman Pearson Education.

Norton, B. (2001) Non-participation, imagined communities and the language classroom. In M.P. Breen (ed.) *Learner Contributions to Language Learning: New Directions in Research* (pp. 159–171). Harlow: Longman Pearson Education.

Stockwell, G. and Levy, M. (2001) Sustainability of e-mail interactions between native speakers and nonnative speakers. *Computer Assisted Language Learning* 14 (5), 419–442.

Storch, N. and Wigglesworth, G. (2003) Is there a role for the use of the L1 in an L2 setting? *TESOL Quarterly* 37 (4), 760–770.

Van Leeuwen, T. (2004) Metalanguage in social life. In A. Jaworski, N. Coupland and D. Galasinski (eds) *Metalanguage: Social and Ideological Perspectives* (pp. 107–130). Berlin–New York: Mouton De Gruyter.

Van Lier, L. (1996). *Interaction in the Language Curriculum – Awareness, Autonomy and Authenticity.* London: Longman.

Verschueren, J. (2004) Notes on the role of metapragmatic awareness in language use. In A. Jaworski, N. Coupland and D. Galasinski (eds) *Metalanguage: Social and Ideological Perspectives* (pp. 54–73). Berlin–New York: Mouton De Gruyter.

Yonge, C. and Stables, A. (1998) 'I am it the clown': Problematising the distinction between 'off task' and 'on task' classroom talk. *Language and Education* 12 (1), 55–70.

Appendix 12.A: Metatalk

'Apprivoiser' conversation, with English translation below.

Learner 1	Le mot 's'apprivoiser' m'intéresse. Apprivoiser veut dire 'to tame, domesticate or to make more sociable' et s'apprivoiser, 'to become more tame or sociable or to become accustomed to'. Je l'ai chercher dans le Petit Robert [...] Mais je fais une digression. Que veut dire, 'à tout ce qui, s'apprivoise pour l'éternité'
Learner 2	Peut-être le fait qu'il risquait sa vie tous les nuits qu'il volait, et lentement il s'accoutumait à l'idée d'une autre vie qui durait plus longtemps. Je ne suis pas sûr. à bientôt. A
Learner 3	[...] Je voudrais proposer que dans le contexte vous citez des pensées de Fabian, St Ex. l'utilise en façon très ironique, ou, peut- être philosophique. [...] Donc ma traduction de votre phrase 'à tout ce qui, s'apprivoise pour l'éternité' est

	'everything that prepares us for death' ou 'everything that gets us ready for eternity'. Sans aucun doute, tout cela est bien évident à vous et soit il y a des autres interprétations, soit je me trompe. Amitiés, R
Learner 1	[...] Merci de vos idées pour la traduction de la phrase que j'ai citée. C'est intéressant. Richard a proposé quelque chose d'autre. Toujours, on peut lire St. Ex aux niveaux différents. [...]

Learner 1	The word 's'apprivoiser' is interesting to me. Apprivoiser means 'to tame, domesticate or to make more sociable' and s'apprivoiser, 'to become more tame or sociable or to become accustomed to'. I looked it up in the Petit Robert dictionary [...] But I digress. What is the meaning of 'à tout ce qui, s'apprivoise pour l'éternité'?
Learner 2	Maybe the fact that he risked his life whenever he did a night flight and slowly he was getting used to the idea of some other life, lasting much longer. I'm not sure. Bye for now, A.
Learner 3	I'd like to propose that in the context that you mention, the thoughts of Fabian, St Ex is using irony or may be is talking philosophically. [...] So my translation of your quotation 'à tout ce qui, s'apprivoise pour l'éternité' is 'everything that prepares us for death' ou 'everything that gets us ready for eternity'. No doubt this is all very obvious to you. But I think, although I may be wrong, that there are different interpretations. All the best, R.
Learner 1	Thank you for your ideas for the translation of the sentence that I quoted. It's interesting, R. has come up with yet another idea. St Ex may always be read at different levels.

Index

Accuracy viii, ix, 2-4, 12, 21-22, 28, 30, 34-35, 37-40, 43, 46-47, 49-53, 56, 58, 60, 62-65, 68, 109, 117, 119-133, 137-138, 140, 142-143, 146-147, 150-155, 158-161, 163, 165, 167-168, 171-174, 203-206, 212-213, 217

Adult learners 242

Agency 256, 258, 261

Attention v, viii, 3, 17, 21, 26, 28-29, 41-44, 46-53, 61-65, 67-69, 71, 74, 77, 91-93, 95-98, 100-101, 105, 107-112, 114, 117, 119, 122, 130,133, 137-138, 140, 150-151, 154, 167, 171, 173, 178-180, 185, 191-95, 199, 203-205, 207, 211-212, 219, 222-224, 227, 231, 234-236, 238-239

Attentional capacity 22, 120, 124, 137

Attentional resources viii, 2, 21, 48-49, 64, 117, 119-120, 137, 139-140, 178-179, 181-182, 191-192, 195, 204

Capacity Hypothesis viii, 2, 21, 137-138, 151

Code-complexity 14, 22, 40, 46, 179, 205-207, 217

Code-strategies 200, 206, 208-209, 218

Code-switching 200, 203, 206, 208-211, 213-214, 216-217, 251, 258

Cognition Hypothesis viii, 2-3, 20, 22-23, 117, 119-122, 130, 137-138, 140, 151-152, 204

Cognitive factors 14, 18-19, 120, 205

Cognitive processing 17, 25, 119, 178, 180, 205

Cognitive complexity x, 6, 22, 26, 44, 46-48, 52, 65, 68, 117, 121-123, 129-130, 132, 155, 178, 180, 198, 202-203, 205, 207, 219

Collaborative tasks v, ix, 3, 91-93, 112

Collaborative writing 4, 92-93, 95, 117, 158, 171-174, 246

Communicative effectiveness 200, 208

Communicative pedagogies 256

Complexity v-vi, viii-x, 2-6, 12, 14-16, 19-26, 28-30, 34-36, 38-40, 43-50, 52-53, 55-68, 72, 75, 86-87, 90, 94, 117, 119-131, 136-156, 160-161, 163, 165, 174, 178-181, 183, 186-187, 189, 191, 193, 197-198, 202-206, 208, 212-213, 217, 219, 251

Comprehensible input 24, 70, 89-90, 114, 173

Competition for attention 47-49, 53, 62-63

Conversations ix, 5, 48, 77, 88, 90, 242, 245, 256, 261-263

Dual task 4, 179-180, 182

Effort 7, 17, 46, 62, 64, 67, 139-140, 148, 201, 202, 204, 212-213, 216

EFL v-vii, ix, 2-5, 9, 13-14, 91, 92, 95-96, 108, 111, 113, 152-153, 197, 221-224, 236-239

ESL 24, 40, 67, 69, 113, 153-154, 173, 237-239, 263

Feedback 3-4, 25, 35, 43, 56, 67, 69-71, 74-75, 81-83, 85-87, 89-90, 92, 97, 110-112, 157-159, 168-172, 202, 212, 216-217, 223, 225, 233-234, 236, 238, 246

Fluency viii, ix, 2-3, 12, 20-22, 28-30, 34-40, 44, 46-47, 49-53, 58-59, 61-64, 66, 68, 119, 132-133, 140, 142-143, 146-147, 149, 150-152, 155, 159-161, 163, 166, 174, 200, 203-204, 213, 223, 238

Foreignizing 200, 208, 210

Focus on form viii, x, 3, 20-21, 23, 43, 50, 67-68, 91, 96, 100, 104, 108, 113-114, 136, 152, 154, 179, 191, 223-225, 228-229, 231-232, 236-238

Group work 171, 262

Here-and-Now v, viii, 2-3, 7-8, 44-45, 47-48, 51-58, 60-63, 120-121, 136-150, 155, 179, 205

Socio-cognitive 112
Structural complexity 2, 50-53, 56-58,
   60-61, 64, 120, 142, 145, 147-148
Syllabus design vii, x, 5, 9-12, 23-26, 43,
   44-46, 65-68, 132, 136, 154, 197
Syntactic complexity 55, 119, 122,
   123-125, 127-131, 139, 212

Task-based learning vii, 6, 19-20, 23, 43
Task classification 1-2, 9, 13, 15, 19, 20, 24
Task complexity vi, viii-x, 2-5, 12,
   15-16, 19-26, 43-48, 50, 53, 56, 58, 60,
   62, 65, 68, 72, 90, 117, 119, 120-132,
   136-138, 140, 143-149, 151-154,
   178-187, 189, 191, 193, 197-198, 203,
   205, 212, 219
Task design v-vi, viii-x, 1-2, 5-7, 9, 11,
   13, 21-22, 26-28, 41-46, 67-68, 72,
   132, 153, 155, 198, 219, 222, 242, 245,
   250, 251, 254, 258, 260-261
Task instruction 4, 178, 180-181,
   186-188, 191-192, 195, 253, 254, 260
Task performance ix, 2, 5, 9-13, 18-21,
   23-24, 34-35, 44-45, 47-49, 51, 54, 62,
   64-66, 98, 120-121, 133, 139-140,
   153-154, 196, 203, 206, 226, 238-239
Task sequencing viii, x, 2, 6, 9-10,

20-22, 26, 68, 132, 155, 198, 218,
   258-259
Task type viii-ix, 4, 10-11, 14, 29-30, 39,
   49-50, 50, 66, 68, 71-73, 77, 80, 82-84,
   86-87, 91, 93, 95, 98, 101-102, 104-109,
   111-112, 128, 150-151, 155, 167, 173,
   202, 206, 208, 210-11, 214, 217, 219
Teaching pragmatics 234
There-and-Then viii, 7-8, 18, 51, 52-54,
   56-61, 61, 63, 179
Threshold Hypothesis 122, 130
Trade-off effects 63, 137, 150-151, 204

Vocabulary acquisition v, 4, 132, 178,
   179, 180, 181, 191, 197

Word coining 202, 206, 208-214, 216-217
Word retention 4, 178, 180-181,
   187-188, 190-192, 194-195
Writing v, viii-ix, 3-4, 24, 67, 89, 92-95, 97,
   115, 117, 121, 123, 133, 138-1142, 146,
   148-149, 153-156, 158-159, 161-162, 164,
   166-168, 171-175, 197, 246
Writing processes 158

Zone of Proximal Development (ZPD)
   93